Negotiating Identity

CATHOLIC
HIGHER EDUCATION
SINCE 1960

Alice Gallin, O.S.U.

UNIVERSITY OF NOTRE DAME PRESS

Notre Dame, Indiana

Copyright 2000 by
University of Notre Dame Press
Notre Dame, Indiana 46556
All Rights Reserved

Manufactured in the United States of America

Library of Congress Cataloging-in-Publication Data

Gallin, Alice.
    Negotiating identity : Catholic higher education since 1960 /
Alice Gallin.
      p.   cm.
    Includes bibliographical references (p.) and index.
    ISBN 0-268-01489-2 (cloth : alk. paper)
    1. Catholic universities and colleges—United States—
History—20th century.   I. Title.
    LC501.G36   2000
    378'.071'273—dc21   99-088281

∞ The paper used in this publication meets the minimum requirements of the
American National Standard for Information Sciences—Permanence of
Paper for Printed Library Materials, ANSI Z39.49-1984.

Errata
p. 29, line 9: "synthesizing" should read
  "synthesizing power"
p. 47, line 23: "88,000" should read
  "231,000"
p. 106, line 1: "Wulff" should read "Wolff"

*In gratitude for the Catholic intellectual tradition
which links so well the "love of learning"
and "the desire for God."*

Contents

Acknowledgments

The inspiration for this book came from my fifteen years with the Association of Catholic Colleges and Universities. Introduced to the complicated concerns of a membership of over two hundred colleges and universities by the Executive Director of the Association, Rev. John F. Murphy, I came to know and appreciate most of the presidents of these institutions. They comprise a long list of those to whom I am indebted. In the 1980s, when I served as Executive Director, I also came to know the leaders of the other higher-education associations, state, private, and church-related, and from them learned a great deal about American higher education, which was, after all, the context for Catholic higher education. Beginning in the fall of 1992, a support group of leaders evolved: Rev. Theodore M. Hesburgh, C.S.C., Mr. Edward Stephan, Rev. Paul Reinert, S.J., Mr. Daniel Schlafly, Ann Ida Gannon, B.V.M., Dr. David O'Brien, and Dr. Philip Gleason. Their doors were always open to me as I sought clues about the changes that occurred in the late 1960s and 70s.

Since very little has been published on the history of Catholic higher education in this recent period, I was dependent on the archives of Catholic colleges and universities. I received the most courteous and helpful assistance from the archivists and staffs at Notre Dame, St. Louis, Mundelein, Loyola of Chicago, the College of New Rochelle, Fordham University, College of the Holy Cross, Trinity College, Saint Michael's College in Vermont, St. Bonaventure University, and The Catholic University of America. I am also grateful to the administration of CUA for its willingness to administer the grant I received from the Lilly Endowment and to grant me the status of Visiting Research Scholar in 1992 and subsequent years. To Dr. Adele Chwalek, Director of Libraries at CUA, and Mr. Edward Bellanger of her staff I extend special words of appreciation for their patience and perseverance in administering the grant despite my mathematical deficiencies.

The libraries and files of the Association of Catholic Colleges and Universities, the Association of Governing Boards, the American Association of Colleges and Universities, and the American Association of University Professors were also placed at my disposal. At each library I met a number of persons interested in my work and willing to assist me in any possible way.

In the academic year 1996–97, through the good offices of Professor William M. Shea, I was invited to Saint Louis University as a Visiting Professor to utilize the archives there and to conduct a seminar with faculty and graduate students on the topic of my book. Dr. Shea and I collaborated in running the seminar and invited scholars from elsewhere to join us for two separate colloquia during the year. I am grateful for the support of the administration of Saint Louis University, especially the Provost at the time, Dr. Richard Breslin. During one of the colloquia I asked for suggestions for the title of the book; it was Rev. John Padberg, S.J., who responded with *Negotiating Identity*.

In dealing with the legal issues, canonical and civil, I needed a great deal of wise and knowledgeable counsel, and I received it over the years from Msgr. Frederick R. McManus and Rev. Robert Kennedy and in several conversations with Mr. Charles Wilson. Service with the Implementation Committee of *Ex Corde Ecclesiae* gave me an opportunity to widen and deepen my appreciation of the concerns of both bishops and presidents.

The funding provided by the Lilly Endowment was crucial, and I am especially indebted to Dr. Jeanne Knoerle, S.P., for her assistance and unflagging interest in my work. The book would never have been possible without the support and encouragement of my religious community, my family, and my friends. To all of them I am deeply grateful. And the final word of thanks goes to Rebecca DeBoer, my editor at the University of Notre Dame Press, who made the hard part of writing a book very easy by her skillful and gentle interventions.

Preface

I do not believe that the Catholic University as such has a future.
—John Cogley, "The Future of an Illusion,"
Commonweal, June 2, 1967

Was this well-known Catholic writer prescient about the future of Catholic higher education? Or did his emphasis on "as such" simply indicate that the Catholic identity of colleges and universities would no longer be taken for granted and would not continue in its present form?[1] As the twentieth century draws to a close, a glance back over the last forty-odd years of Catholic higher education in the United States reveals radical changes in the approximately 250 institutions considered Catholic in the early 1960s. While there were questions about the direction in which these colleges and universities were heading, nevertheless the various constituencies that supported them agreed that the institutions were "Catholic." Much of this certitude came from the presence of large numbers of priests, brothers, and sisters on these campuses and their control of the government of these institutions. In the case of The Catholic University of America and the dozen or so diocesan colleges, the clear relationship to the bishops was the basis for their recognizable Catholicity. But such clarity gave way to cultural realities that in turn resulted in a process of negotiating identity with a number of constituencies. Negotiation replaced the assumption that the institution as it had once existed was normative for all time.

---

1. Cogley's paper was originally presented at Marquette University. Cogley maintained that the Catholic colleges and universities would "some day seem as anachronistic as the papal states." However, he argued that they should not be "dismantalized [*sic*] or secularized but pluralized, ecumenicalized, and universalized." In the mid-sixties Cogley was religious editor of the *New York Times* and an avid supporter of Vatican Council II. He later left the Roman Catholic Church and became an Episcopalian (Obituary, *New York Times*, March 30, 1976).

The colleges' self-understanding as well as their public image as "Catholic" suffered from ambiguities consequent upon the changes in philosophical and theological methodologies which became evident in the documents of Vatican Council II (1962–65). If it was no longer easy to identify a Catholic by observing his or her attendance at weekly mass or abstinence from meat on Friday, it was also no longer easy to identify a university as Catholic by visible symbols of belief, required courses in theology, or a code of behavior based on Catholic moral teaching. The question "What makes a university Catholic?" would be revisited constantly in the decades under study in this book.

To define institutions as Catholic colleges and universities in relation to the modern world was evidently the task of their leaders, but these leaders could not act in isolation. Their task would have to be pursued through negotiation with a number of important and very complex constituencies: (1) civic and governmental officials, (2) the American higher education community, (3) the Roman Catholic Church, and (4) the internal constituency of faculty, students, administration and trustees. As with all historical studies, the complexity of the process of "negotiating identity" far outweighs any simple interpretation of the facts. How and why such a process occurred is the subject of this book. The task these Catholic colleges and universities faced was to adapt to the standards of American higher education, meet legal demands consequent on government funding, satisfy the expectations of students, parents, faculty, and alumnae/i, and do all this without losing their Catholic character.

The book proceeds chronologically, relating historical events to the ongoing effort of the institutions to arrive at a clear self-understanding. It is basically a history of the American Catholic colleges and universities engaged in educating laypersons. It does not include seminaries, theologates, sisters' colleges, or junior colleges, since their histories arise from different missions and they relate to another set of constituencies. While there is some overlap in the telling of the story, the goal is to view the scene from different perspectives. As with all history, the account reflects the knowledge and experience of the author. I have benefited from the questions of those who have read the manuscript and hope that I have sufficiently separated fact from personal opinion in the final work. Because the topic deals with such a recent period of history, there is a dearth of secondary literature and not all archival materials are available. Most of the archives on which I rely belong to the universities and/or the religious communities that sponsored them. Vatican and diocesan archives have not been used. Presumably, later historians will have access to those, and our understanding of the events and issues under study will be enriched.

There is no attempt by the author to predict the future of Catholic higher education, but it is my hope that serious reflection on the history of the many institutions will illuminate and color future decisions by those who now govern them. The oft-expressed desire of the presidents that their institutions be truly Catholic, and at the same time, truly universities and colleges, will be realized only if there is sufficient courage to communicate the Catholic intellectual tradition to administrators, faculty, and trustees and to offer intelligent critiques of some aspects of American higher education. The conscientious setting of priorities and policies to further the Catholic mission of the institutions will determine the outcome in the twenty-first century.

Negotiating Identity

ONE

The Winds of Change

In the year 1960 could anyone have envisioned the American Catholic college campus of 1990? While the approximately 250 Catholic colleges and universities in 1960 were not identical, they clearly had a common culture. Their mission statements were almost interchangeable, and their commitment to liberal arts, character formation, and a sense of campus community as spelled out in their annual Bulletins was openly proclaimed as rooted in their Catholic faith. Their environment was already being challenged by many as a "ghetto" that lacked connection to the real world, but it was treasured by many others. Undoubtedly, the rhetoric of the college Bulletins presented the ideal rather than the day-to-day reality, but it was an ideal that reflected a conviction on the part of those who had founded and still governed the institutions. Alumni/ae testify to the deep sense of "belonging" which made their college years a treasured memory. For others, of course, the education provided by Catholic colleges and universities sometimes lacked intellectual excitement, personal freedom, and real experiences of life.

The coming years of growth, diversification, and an economic roller coaster witnessed spectacular changes in all of American higher education. For Catholic colleges and universities there was an added factor: fundamental change in what they regarded as their "distinctive" mission precisely as Catholic. During these years they would struggle to improve their status in the academic world and at the same time find new ways to understand and articulate a special task for a Catholic university. Earlier generations of college faculties had provided an education for Catholic young men and women whose parents, often immigrants or children of immigrants, sought the advantages of higher education without exposure to dangers to their faith. They wanted a Catholic campus that would replicate a Catholic family environment, and they were not especially concerned about the level of advanced degrees or scholarly publications of the faculty. According to Philip Gleason, in his excellent history of the period, Catholic higher education believed its distinctive mission was to produce a culture that would confront and contradict modernity.[1] But in the sixties, as Andrew Greeley noted in the title of his 1969 work, *From Backwater to Mainstream,* Catholic colleges were determined to leap into the culture of the modern world.[2]

To appreciate that "sea change" in attitude and to explore the consequences, we must first consider prior developments in Catholic intellectual circles. Especially important was the work of scholars in the fields of philosophy and theology, their growing recognition of the role of the laity in the church, and the new awareness of human freedom and personal responsibility. At the same time, the traditional understanding of academic freedom in Catholic colleges came into conflict with the definition upheld by the American Association of University Professors (AAUP).[3] The context for this sea change is found in changing relationships with each of the four constituencies of Catholic colleges and universities: government, higher education, the Roman Catholic community, and the internal campus community.

Intellectual Environment in Catholic Circles

Undoubtedly a major cause for the new mentality which developed in Catholic higher education after 1960 was Vatican Council II, but the documents produced by the fathers of the Council did not emerge from an intellectual vacuum. The foundations were laid in the post–World War II universities and theologates by scholars such as Henri de Lubac, Yves Congar, M. D. Chenu, Karl Rahner, Pierre Teilhard de Chardin, and John Courtney Murray, as they struggled to give expression to the truths of the Roman Catholic tradition in contemporary concepts and language. Their writings made a major contribution to the winds of change. Indeed, Bryan Hehir claims that their theological reflection "led directly to Vatican II," and that although "the architects of this theological renewal had no sense that an ecumenical council was just over the horizon, in retrospect we can see the direct and substantial connection between the theology of the 1930s through the 1950s and the documents of Vatican II."[4]

The shift in the theological understanding of the relationship between the church and the world, an understanding that would be incorporated into *Gaudium et Spes* (*The Church in the Modern World*), had a profound impact on the way in which the Catholic university would struggle to articulate its own task of harmonizing scientific knowledge of the "natural" world with the religious understanding of the human person. As Hehir points out, this document gave "clear recognition of the intrinsic value and validity of secular institutions and secular disciplines."[5] Hence, it became a chief point of reference for university leadership in the three decades ahead, providing a solid foundation for arguments favoring conformity to "secular" standards in higher education.

Linked to this new theological understanding of the secular world was the declining interest in Catholic philosophical thought, as philosophers abandoned the neo-scholastic approach to reality.[6] Central to the "new philosophy" of the forties and fifties was a personalist and existentialist appreciation of the dignity of the human person and consequently a great emphasis on human freedom. The effect on traditional methods of theological research has been well described by de Lubac in his reflections on his own work.[7]

In the decade before Vatican II there was a growing awareness of the tensions involved in the teaching of philosophy and religion in Catholic colleges and universities. Rev. Gustave Weigel, S.J., questioned the assumption that a commitment to scholastic philosophy was a *sine qua non* for the study of theology. In an address to the Catholic Commission on Intellectual and Cultural Affairs in 1957,[8] Weigel traced the history of the Catholic intellectual tradition from Origen through Aquinas and pointed to the continuous efforts made by Christian philosophers to reconcile faith and reason, or, in other words, to understand the relationship of theology to science, a word used in medieval times to describe all secular knowledge. After Aquinas, revolutionary developments in the world of science created far greater challenges for the scholar working within the Christian tradition. Catholic thought, in a defensive posture after the seventeenth century, tended to make theology the reigning judge of all other disciplines, and this approach led to a situation in which the autonomy of secular science was denied. The basic attitude of Catholics in the first half of the twentieth century was one of apologetics; every new scientific or literary discovery had to be reconciled with an already defined "truth." By 1957, according to Weigel, the failure of Catholic scholars to distinguish themselves in American university circles was deplorable and was due, at least in part, to their "apologetic" approach to knowledge.

In the fifties a struggle emerged between clergy, educated mostly in seminaries, and a new breed of Catholic lay people, educated in universities. Many young Catholic philosophers were receiving their degrees at Louvain and other European universities, and they were acquiring an interest in the work of Hegel, Marx, Marcel, Sartre, Heidegger, and other exponents of phenomenology, existentialism, and personalism, as well as socialism and Marxism. They rejected the notion that Thomistic theology/philosophy was the basic criterion by which to judge all other systems of thought.

A survey by Ernan McMullin[9] showed that by 1966 a quarter of the Ph.D.-holding philosophy teachers in Catholic colleges had earned their degrees in Europe, and a fifth of those teaching philosophy listed themselves as existentialists or phenomenologists. The impact on the curriculum of many Catholic colleges and universities in the United States was self-evident. Many of the leading European philosophers and theologians, under whom these young American Catholics had studied, were guest lecturers on Catholic campuses in the fifties and sixties.[10] In 1950 a publication had been founded by lay men and women precisely to explore these scholarly trends. Called *Cross Currents*, it published translations of European authors and promoted dialogue that was both Catholic and ecumenical. However, its avant-garde selection of writers was not always well received by critics of a more conservative mind.

Among the critics were several converts to Roman Catholicism who had entered the church because they found there "a pattern of beliefs, ritual actions, liturgical practices, food taboos, and even a distinctive view of the nation's history and its place in Western civilization."[11] Many of these lay converts had attended secular universities and now denounced them for their godlessness.[12] Patrick Allitt includes in this group William Buckley, Anthony Bouscaren, Brent Bozell, Louis Budenz, John Lukacs, and Thomas Molnar. They had come to the Roman Catholic tradition for its clarity and security of faith, and they had a strong suspicion by the late fifties that the moorings were slipping.

The "secular" and "liberal" philosophical positions of the non-Thomists were seen by the converts as a means of buttressing radical leftist positions of socialist and communist political philosophy. Indeed, the fear of communism was ubiquitous on the American scene in the fifties. The anti-communist climate made creative thought dangerous and hindered honest public discussion on basic philosophical and political topics. Under the leadership of Senator Joseph Mc-Carthy and the House Committee on Un-American Activities, faculty members, like many other Americans, were interrogated and often denounced on little or no evidence of communist persuasion.[13]

Although Americans in general regarded Catholics as immune to the communist virus because it was atheistic, the requirement that all teachers take a loyalty oath did not exclude Catholics. Such action on the part of the state was regarded by many, especially in private universities, as an infringement on the recognized autonomy of academia with its guarantee of freedom to teach and to learn. In response to the repressive McCarthy era, the proponents of academic freedom led a strong counterattack in the late fifties and early sixties. For Catholic institutions, this had both civil and ecclesial ramifications.

Academic Freedom

In 1955 it was still mandatory in several states to take a loyalty oath before entering the classroom as a teacher on any level. Faculty contracts at many Catholic colleges specified that nothing should be taught contrary to the United States Constitution or the teaching of the Roman Catholic Church. One could say, as Gleason pointed out in a speech in 1967, that the general attitude prior to that time was that Catholic colleges favored academic freedom, by which they meant the "freedom to teach what is true and to receive instruction in what is true."[14] A less limiting definition, such as that of the AAUP, was deemed "incompatible with the nature and purposes of Catholic higher education."

Faculty handbooks and contracts made the limits on academic freedom quite clear. One example is Duquesne University's, *Policies and Regulations concerning Appointments to the Faculties* published in 1940. In Section III, entitled "Academic Freedom," we read:

> Academic Freedom, like all things finite, has its limitations. To transgress those limits is not freedom but license. For there is such a thing as objective reality, truth that is truth regardless of what any particular human mind may think to the contrary. Consequently no man is free to teach objective falsehood simply because subjectively he fancies it to be the truth. In questions of fact there is no such thing academic freedom. The truth limits the human intellect within limitations that connote true freedom— freedom from error. . . . [Duquesne's] position is that the Deity in the person of the historic Jesus Christ made very definite pronouncements as

regards belief, worship and ethics. . . . True, the practical application of this principle is confined to the department of religion at Duquesne University; but just as it would be incongruous for a teacher of history to question or minimize the basic facts in the department of mathematics, so too, philosophically and ethically it would be inconsistent with the purpose of the University to concede to her teaching staff a type of freedom that is not at her disposal to give. . . . any overt act even extra-mural that might compromise Duquesne University's ideals is sufficient grounds for Duquesne University to terminate immediately any agreement as to tenure previously entered into. . . .

There follows a list of sixteen "discrediting acts," including: questioning the existence of a personal God and the immortality, spirituality, and individuality of the human soul; questioning the physical freedom of the human will; and finally, as no. 16, "to teach any other proposition inconsistent with Catholic Doctrine."[15]

Limitations such as these were not unusual. Another example can be found in a "Faculty Rank and Tenure Policy" of the University of Scranton in effect in 1955.[16] After defending the freedom to search for and communicate truth, the statement discusses the limits to such freedom: the impassable barrier of positive facts, a recognition that sincerity is not a guarantee against error, and a realization that unaided reason "will not carry him [the scholar] very far in these days of complex and extended knowledge." The faculty member "can never teach anything that contradicts certain truth, whether that truth be known to him from his own evidence, from reliable human authority, or from the Catholic Church speaking within its legitimate scope."

Such an open statement of limitation on speech and behavior was acceptable under the AAUP principles issued in 1940:

> The teacher is entitled to freedom in the classroom in discussing his subject but he should be careful not to introduce into his teaching controversial matter which has no relation to his subject. Limitations of academic freedom because of religious or other aims of the institution should be clearly stated in writing at the time of the appointment.[17]

Using this principle, AAUP took cognizance of only one or two complaints from Catholic colleges in the pre-1965 days (Mercy College in 1963 and Gonzaga in 1960). Nevertheless, the higher education community often criticized the lack of freedom at denominational schools. It assumed that they were not "real" universities or colleges because they were Catholic and therefore subject to control by church authorities.

Scholars such as Sidney Hook and Robert MacIver insisted that the ideal of free inquiry and instruction was incompatible with denominational education. Hook wrote: "Of course in Catholic institutions, the Church dogma is the decisive matter. There is no academic freedom in Catholic colleges and were Catholics to constitute a majority of the population, education would in all likelihood lose its secular character."[18] Even among Catholics there were those, such as John Cogley, who saw an incompatibility between a true university and a commitment to Catholicism on the part of the university.[19] Sister Jacqueline Grennan, S.L., in separating Webster College in St. Louis from the Sisters of Loretto and any sort of church relationship, claimed that only a truly "secular" institution could give adequate freedom to teachers and scholars.[20]

Journet Kahn of the University of Notre Dame, speaking at the American Catholic Philosophical Association in 1957, complained that Catholic universities were still operating on the assumption that the "primary goal of higher education is the development of religious piety."[21] Hence, the parameters were clear and academic freedom was limited.

It must be admitted that on Catholic campuses there was a latent desire on the part of some self-appointed guardians to ferret out unorthodox teachers and report them to church authorities. The way in which such matters were handled often created an atmosphere of suspicion because there was no opportunity for a public defense of one's position. In the fifties such cases were generally handled behind closed doors by conversations among college administrators, religious superiors, and church officials. Together, they would find a way of convincing the "problem" professor that he (seldom she) would be "happier on a different kind of campus." Religious superiors did not hesitate to use their authority to remove a troublesome member of the community from the faculty at the president's request, or even without it. In many cases the superior of the religious community was also the president of the college and simply took action. Because the solution was so informal and the government of college and community so intertwined, there is little documentation in university archives of this unfortunate way of dealing with critical or nonconforming faculty members. However, this kind of quiet pressure on faculty, testified to orally by those who experienced it, should be kept in mind as we note the absence of "cases" of violation of academic freedom at Catholic colleges and universities in the AAUP files prior to 1965.

A good example of a purely internal conflict over academic freedom is one that arose at the College of New Rochelle in 1955–56. It illustrates problems already existing on some Catholic campuses where the winds of change were blowing strongly and the colleges were not always able to cope with them. Lay faculty concerns at New Rochelle foreshadowed problems that would be common experiences in the sixties.

The mission of the College of New Rochelle, since its foundation in 1904, was always stated not only in terms of the intellectual development of the students, but also in terms of their moral character and religious faith. The educational philosophy which predominated was that of a classical liberal arts program with heavy requirements in philosophy and religion. In the early fifties, new faculty members in the philosophy department included John Bannan and Eugene Fontinell. Joseph Cunneen, the founder of *Cross Currents,* had recently joined the English department, and Francis Sullivan was a new faculty member in education. All of these men were impressed by the intensely academic environment of the college and took seriously the task of developing Catholic lay women as critical thinkers for contemporary society.

Deep disagreements between the clerical and lay faculty surfaced in the spring of 1955 precisely around the question of how best to achieve that result. Several members of the faculty and administration (two lay men and two Ursuline nuns), understanding the need for the college community to discuss questions related to the integration-concentration curriculum that had just been introduced, invited their colleagues to a study day on the topic "A Consideration of Intellectual Freedom in the Catholic College" on May 19.[22] The invitation stated that the way in which the mission of the college—"the pursuit and communication of knowledge"—would be achieved depended on the "variety of experience and insight which exists among faculty members." A Catholic college, it pointed out, has the benefit of some members who are lay and some religious, a reality which was seen as producing complementary views of its task. The invitation continued: "One of the essential features of this community is its intellectual freedom," and this needs to be discussed by the community so as to achieve a common understanding of what it means.

What began as a day of conversation among faculty turned into an unpleasant confrontation between the clerical members of the faculty and the lay defenders of academic freedom. Reference to the 1950 encyclical *Humani Generis* by one of the priests led to argument about the binding force of papal letters regarding the teaching of philosophy. One of the priests, Rev. Thomas Maher, a political scientist, insisted that not only the pope's but also the bishops' authoritative judgments regarding economic and social issues must be upheld by teachers in every discipline. John Bannan retorted, "Then it's *your* church," explaining later in his written defense that such an understanding of authoritative teaching by bishops would leave "the lay Christian totally inert and completely without initiative."[23] The disagreement was thus framed in terms of different understandings of "the church," especially the role of the laity, as well as different perceptions of the education that should be given to the students at a Catholic college in 1955–56. The lay men had high regard for the quality of students they found at New Rochelle and the toughness of the curriculum, and they thought that the clerics underestimated the students' intellectual sophistication.

For most of the college's history, lay faculty had outnumbered clerical and religious members. From the beginning of the college in 1904, outstanding men and women from leading secular universities were hired to assist the nuns in building a demanding curriculum and setting the high standards of achievement which characterized the college by the mid-fifties. The chaplain of the college, Rev. John Quinn, appointed by the cardinal in 1950, was well suited by his own education and interests to collaborate in such an effort. His religion course for seniors moved away from apologetics into the newest commentaries in biblical studies. Hence, he easily became friends with the new lay members who joined the faculty in 1953 and 1954, and was invited by them to lead a Scripture study group and to engage in discussions about liturgical changes. According to Joseph Cunneen, Father Quinn had often visited his bookstore and was one of the early subscribers to *Cross Currents*, the new journal of opinion in the fifties. The general atmosphere among lay and religious faculty was one of mutual respect and collaboration, that is, until May 1955. The angry confrontation took everyone by surprise.

In retrospect, it is clear that the educational experiences of the two groups led them to contradictory opinions, strongly defended. The priest-faculty members, all priests of the Archdiocese of New York, had received most of their education in the seminary system, a program heavily dependent on neo-scholastic philosophy. Two of them, Rev. Thomas Darby and Rev. Thomas Moriarty, were part-time faculty in the religion department, while Rev. Thomas Maher was a member of the history and political science department. The chaplain's

expertise was in liturgical matters, and he was suspicious of new philosophical trends in European thought. On the other hand, the new lay
members of the faculty in philosophy, education, and English were attuned to trends in modern secular fields. John Bannan had just completed his doctoral studies at Louvain and had written his dissertation
on the thought of Merleau-Ponty, while Eugene Fontinell was com-
pleting a dissertation at Fordham University on Royce. Francis Sullivan, in education, was a specialist in the thought of John Dewey, and
Joseph Cunneen of the English department was also the editor of *Cross
Currents,* as mentioned earlier.

The young men clearly did not fit the description of faculty
on Catholic campuses given by Gleason in his 1967 address: "Catholic
educators [in pre–Vatican II days] were in practically universal agreement that they already had the truth—that they understood the knowledge, skills, values, and religious truth that collegians needed to learn."[24]
On the contrary these "Young Turks" (as some saw them) conceived
their task as one of stimulating critical questions and suggesting new
horizons of thought, certainly not one of developing piety, even though
they were all serious Catholics in their personal lives. They resisted any
McCarthy-like thought control, whether by state or church authorities.[25] The chaplain, interestingly, was ahead of the times in his liturgical reforms and extremely well-read in a variety of theological areas,
but he did not extend his "liberal" positions into areas of philosophical
exploration.

To put the conflict over academic freedom at New Rochelle in context, we should recall that in the 1950s the stated goal of Catholic colleges was to present a unifying synthesis of all knowledge and values,
one which required acceptance of the boundaries set by both church
and state regarding the rights of individuals vis-à-vis the common good.
It also assumed the central "integrating" function of neo-scholasticism.
However, this goal was now being challenged.

The young lay faculty members raised a critical question: Should
the students be informed and guided only according to the traditional
understanding of Christian life and leadership, or should they be stimulated to criticize some elements of the tradition? The conflict also represented a struggle on the part of these lay faculty members to become
free from clerical control in what pertained to their scholarly careers,
and to be recognized as equal partners in the work of the church.

The public argument that developed in May 1955 colored all relationships in the year that followed. The clerics' complaints about these

particular lay members of the faculty multiplied. Various charges, without explicit evidence, were leveled against them by the priests. They were referred to as heretics because of the way the Thomistic proofs for the existence of God were handled in philosophy courses. Specific articles in *Cross Currents* were cited in support of a charge that the students were being exposed to scandal. One example was an article entitled "The Temptation to Do Good" (*Cross Currents*, Winter 1956). Although Cunneen denied ever assigning readings from this source, the chaplain claimed that this particular article would reveal to students "recent scandalous incidents which, if they are true, are not commonly known." Furthermore, he charged that books on the Index[26] were sold in the *Cross Currents* bookstore, a store managed by Cunneen but located nowhere near the college.

Some complaints from the priests dealt with comments made by the men, sometimes facetiously, outside the classroom. Read forty years later, these complaints are (to use Father Quinn's own assessment) "anachronistic." From the point of view of academic freedom, perhaps one of the more serious incidents regarded the interference by the chaplain in the publication of a student essay on Gabriel Marcel, which was submitted to the student magazine, *Quarterly*. Although the Ursuline moderator of the publication, Mother Christopher Pechaux, had submitted the article to an outstanding philosopher at Fordham University and been assured of its value, the president of New Rochelle was pressured by the chaplain into overriding the decision to publish. Another student essay, this one on Emerson, was denounced by the chaplain as demonstrating an unnecessary reliance on a non-Catholic philosopher.[27]

All of these charges were brought to the dean's office, where an attempt was made to distinguish justifiable criticism from bias against new ways of studying philosophy and/or theology. Further study days in the fall of 1955 and in May 1956, as well as monthly faculty colloquies, only deepened the chasm. By the fall of 1956 the complaints against the laymen occurred almost daily.[28] There were public accusations of heresy and a demand that the offending lay faculty be dismissed from the college. Clearly, academic freedom was under siege. At the close of the school year, in June 1956, the four priests most involved met with the Ursuline administrators (the president, acting dean, and the superior of the community, who also chaired the board of trustees). No resolution of the situation could be reached.

At the beginning of the new academic year, Bannan requested the acting dean to have the charges put in writing; the faculty could no longer deal with informal comments and rumors. The administration then referred the matter to the Chancery[29] and sometime in the late fall of 1956 Cardinal Spellman requested, through the office of the president, that the priests put all their charges in writing, and directed that the lay men be asked to respond in writing as well. There is, unfortunately, no available record of the process followed by the Chancery, but the principals are of the opinion that these documents were submitted to a committee of theologians for their review. In the typical "behind closed doors" kind of decision-making of that era, a judgment was reached and communicated to the president, who summoned the men to her office in early January and announced that "the charges had been dropped" and "there is to be no further discussion of the matter." The faculty members, all of whom were untenured, were given normal two-year contracts, except for Cunneen, whose contract was for only one year; Cunneen had originally taken the position with the understanding that it existed only until one of the sisters, who was getting her Ph.D., returned to the faculty. Bannan, with encouragement from the president, later accepted an offer from Loyola University in Chicago. Fontinell remained at New Rochelle, becoming chair of the philosophy department until 1962, when he accepted a position at Queens College.

There is no record of this entire matter in the AAUP files or in the trustee minutes of the college. An aura of mystery surrounded the "charges" in both the college and the Ursuline religious community, since nothing was ever explained. The tragedy was that the infusion of intellectual strength which had come with these young lay faculty was derailed, and the reputation for academic freedom at Catholic colleges was further tarnished.

In one of the ironies of history, a bequest was used to set up the Anna V. McCarthy Visiting Professorship a few years later, and the first occupant of this Chair was Rev. Guy Léonard, O.P., who had had several articles published in *Cross Currents* on the subjects of freedom and the role of the laity. By that time the chaplain, Father Quinn, had been reassigned (not because of the academic freedom issue but because of his own avant-garde liturgical experiments). The events of 1955–57 were a thing of the past. Father Léonard later evaluated his experience at the College of New Rochelle and commented that the "outstanding intellectual climate" was certainly not something he had expected to find at a "small college for women."[30] That climate was due, in large part, to the wisdom of those who had hired the "Young Turks" of the fifties and who expected others on the faculty to respect their ability to stimulate critical thinking and independent judgments in their students. The violation of their academic freedom by clerical colleagues, while not upheld by the Ursuline administrators or the Cardinal-Archbishop of New York, was nevertheless seen as an interference by the church in the affairs of the college.

Another type of interference with intellectual freedom was the case of Rev. John Courtney Murray, S.J. Father Murray taught at Woodstock College, the Jesuit theologate, and was esteemed as a scholar by colleagues on many Catholic campuses. He was also a frequent lecturer at Fordham, Georgetown, and other universities. In the late forties and early fifties he published several articles in *Theological Studies* exploring contemporary issues in church and society, especially from an ecumenical point of view. He was dissatisfied with the traditional Catholic theory of the relationship between the state and the church and sought to develop a theoretical framework more suited to the American experience. However, his work was refuted as unorthodox by two professors at The Catholic University of America, Msgr. Joseph Fenton and Rev. Francis J. Connell, C.S.S.R. They published several acrimonious reviews of his work in the *American Ecclesiastical Review* and took steps to make sure that authorities in Rome were informed of Murray's position.[31]

Despite the fact that Murray was not affiliated with a particular Catholic university, two universities became involved in the debate: The Catholic University of America, where Murray gave a lecture to which Fenton and Connell took great exception and so reported to Rome, and the University of Notre Dame, where Murray was one of the participants in a symposium on academic freedom. Advance review copies of the publication of the proceedings, including Murray's presentation, reached Rome and caused officials in the Holy See to bring pressure on the Father General of the Holy Cross Fathers who governed the University of Notre Dame, to withdraw it.[32] For over a year the struggle about the book continued and President Hesburgh, who was unwilling to withdraw the 1954 publication, finally agreed not to do a second printing. However, in his account of the affair he cannot refrain from pointing out that Notre Dame subsequently gave Murray an honorary degree.[33]

Between these events and the 1965 faculty strike at St. John's University, New York,[34] lay faculty at most Catholic colleges developed a sense of their own professional rights and were ready for public confrontation over perceived violations of academic freedom, especially lack of due process. In this, they could rely on support from AAUP and on a network of colleagues in other institutions. By the mid-sixties most administrators of Catholic colleges and universities had accepted the AAUP principles as normative, whether they liked them or not. Faculty could also rely on the official teachings of Vatican Council II to buttress their arguments. One of the most quoted passages from *Gaudium et Spes* was: "It is, however, only in freedom that man can turn himself towards what is good." Furthermore, "man's dignity therefore requires him to act out of conscious and free choice" (no. 17).[35] This emphasis on personal freedom highlighted an area in need of reform in Catholic universities and colleges, one that would receive great attention in the decade ahead.

Countercurrents from Rome

Conflict between American Catholic universities and Roman authorities in the church, already present to some degree in the struggle over the publication of Murray's symposium essay, was also foreshadowed by two "red flags" involving institutional autonomy, the companion of academic freedom. The first was the contested election in 1963 of Rev. Theodore M. Hesburgh, C.S.C., as president of the International Federation of Catholic Universities, and the second, a decree from the Sacred Congregation for Seminaries and Universities mandating permission from the Holy See for all honorary degrees. Among the winds of change, there were obviously countercurrents.

A Red Flag: IFCU

The post–World War II environment was highly supportive of international efforts at cooperation. The United Nations and its various subgroups, such as the United Nations Economic and Social Organization (UNESCO), provided a vigorous vision of a world of peace and justice. In 1948 Pius XII and the Sacred Congregation of Seminaries and Universities (renamed the Congregation for Catholic Education in 1967) proposed the creation of a federation which would provide a "university presence in international matters." Although there had been an "informal group" of the rectors of some thirty universities erected by the Holy See, which had met occasionally prior to World War II, the pope now asked that an "International Federation of Catholic Universities" be formed. In his decree of July 27, 1949, he "erected and constituted the Federation of Catholic Universities" and ruled that the members would be "those higher institutions which have been canonically erected or may hereafter be erected by the Holy See in any part of the world, and also ... those institutions which shall publicly be recognized as fully in accord with norms established by it and governed according to them."

Within the International Federation of Catholic Universities, almost from the time of its formal foundation,[36] these criteria for membership were a subject of disagreement.[37] If applied strictly, only The Catholic University of America and possibly one or two others which had been "canonically erected" in the United States qualified as members. Yet American leadership in the United Nations was extremely important. Hence, some nonecclesiastical American Catholic universities were admitted to membership: Notre Dame, Fordham, and Boston College were among the first.

Under the presidency of the rector of The Catholic University of America, Msgr. Joseph McDonald (1960–63), the Federation found itself in a "do-nothing" mode. McDonald's lack of leadership had dire consequences on the Federation's role in international academic circles. The original goal of the Federation to exert influence by participation in the International Association of Universities (IAU) and in UNESCO suffered eclipse. In 1963 the IFCU met in Washington, D.C., voted on new statutes that would open membership to a wider group, and elected Father Hesburgh as president. There was surprise and anger when the Sacred Congregation refused to acknowledge these actions. Hesburgh, according to Msgr. Staffa of the Congregation, was not the rector of a *true* Catholic university, by which he meant that it was not canonically erected. Staffa announced that a special commission would be appointed by the Congregation to govern the association until new elections could be held. Those who had been elected to the IFCU Council in Washington refused to serve under such an arrangement.[38] Hesburgh and the new Council were supported by Cardinal Spellman, by the head of the Jesuit Educational Association, Edward Rooney, S.J., and by Msgr. Paul Marcinkus at the Secretariat of State. European bishops such as Leon Josef Suenens of Belgium and Franz Koenig of Austria also expressed their support.

The proposal put forth by Staffa at his meeting with the IFCU officials on November 16, 1963, led to a stalemate. A further meeting on November 28 still failed to produce mutual agreement. The affair was ended only after the personal intervention of Paul VI; on February 1, 1964, the Prefect of the Congregation, Cardinal Pizzardo, confirmed the elections and opened the door to discussions about the statutes.

In his letter of July 15, 1964, to the rectors and representatives of IFCU, Hesburgh discussed plans for the future. He quoted Pizzardo asking in a special letter to Hesburgh that all members work together "in the great task at hand: to give Catholic universities a vital corporate presence in the modern world." But could such a task be accomplished without the universities' necessary freedom and autonomy? This question, Hesburgh argued, should be considered by the Council and by the IFCU Assembly at Tokyo in August 1965.

Hesburgh also informed IFCU members that Paul VI had spoken to him at a meeting on April 27, 1964, about a special project (at the moment confidential) which he wished IFCU to undertake.[39] This gesture of papal confidence in the leadership of IFCU was congruent with the pontiff's suggestion that the IFCU set up headquarters in Paris, supporting the IFCU's desire to interact with IAU and UNESCO and to avoid a direct relationship with the Congregation in Rome.

In preparing for the 1965 IFCU Assembly in Tokyo, the Council agreed to focus on the same topic that the International Association of Universities was considering: the autonomy of the modern university. Since one of the purposes of IFCU was to influence IAU by participation in their meetings, the schedule was arranged to precede that of IAU so that the IFCU might better prepare to contribute to the discussion. The members of IAU were concerned with interference and/or censorship on the part of governments; IFCU had the additional problem of church interference. To discuss the issue from a specifically Catholic point of view, the Council invited Dr. Charles DeKoninck, Dean of the Faculty of Philosophy at Laval University, to give the keynote address. Such a presentation, the Council believed, would link current thought with that of the Catholic philosophical tradition regarding freedom. Unfortunately, Dr. DeKoninck died before the August meeting.

The keynote address was given instead by René Thery of the University of Lille, and perhaps because of his European location rather than DeKoninck's Canadian one, he focused on autonomy more than freedom.[40] However, by thus linking discussion at the IFCU Assembly directly to that of the subsequent IAU meeting, the Council made a clear statement about the goal of the IFCU. Catholic universities needed autonomy if they were to be accepted as partners in the international academic community, and the Tokyo Assembly wanted to move in that direction.[41] According to Hesburgh, such status would assist the Catholic universities in their role of solving "the enormous intellectual problems today regarding social justice and social charity." By referencing the papal documents *Mater et Magistra* and *Pacem in Terris,* he emphasized the connection that he saw between the Catholic university and service to society through the church. Recognition of the university's freedom and autonomy, he believed, would not lessen its commitment to the mission of the church.

When one reflects on these difficulties concerning the membership and leadership of IFCU, it is clear that there was a fundamental difference of opinion about the meaning of the word "Catholic" when used to modify the word "university." This definitional problem would recur over and over again in the dialogue between Rome and the American Catholic higher education community for the next thirty-five years. The discussions at Tokyo in 1965 enabled the Americans to view the question in a broader international context, and initiated a collaboration with colleagues from other countries that would have significant results. It also shed light on the differences between American higher education and European universities or those influenced by Europe in their academic structures.

A Second Red Flag: Honorary Degrees

As can be seen from the 1949 Statutes of IFCU, the "Catholic university" was defined as one erected by the Holy See or, at least, governed in accordance with the norms dictated for such institutions. There was a move in the fifties to "raise" all Catholic universities to the status of canonical "erection," a change which would have brought American Catholic universities into a new relationship with the Vatican. In 1955 the Sacred Congregation of Seminaries and Universities had been urging all "true" universities to seek formal pontifical recognition, a common course of action followed by many Catholic universities in other parts of the world, but not in the United States. Such recognition was generally desired as a protection against an unfriendly State. Americans, however, considered themselves protected by the First Amendment to the Constitution and did not want such pontifical status. They based their claim to Catholicity on the founding purposes of the religious communities and the general recognition of their character by the Catholic community and the hierarchy.

In 1962 it was rumored that the Congregation was about to issue a decree which would require approval by the Holy See for *any* honorary degrees that might be granted by *any* Catholic university. Even before the actual decree was issued, Cardinal Spellman rose to the defense of the universities. He insisted that he was tired of explaining over and over again to the Sacred Congregation that Catholic universities in the United States were chartered by the state governments and had no desire to be chartered again by the Vatican. In a letter to Cardinal Pizzardo, Prefect of the Sacred Congregation, on June 18, 1962,[42] Spellman wrote that "it is with deep regret" that he had heard that the Sacred Congregation was still pushing for the canonical erection of American universities. He argued strongly that such a move on Rome's part would have dire effects in the United States in view of the current controversy regarding federal aid to Catholic schools. Pizzardo responded (June 23, 1962) that he understood the situation but that the Jesuits wanted to be listed as "Catholic" in the *Annuario Pontificio*, and for that citation canonical status was necessary. Spellman replied that he was pleased that the Sacred Congregation now understood the situation, but he doubted that the Jesuits still wanted this status, if they ever did. At the same time, showing the political skills for which he was known, Spellman informed both the Secretary of State, Amleto Giovanni Cicognanni (formerly Apostolic Delegate in Washington), and Paul VI of his correspondence with Pizzardo.

Nothing, however, changed in the attitude of Pizzardo and his confreres. The following year, the same year that Hesburgh was rejected as IFCU president by the Sacred Congregation, the threatened action on honorary degrees was taken. On May 23, 1963, the Sacred Congregation issued a decree that all honorary degrees awarded by Catholic universities must be approved by the Holy See. Evidently this was the price to be paid for recognition as "Catholic." It was also interpreted as a slap on the wrist of Saint Louis University for having awarded a degree to Rev. Hans Küng of the University of Tübingen, whose work, *The Council, Reform and Reunion,* was highly popular in the United States but was frowned upon by the Congregation.[43]

This decree was clearly an attack on the autonomy of the university. Once again, it was Spellman who insisted to Rome that such a decree was indefensible. In October the Sacred Congregation modified the decree to state that although theological degrees needed Roman approval, honorary degrees in civil subjects needed only the approval of the local Ordinary. Again, Spellman protested, pointing out that for him, as an American bishop, such an exercise of authority would be illegal under American law since it would violate the autonomy of the university. For the next two years (the years when Vatican Council II was in session), correspondence and phone calls were numerous among the major players: Spellman, Edward Rooney of the Jesuit Educational Association (JEA), Father General John Baptist Janssens of the Jesuits, Archbishop Cicognnani of the Secretariat of State, Rev. Laurence McGinley, S.J., president of Fordham, the Father General and Provincial of the Holy Cross Fathers, and Brother Gregory Nugent, president of Manhattan College and the president of the College and University Department of NCEA.[44]

On March 24, 1964, Archbishop Cicognnani sent a strong letter of protest to the Sacred Congregation of Seminaries and Universities, a copy of which he sent to Cardinal Spellman. He insisted to Pizzardo that universities in the United States had to comply with their own civil charters. As Catholic, he wrote, "they are animated by and conform to Catholic doctrine; they esteem and profess Catholic principles." He argued, moreover, that such universities could not be subject to further control: "since a proper liberty and autonomy in making decisions increases a sense of responsibility and augments the importance of the work of those to whom is entrusted the destiny and prosperity of such institutions, they should be left free to follow their own traditions and in common with other universities, govern their institutions in accordance with their own rules."[45]

Spellman assumed that this was the end of the controversy, but the Prefect of the Congregation continued to insist that the decree was still in effect. In July 1964 Pizzardo sent a directive to the Father General of the Jesuits insisting that the decree be implemented by the provincials. By February 1965 Spellman had really lost patience. He insisted that the danger to American colleges was clear from the *Horace Mann* case now under litigation.[46] Pizzardo then suggested that the American bishops could exempt their institutions from the decree if they chose; Spellman replied that there was no basis for such a proposal since the decree did not come from the bishops. He wanted a clear statement from the Congregation that the decree applied only to pontifical honorary degrees.

Finally, in a letter of July 21, 1965, Cicognnani informed Spellman that he had referred the matter to the pope, who had directed the Sacred Congregation to reexamine the decree. Evidently this killed the decree, but Spellman was still concerned that there was no public withdrawal of it; he was aware of the negative effect such evidence of control by the Vatican would have on current efforts to obtain federal aid for Catholic schools. Fortunately, there had never been a public proclamation of the original decree and, except for one article in *Time* magazine, it seemed to have escaped notice. Although some presidents protested, and one even said he would not award any honorary degrees under those conditions, others seem to have quietly asked for and received the Ordinary's permission.[47] Many of the smaller colleges at that time did not award honorary degrees, and others apparently paid no attention to the whole affair. Perhaps they considered their trustees, who were all members of the religious community, competent to act on behalf of "the church." Presumably the diocesan colleges would have complied by having their bishop-chair approve honorary degrees, thus keeping it an internal matter.[48] Nevertheless, the imperial style of Roman ecclesial operation, so anachronistic by the 1960s, had to be resisted, and the American Catholic universities and hierarchy did so.

Church and Secular Society

Reflection on these events suggests a tension in the understanding of the role of church authority in matters generally acknowledged to be part of the secular order. Should the granting of an honorary degree in chemical engineering somehow be screened by members of the Curia or by the local Ordinary? Should a university, chartered by the state and accredited by a secular agency, be limited by church authority in its power to grant degrees? Up to this point the governance of Catholic colleges and universities was in the hands of religious communities; hence, church authority was often exercised through higher superiors, often resident in Rome. But the increasing inclusion during the 1960s of lay men and women on governing boards of these institutions, as well as on their faculties and in administrative posts, complicated and even made impossible the exercise of authority in that mode.

The need to understand with greater sensitivity the vocation of the layperson in the church and his or her work in and through its institutions became a major priority in the preparation of the documents of Vatican Council II. Although ecclesial letters and papal pronouncements had often affirmed the lay vocation, it was never very clear just what was meant by that term; the definition given in the context of Catholic Action was "the participation of the laity in the apostolate of the hierarchy."[49] Movements such as the Catholic Worker and the various forms of Catholic Action such as Young Christian Students existed in the thirties and forties, but after World War II the understanding of these lay movements in the church took on a new coloring. According to one author, the post-war debate now focused on the layperson's relation to the modern world: should it be embraced and shaped, or rejected?[50]

Links were established between the Liturgical Movement, the Catholic Family Movement, and the various forms of Catholic Action. On campuses in the fifties many young people volunteered to serve as "lay missionaries" for a year or two.[51] Beginning in 1951 there were international Congresses for the Laity, which gave a voice to lay men and women in the church.

The recognition of the lay vocation as a special call to serve in secular surroundings presented an implicit challenge to the negative overtones in ecclesial references to the secular world. If the secular world was the place in which the lay vocation was exercised, then it ought to be perceived as a gift rather than an obstacle to personal holiness. In his 1959 work, Yves Congar, O.P., called attention to the need to appreciate the secular world to which the laity were "missioned." "To be secular," he wrote, "is to use all the resources within us in that pursuit of justice and truth for which we hunger, the very stuff of human history."[52]

The fundamental goodness of the secular world and the necessity of a positive appreciation of its distinctive reality furnished the subject matter for the extensive literature on the role of the laity which appeared in the late fifties and early sixties.[53] Searching for the proper way to explain the basic vocation of the layperson in the church, theologians had to rethink much of the anti-secular language in earlier writings. Not only *Cross Currents* but other publications, such as *America* and *Commonweal,* reported frequently on work being done in France, Germany, and Belgium on the "new theology" of the laity. The attention given in book reviews in these journals to the works of Yves Congar, Pierre Teilhard de Chardin, Walter Ong, Thomas O'Dea, Justus Lawler, Donald Thorman, and others testifies to the fascination of the Catholic community with a somewhat revolutionary understanding of the role of the laity as having a distinct mission within the church, rather than simply participating in the "apostolate of the hierarchy."[54]

At the same time, the new appreciation of the "secular" world made deep inroads into the interests and lifestyle of religious communities, urging them to change customs that had stemmed from the monastic (often anti-secular) form of religious life. In many cases, unfortunately, the new appreciation of the secular world and the role of the laity in it led to individual departures from the priesthood and religious life.[55] The loss of many gifted religious from faculties of Catholic colleges and universities would have a profound impact on the future of these institutions.

Two major themes that emerged from the intellectual ferment preceding and incorporated into the work of Vatican Council II and would make deep inroads into Catholic higher education in the United States were (1) the necessity for the church to recognize the autonomy of scientific knowledge in the search for truth; and (2) a conviction that the gift of human freedom demanded respect for individual consciences even in the process of evangelization.

Both of these themes had their origin in the work of the theologians cited above. While they were often censured in the late forties and throughout the fifties, their writings inspired important debates among theologians and bishops. Ultimately, their insights found their way into the documents of the Vatican Council II, particularly those dealing with the nature of the church and its relation to the modern world: *Lumen Gentium, Gaudium et Spes, Apostolicam actuositatem,* and *Dignitatis humanae.* By the end of 1965 a whole new ecclesial canon was presented to Roman Catholics for their reflection, a list of required readings which colored their thinking in a dramatic way.

The work of the theologians who had once been under censure now received a benediction from the Council fathers. John XXIII signified papal atonement to de Lubac and Congar by naming them to the Preparatory Theological Commission for the Council, and Francis Cardinal Spellman of New York did a major service to the church by inviting John Courtney Murray to be one of his *periti* at the second session of the Council. The indirect influence of many other theologians, especially in Europe, on their own bishops during the days of the Council is hard to report on in detail, but it is described in some of the work now being published on the debates at the Council.[56]

Since American Catholic colleges had been founded for the education of young Catholic *lay* men and women, and a growing proportion of their administrators and faculties were laypersons, the impact on the campus of the new teaching on the role of the laity in the church was almost instantaneous.[57] While there were other societal factors at work in changing the campus climate of the sixties, the ecclesial revolution in the church's self-understanding furnished the basic justification for many of the "liberal" changes already underway. Presentations made by many European visitors to the United States during the Council, especially in 1963 and 1964, found receptive audiences even prior to the publication of the documents.[58]

In his address at NCEA in 1967, Philip Gleason could say with some assurance: "It will suffice here merely to call attention to this factor [impact of Vatican Council II] since the influence of the Council and the postconciliar atmosphere, and its relationship to the new emphasis on freedom in Catholic institutions, is so obvious that discussion would be superfluous."[59] While recognition of the fact that the Council placed a high priority on individual freedom may have been present in 1967, the consequences of the new emphasis on freedom would only gradually be realized over the next three decades.

Spirit and Practice of Ecumenism

Once respect for individual consciences was fostered, Catholics began to have a wider vision of society and a changed perception of non-Catholic Christians. The Catholic church in the United States had a history of involuntary subordination to the dominant Protestant culture. In reaction, there were episcopal strictures against mingling with non-Catholics, participation in events sponsored by Protestant churches, membership in organizations like the YMCA, and above all, perhaps, against attendance at nonsectarian colleges or universities. As late as 1960, Archbishop Ritter, known in general as a progressive pastor, informed the people of St. Louis that no one might send a child to a non-Catholic college without his explicit and written permission. "We are alarmed and grieved," he wrote on June 17, "at the number of graduates who are selecting secular and non-Catholic colleges. . . . Many do not follow the requirements of the law that they seek our permission which is to be secured through their devoted pastors to attend these secular schools." Only a "grave reason" could excuse parents and students from choosing a Catholic college, since "when they come to the selection of a college their Faith and religion must be foremost in their minds."[60] It was well known that priests and religious, not only in St. Louis but elsewhere, often refused to send recommendations for graduating seniors in their high schools to non-Catholic institutions.

Here again the winds of change were strong. The theological groundwork had been laid to overturn these judgments. The work of Yves Congar furnished an understanding of church unity which challenged others to rethink their attitude toward the "separated brethren." Congar called on Catholics to focus on the second word, "brethren," more than

on the first, "separated." Exploring the meaning of the church in the
thought of Aquinas and extending it through the concept of the Mys-
tical Body of Christ, Congar, in the 1953 work *Esquisses du Mystère de
l'Église* and a companion volume, *La Pentcôte Chartres,*[61] examined the
roots of the Protestant Reformation and the Orthodox schism so as to
understand better the decisions of the Council of Trent and the resulting discipline in the Roman church.

A practical illustration of Congar's understanding of Christian unity
can be seen in Pope John XXIII's *Pacem in Terris,* issued just two months
before his death in 1963. The pope began by addressing his words not
only to those in communion with the Apostolic See but also to "all
men of good will." Much of what he wrote about justice and peace was
based on natural law and the Gospel, and he hoped that such an approach would provide a basis for collaboration among Christians as well
as with those outside the Christian tradition. While he in no way diminished the need to avoid compromise in matters of faith, he urged
Catholics to "show themselves to be animated by a spirit of understanding and detachment, and disposed to work loyally in the pursuit of
objectives which are of their nature good, or conducive to good."[62] Contrary to earlier practice, he urged joining with non-Catholics in discussion: "Meetings and agreements, in the various sectors of daily life, between believers and those who do not believe or believe insufficiently
because they adhere to error, can be the occasions for discovering truth
and paying homage to it."[63]

This was a revolutionary bit of advice for American Catholics who
had been taught to avoid contact with non-Catholics and their institutions. Within a decade the impact on Catholic higher education was
widespread and significant. Pope John's invitation to the other Christian churches to send observers to Vatican Council II, his establishment
of the Secretariat of Christian Unity in 1960 with Cardinal Bea at its
head, and his reception of the Archbishop of Canterbury at the end of
that same year gave a signal that was loud and clear.

Almost overnight the ecumenical outreach transformed the Catholic colleges in a way they could not have foreseen. Fewer religious regis-
tered at Catholic universities once they could receive permission to
study at Harvard or Yale;[64] students' applications were no longer held
up by vigilant principals in Catholic high schools; enrollments from the
Catholic high schools notably declined; and Catholic college curricula
were revised in order to offer theology or religious studies options to
both Catholic and non-Catholic students. As time went on, liturgies on

campus were sometimes altered in order to be more "ecumenical." Hiring policies, especially in religious studies departments, now advocated seeking out non-Catholic faculty in order to offer greater variety of content as well as different points of view. Admissions offices gave new attention to non-Catholic students.

Leaders in Catholic higher education had already begun to mingle more freely with their colleagues in other colleges and universities and in professional associations and civic groups. In 1957 Sister Ann Ida Gannon, president of Mundelein College, had been the keynote speaker at the Religious Education Association meeting and Father Theodore Hesburgh had been appointed to the national Civil Rights Commission. Hesburgh served as chair of the Association of American Colleges from 1961 to 1962, a position later held by Rev. Paul Reinert, S.J., of Saint Louis University and by Rev. Vincent Flynn and Rev. James P. Shannon, presidents of the College of Saint Thomas. The latter was also president of the Higher Education Committee of the Minnesota Education Association. Rev. Laurence McGinley, S.J., president of Fordham University, was an early participant in the leadership of the Middle States Association of Colleges and Universities, and Sister Ann Ida Gannon was the first woman to serve on the North Central Association Board. Roman collars and religious habits now were very visible at higher education meetings, and many of the presidents made it a point to be heard as well as seen. One notable attendee was Mother Elinor O'Byrne, R.S.C.J., president of Manhattanville College of the Sacred Heart, whose knitting marked her place in the front row of many such gatherings and whose comments on the topic under consideration never resulted in even one dropped stitch.

All of these moves into the mainstream of American higher education had the concomitant effect of providing opportunities for interdenominational dialogue. Especially in the Association of American Colleges, bonds were forged among the church-related colleges that would strengthen their influence as a particular cohort in the private college sector. Working with non-Catholic colleagues in higher education, the presidents and others in administration and on faculties of Catholic colleges soon saw the commonalities in their missions.

In the spirit of John XXIII, presidents of Catholic universities encouraged invitations to speakers from other churches. In 1960 Rev. Gustave Weigel, S.J., Dr. Will Herberg, and Rev. J. V. Langmead Casserly, an Anglican priest, were the presenters on a panel discussing "Toward Greater Understanding" at the annual alumnae college at the College of

New Rochelle. In 1962 there were symposia on ecumenism at St. Xavier College in Chicago, Saint Mary of the Woods (Terre Haute, Indiana), and Alverno College in Milwaukee. The NCEA College and University Department, Eastern Division, made ecumenism its topic for the meeting in 1962. In 1963 there were inter-faith meetings at Merrimack (Massachusetts) and Saint Edward's College (Austin, Texas) to discuss Hans Küng's *The Council, Reform and Reunion.*[65] Protestant theologians were added to faculties at colleges such as St. Norbert's (Wisconsin) as well as at major universities such as Fordham. In 1964 the *Journal of Ecumenical Studies* was initiated at Duquesne University. *Cross Currents* continued its work of bringing authors of other traditions to the attention of Roman Catholics. *Commonweal* and *America* filled their pages in the early sixties with book reviews and articles dealing with ecumenism. The journey to Vatican Council II and its final declarations on the subject was well prepared for, indeed, had already begun.

John XXIII's approach to the "separated brethren" was already clear in *Pacem in Terris.* His openness to the other Christian traditions was endorsed by Vatican Council II in its 1964 Decree on Ecumenism.[66] Subsequent documents on mixed marriages, ecumenical liturgical services, and theological studies were followed by a Directory on Ecumenism in Higher Education (April 16, 1970). Bishops were urged to implement the general principles enunciated in the decree and, in the spirit of Vatican II, to include in carrying out their task religious superiors, rectors, administrators, specialists in religious education, and practicing teachers—and should "bring representatives of the students into consultation when necessary."[67] All those engaged in higher education were strongly encouraged to support joint efforts by the various communions in areas of theological inquiry, study of history, and socially benevolent activities. Students should be brought into contact with those of other faiths and work together with them in various ways. This Directory on Ecumenism in Higher Education is an enlightening resource for those attempting to understand the rapid change in Catholic universities' attitudes toward non-Catholics.

Many statements in the Council's Decree on Ecumenism itself were revolutionary:

> Moreover, some, even very many, of the most significant elements and endowments which together go to build up and give life to the Church itself, can exist outside the visible boundaries of the Catholic Church. (Chapter 1)

> The brethren divided from us also carry out many liturgical actions of the Christian religion. In ways that vary according to the condition of each

Church or community, these liturgical actions most certainly can truly engender a life of grace, and, one must say, can aptly give access to the communion of salvation. (Ibid.)

Sacred theology and other branches of knowledge, especially those of a
historical nature, must be taught with due regard for the ecumenical point
of view, so that they may correspond as exactly as possible with the facts.
(Chapter 2, 10)

These statements reenforced the effects of *Pacem in Terris*. One of
the results which would prove detrimental for Catholic colleges, however, was the new freedom of students and their parents to choose
non-Catholic colleges and universities. For example, a report by Eugene
Grollmes, S.J., on fourteen "feeder" schools (all in the Saint Louis Archdiocese) for Saint Louis University during the years 1959–69, points out
that although there was a 33 percent increase in Catholic high school
graduates in the archdiocese going on to college, there was a 43 percent
decrease in the number going to Catholic colleges. From 1964 to 1969
there was a 38 percent decrease of enrollment from these feeder schools
for Saint Louis University.[68]

The NCEA *College Newsletter* for the late sixties and early seventies
reports on a variety of collaborative arrangements between Catholic
colleges and nondenominational or public institutions. Santa Clara
College was working with Stanford (vol. 27, no. 4); Fordham University
announced an agreement with Union Theological School (vol. 28, no. 3);
the New York Province of Jesuits announced that it would make more
men available for teaching posts at secular colleges, at the expense of
staffing Jesuit colleges and high schools (vol. 31, no. 2); Rev. Timothy
Healy, S.J., was named Vice Chancellor for Academic Affairs at the
City College of New York (vol. 30, no. 2, 1969). Cross-registration with
non-Catholic schools permitted students to explore various religions,
and several Catholic colleges began to hire non-Catholic faculty in their
theology or religious studies departments.

By 1970 the ecumenical movement was alive and well on most Catholic campuses. Student organizations such as the National Federation
of Catholic College Students gave way to broader-based national associations, where the interaction among students of many faiths (or
of none) gave students an environment which was different from that
experienced in an exclusively "Catholic" culture. In the summer of 1970
a large convention was held at St. Mary's College, Notre Dame, called
"Campus '70." It was a successor to the Quadrennial Convocations
of Christian Colleges, but this time was cosponsored by the NCEA

College and University Department and the Council of Protestant Colleges and Universities.

This new bonding with students from all types of colleges and universities flowered during the days of the anti-Vietnam protests. On a faculty level something similar happened under the leadership of the "Clergy and Laity Concerned" organization. Barriers were broken in the rush to join hands in opposing injustice and war; actions ran ahead of theological reflection, a reflection, we should note, that was urged by all the various decrees on ecumenical endeavor.

Indeed, such theological reflection was clearly needed. Ahead lay a troubling contrast between the rhetoric of Christian faith and fellowship (including concern for the marginal groups in society) and a lifestyle among students which ignored the moral teaching of the Gospel.[69] In the drive to overcome Catholic separatist patterns of the preceding generations, many young people abandoned fundamental Christian values. In urging a less rigid kind of Catholicism, Vatican Council II had not intended to negate the traditional understanding of right and wrong or to deny the effects of original sin. However, it would take time to create models and structures supportive of a new vision of grace and freedom in the living out of the Christian message.

The typical Catholic college of the fifties, intrinsically related to a Catholic culture of home, school, and church, was fast disappearing in the wake of societal and ecclesial changes. Decisions made and actions taken by the leaders of Catholic higher education between 1960 and 1965 would have serious consequences.

Concern about the dramatic changes appearing on the campuses of Jesuit colleges, for example, led the Board of Governors of the Jesuit Educational Association to establish a committee in May 1960 to study the "objectives" of American Jesuit universities. A draft report submitted to the board in 1962 by the chair of the committee, Rev. Robert F. Harvanek, S.J., explained the difficulty of the task given to the committee. It pointed out that in 1958 the Father General had approved the guidelines submitted by the provincials for the expansion of the universities in keeping with Jesuit educational tradition, but recent decisions seem to go in a different direction. "We are building autonomous expanding universities," said the committee. "Many of the decisions have already been taken." Harvanek saw little point in trying to establish "principles" for decision making when the decisions were already made.[70] By the end of the decade, this was even more true.

Similar acceleration in the rate of change could be observed on the campus of the University of Notre Dame. In 1961 a committee was appointed to "suggest ways for improving the intellectual substance of the College." The previous review of the curriculum (1953) had urged greater integration of the curriculum around neo-scholastic philosophy and theology; now, in 1961, the approach was highly departmental and specialized. This approach, according to Philip Gleason, "represented a significant movement in the direction of secular norms of excellence and away from the older belief that Catholic higher education should embody and make available to its students a distinctive Catholic intellectual vision whose most characteristic mark was its synthesizing."[71] Most college presidents at the time seem to have been unaware of the drastic movement away from a Catholic intellectual vision which Gleason perceives.

Despite the secular norms, the "Catholic" character of the university was palpable to at least two new faculty members at Notre Dame in 1962, Timothy O'Meara, newly arrived from Princeton University as a professor of mathematics and later to be provost of the university, and Morris Pollard, a Jewish biologist from the University of Texas who would spend the next thirty-two years at Notre Dame.[72] The faculty at Notre Dame already included members of almost every religious tradition, a decision seen by Hesburgh as necessary to the realization of his dream of Notre Dame becoming "a great Catholic university," bringing together a community of scholars and giving them the "elbow room" advocated by Cardinal Newman so that the church could do some of its best thinking, while the faculty and students would grow in their search for wisdom and in their commitment to work for the welfare of the global community.[73] Hesburgh's vision was never to waver in his pursuit of excellence, ecumenism, and firmness of faith. Other presidents would count heavily on his leadership in the coming years.

Newly confident in their "manifest destiny" of playing a significant role in American higher education, the Catholic colleges and universities were to evolve with the determination that had characterized each phase of their earlier development. The pioneer spirit which had animated them from the time of their feeble beginnings through fires, economic disasters, and anti-Catholic prejudice, would now enable them to meet a host of new challenges, challenges that arose from their desire to be significant players in the *modern* academic world.

TWO

The Americanization of Catholic Colleges and Universities

The movement toward greater assimilation into American culture did not immediately find itself welcome in the existing structures of school or church. The emphasis on human freedom and the dignity of each person which was at the core of the new philosophical and theological scholarship, and so congruent with American thought, inevitably meant a search for horizontal as well as vertical modes of decision making. Authority would come to be exercised more and more through the collaboration of the various constituencies within the university structure. This meant continuous consultation with all those who had a stake in Catholic higher education: government on both state and federal levels, the other institutions in American higher education, the Catholic community, and the trustees, administration, faculty, and students of the university or college. Since each of these groups was itself undergoing significant changes, a study of their evolution must accompany our attempt to understand Catholic higher education's search for its proper identity. The various partners to the dialogue would come to the table with their own interests, agenda, and power; the task would be to discern the proper mode of action if both terms in the description "Catholic university" were to be maintained.

The Mood of the Sixties

The passage from the fifties to the sixties was symbolized by two new leaders: the young John F. Kennedy and the aging John XXIII. Both inspired men and women from every walk of life and in their short reigns as president and pope gave birth to a new generation. It was a genera-

broadest possible participation of the members of the academic community."[66] In order to achieve such participation, some institutions created structures of internal government wherein faculty, students, and administration met together about policies. In some cases students and faculty were also given places on boards of trustees, on committees of the board, or as "young trustees" soon after graduation.[67]

Some faculty took a dim view of the "new" students, who often saw themselves as "consumers." The rising unemployment rates in the seventies put pressure on these students to take more "practical" courses and fewer of the liberal arts courses to which most of their professors were devoted. Since nationally, only about one-third of all students lived on campus, it was difficult to create a sense of community, and student participation in the new committee structures, once greeted with enthusiasm, soon declined. According to one author, collegians of the 1970s "held high hopes for personal achievement at the same time they were deeply pessimistic about the future of the society."[68] Their desire to shape that future was also muted. On the other hand, their self-image as "consumers" led to threats of litigation unheard of in the past.

Enrollment figures for the 1970s began with a decline and then, contrary to predictions, regained strength after 1972. But this is precisely the point at which one can identify the rapidly changing student population. In terms of full-time equivalent students, enrollment in Catholic colleges went from 363,029 in 1970–71 to 407,135 in 1977–78. This growth was not uniform, and in many colleges the growth was almost entirely in part-time students. According to Joseph Pettit, Catholic colleges and universities grew in full-time enrollment from 1970 to 1980 by 16 percent while part-time enrollment went up 51 percent. From 1980 to 1988 the full-time increase was by 1 percent and the part-time by 17 percent.[69]

In common with other American colleges and universities, the Catholic cohort had to deal with this changing "market" and the consequent need for more and better facilities and personnel. It was also important for them to do so in a way that responded to contemporary needs without sacrificing traditional values. The larger Catholic universities focused on competing for research grants and winning public recognition for the quality of their programs, while some of the smaller universities and the liberal arts colleges found their market by developing alternative ways of achieving degrees for adult and part-time students and by seeking awards for innovative programs. With less uniform requirements in the curriculum, they needed to develop courses seen as "relevant" by contemporary students in order to attract sufficient numbers of them.[70] With student life no longer supervised by religious mentors acting "in loco parentis," they had to expand the efforts of campus ministry and student-life personnel.[71]

The campus climate in the seventies has never received a commonly-accepted description. According to one author, "For many who were young and idealistic in the 1960's it was a grey and dreary end to an age of dreams and excitement. [But] for those who came of age in the '70's, it was a time of exciting cultural and social experiment and change, although it is often debatable just how deep or long lasting those changes were."[72]

Obviously, it was not easy to know how to respond to the new "market," but it is clear that administrators were impressed by its complexities. The concerns of the Catholic colleges and universities can be gleaned from a communication to the membership of the NCEA College and University Department on April 15, 1971, from its Executive Secretary summarizing the activities of the higher education associations in Washington. In an effort to avoid duplicating the activities of the other associations, especially those whose staff dealt with federal relations, the College and University Department was focusing its small resources on the areas of campus ministry, finances, purpose and identity, and college relations. The latter referred to relations between the colleges and their sponsoring religious communities,[73] and in this area Father Friedman, the Executive Secretary, thought the association needed to take some initiative. The question of "sponsorship" was a distinctly Catholic concern. Nevertheless, it was interwoven with the broader issues and could not be dealt with in isolation from the questions of finances, personnel, and mission as "Catholic," concerns which were intensified by the wave of departures of men and women from religious life.

The calls for reform of Catholic higher education which had appeared in many publications in the late fifties and early sixties had been taken seriously by the administrators of the institutions. Critics such as Andrew Greeley, John Tracy Ellis, and Neil G. McCluskey had urged the colleges and universities into the mainstream of American higher education, and now these institutions were perceived less and less as a subculture with its own symbols and language. In taking steps in this direction, they had been encouraged by the Executive Secretary of NCEA. In a memo to the members on October 24, 1968, Father Friedman called attention to an article by Francis Gallagher, the lawyer defending the Catholic colleges in the *Horace Mann* case, in which Catholic colleges and universities were urged to drop their "devotionalism and sectarianism." Friedman had already urged the president of Manhattanville College of the Sacred Heart to drop the "Sacred Heart" from its title,[74] and he expressed the view that the names of religious communities used in titles of colleges should give way to the more generic name, "Catholic." He also urged more collaborative activities among Catholic colleges and more ecumenical outreach to other independent institutions.[75]

One indication of a desire to move into the mainstream was the constant talk about "academic excellence." As a way of proving that they had demanding programs and high standards, colleges placed renewed emphasis on being admitted to the world of Phi Beta Kappa, the prestigious honor society of liberal arts colleges to which only two Catholic colleges had been admitted before World War II, when a moratorium was placed on new acceptances. Critics accused PBK of discrimination against Catholic institutions, while PBK defended itself on the grounds that the colleges that had applied lacked academic excellence, were too involved in athletics (Georgetown), or were controlled by the church (The Catholic University of America) or religious community. In an article in *America* as early as 1958, Neil G. McCluskey, S.J., had complained about the discrimination by PBK. In the same magazine, others who opposed the move toward PBK recognition insisted they had no desire to give up "Catholic" values in order to be recognized as similar to "secular" universities. Although the College of St. Catherine was given a Phi Beta Kappa chapter in 1938, Georgetown and Catholic University were forced to wait. This is partly explained by the fact that a new chapter had to be approved by neighboring chapters, not by a central office with uniform criteria, and there had to be a number of PBK faculty already at the college requesting a chapter. Many Catholic institutions were hampered by the fact that their faculties, by and large, had been educated in universities and/or theologates lacking a chapter and therefore could not be admitted to membership. (By 1977 a dozen Catholic colleges had been admitted.[76])

Maintaining a high degree of excellence required greater financial resources than most of the Catholic colleges possessed. Funds from governmental sources as well as from private foundations and individual donors were clearly needed.

Bundy Money

Could additional funding be found in the several states? The question of eligibility for state funding was particularly complicated for those

Catholic colleges and universities located in New York State. A leader in private higher education (its state system developed only after World War II), New York was searching for a way to assist private universities faced with the financial pressures brought on by increasing enrollments. In 1967 Governor Nelson Rockefeller appointed a Select Commission on the Future of Private and Independent Higher Education, headed by McGeorge Bundy, whose name became synonymous with the commission. Again we find Father Hesburgh as a member of that commission, a significant recognition of the emerging importance of Catholic colleges. Unfortunately, the recommendation by the commission to Governor Rockefeller to grant "Bundy money" to all accredited institutions according to the number of degrees awarded each year was countered in the legislature by those who regarded the inclusion of church-related institutions as a violation of the Blaine Amendment to the New York State Constitution, which forbade any public funds going to "sectarian" purposes. At this time, voters were being asked to amend the constitution, and it was hoped that the Blaine Amendment would be repealed. When the repeal effort failed, the legislature voted (May 13, 1968) to grant the aid to "all those institutions not covered under the Blaine Amendment."[77]

The State Department of Education prepared to implement the new law. A questionnaire on eligibility was circulated to all presidents of private institutions (August 1968) concerning the degree of relatedness to church bodies.[78] Rather than create its own list of questions, the Department of Education used the criteria developed in the *Horace Mann* case of 1966, which, as we have seen, furnished the basis for the ruling against two Catholic colleges in Maryland.[79] To prepare a response to the questionnaire, presidents and trustees consulted with their legal counsel and attempted to present themselves as religious or Christian but "nonsectarian." When the awards were announced, only Fordham University, St. John Fisher University, and Manhattanville College were among those receiving Bundy money.[80] In the next few years several other Catholic colleges—New Rochelle, Canisius, Iona, and Marymount—sued in the state courts to be declared eligible and eventually won because they were judged to be no longer "sectarian." By 1975 all of the Catholic colleges in the state, with the exception of St. John's, Niagara, and Molloy, had chosen to apply.[81] By 1995 only St. John's, by conscious decision, remained outside the group of Bundy recipients. Its leadership did not want to surrender the right to identify the university in its printed materials as "Catholic."

Other states developed scholarship programs and various means of assisting private higher education through grants and loans, but the Bundy approach was unique. Over the years it resulted in particular sensitivity among the Catholic colleges in New York State to any suggestion of an overtly-stated relationship to the church. One of the conditions for receiving Bundy money was that the college would not call itself a "Catholic" college in its printed materials. The ignorance of officials in Albany was clear when they indicated that colleges could identify themselves as a "Jesuit" or "Franciscan" college but not a "Catholic" one.[82] Obviously, this contradicted the trend promoted by Father Friedman to emphasize the common Catholic identity rather than the individual religious community's charism.

One of the questions that arose was, "Could the New York State Catholic colleges hold membership in NCEA?" Some colleges immediately withdrew, but Brother Gregory Nugent, president of Manhattan College, reported to the 1971 association meeting that the New York State Department of Education did not consider it necessary that the colleges drop membership in the NCEA, since it was a voluntary association and not an instrument of control.[83] Eventually, all the Catholic colleges in New York except Manhattanville (which had publicly asserted its "secular" identity) renewed their membership.

Although no other state had as restrictive a constitution as New York, all of the Catholic colleges in the country shared in the additional ambiguity the Bundy money introduced. It cast a shadow far beyond New York State. In retrospect, we can identify changes that were made in the 1970s out of fear over how "Bundy" would be interpreted rather than because of specific federal or state regulations which mandated certain actions. A reading of the questionnaire makes it clear that the fears were not unjustified.[84] The inferences to be drawn from the questions suggested certain assumptions about "sectarianism" that would determine the state's response to the college's answers. In some colleges the crucifixes were removed from classrooms, and statues and pictures with religious meaning were no longer seen in dining halls and libraries. The fear of a challenge in the courts by those opposed to giving public money to private institutions with a religious heritage may have led to unnecessary adaptations. Not all the fears of colleges were irrational. A list of the supporting associations for the plaintiffs in the *Horace Mann* and *Tilton* cases gave evidence of an ongoing crusade against church-related colleges. Catholic colleges and universities had to walk a fine line between the legal implications of "independent" and the legal implications of "sectarian." This fine line was not always understood or appreciated by their Catholic constituencies: parents, parishes, alumnae/i, and church authorities.

The Catholic Identity Question

What was the distinctive character that the Catholic college or university was attempting to preserve, despite the need to be "nonsectarian" in the legal sense of the term? The visible signs of Catholic faith and practice had already begun to diminish on the campuses, not only in New York but elsewhere, in the early sixties, thus predating the availability of state or federal aid and the legal decisions mentioned above. Daily attendance at Mass, strict rules regarding behavior not only of students but also of faculty, standards of decorum in speech and dress, negative decisions regarding divorced and remarried faculty, denial of tenure to those who publicly disputed church teaching—all these regulations began to be ignored or repealed.[85] By the mid-sixties the administrators in Catholic colleges concluded that they could no longer govern students "in loco parentis"[86] or lay down paternalistic or maternalistic rules for faculty conduct. The university as "family" needed new models of internal governance to cope with the changes present in society.

As late as the 1950s with its strong parochial school system, its loyalty oaths for teachers, and its legion of decency pledges, Catholics knew very clearly what they believed in. Faculty handbooks explicitly required that there could be no criticism of the United States Constitution or the teachings of the Roman Catholic faith. The culture of these years can be viewed in retrospect as a time of harmonious integration of faith and intellectual life, a "Catholic revival" to lead the ever-present battle against secularism.[87] Or it can be perceived as the time when Catholics lived in a ghetto, protected from many social currents and making little dent on the intellectual and cultural life of academia.[88] But whichever view is adopted, the kind of Catholic university that evolved in the late 1960s defined itself in a very new way. Often utilizing the Vatican Council II documents, especially *Gaudium et Spes*, presidential oratory emphasized the need for the Catholic university, as mediator of faith to culture, to carry out its mission in the contemporary world. Such a role required presence in and recognition by that world despite the ambiguities that would result. A distinctly "Catholic" culture would no longer be an option.

The consequent question that would be front and center in the following years, while not a new question, had a new intensity: "What really makes a university Catholic?" If the statement of its mission included the moral education or formation of the student, a formation rooted in Catholic faith, it was difficult to assert at the same time the nonsectarian character of the institution. The questionnaire sent to all New York State colleges in connection with eligibility for Bundy money was a concrete example of the problem. Included in it were questions on the stated purposes of the institution, the relationship of the institution to an ecclesiastical body, and the place of religion in the college program, including character formation and extent of religious observance required, sponsored, or encouraged. While these questions were justified by the State Department of Education as necessary to ascertain the degree of "control" exercised by the church, did they not suggest that the faith that lay at the heart of the university's identity as Catholic was itself the problem?[89]

The attempt to think through this dilemma in terms of the educational tradition of American Catholic colleges, free from state control but now increasingly dependent on the state's financial support, proved to be far more challenging than the somewhat philosophical concerns about autonomy expressed by leaders from Catholic universities in other parts of the world. In traditional European universities, as well as in many South American and Asian counterparts, the faith development and moral decisions of the student were not considered a responsibility of the university. It was assumed that the student of university level (who was generally older than the American college student) had already received whatever religious education was needed. In American Catholic colleges and universities, on the other hand, it was assumed that courses in religion were an important part of the curriculum for all students, and the formation of the student's character was an essential part of the institution's mission. This disparity made it difficult for the IFCU to formulate a statement of mission and purpose for Catholic universities that would be applicable in all countries.[90] The various drafts proposed for the document on Catholic universities in the modern world emphasized the broad questions of autonomy and academic freedom but said nothing of curriculum (except for separate theological faculties) or student life.

In 1965, as we have noted, the International Federation of Catholic Universities met in Tokyo and tackled the question of the nature of a Catholic university from the point of view of its necessary autonomy.[91] Such autonomy concerned the freedom to teach and the freedom to learn, the age-old prerogatives of a university. For some of the IFCU members, the defense of autonomy was mainly needed as a protection against the state; for the Americans, already protected by the First Amendment, it focused more on the institution's self-governance vis-à-vis the church as expressed through the bishops, the superiors of the religious orders, and the Sacred Congregation for Catholic Education. The moment was ripe for a consideration of this question in the light of Vatican Council II and the document *Dignitatis humanae* (December 7, 1965).

Such was the agenda for the regional IFCU meeting convened by Father Hesburgh at Land O'Lakes in 1967. The outcome of this meeting, a document entitled "The Nature of the Contemporary Catholic University,"[92] has often been acclaimed as a statement of independence from the church by Catholic colleges and universities in the United States. Its opening statement, "To perform its teaching and research functions effectively the Catholic university must have a true autonomy and academic freedom in the face of authority of whatever kind, lay or clerical, external to the academic community itself," was hailed by many as a legitimate and necessary claim. Others saw it as a destructive one that would lead the Catholic universities away from the church and down the slippery path to total secularization.[93]

Both groups often ignored the second paragraph: "Distinctively, then, the Catholic university must be an institution, a community of learners or a community of scholars, in which Catholicism is perceptibly present and effectively operative." The document claimed that this presence required outstanding scholars and academic programs in theology. It concluded: "the Catholic university of the future will be a true modern university but specifically Catholic in profound and creative ways for the service of society and the people of God."

The Land O'Lakes statement was partly incorporated into the IFCU Kinshasa paper in 1968 and the subsequent meetings in Rome leading up to the 1972 document "The Catholic University in the Modern World." Perhaps the major struggle occurred after the World Congress of Catholic Universities which met in Rome from April 25 to May 1, 1969.[94]

Freedom on the Campus

While the rhetoric for describing academic freedom and institutional autonomy in Catholic higher education was being hammered out in a series of regional and international meetings, the day-to-day life on campuses already reflected a post–Vatican Council II concept of human freedom. We have mentioned earlier the impact that Pope John XXIII had on Catholic higher education. It was, to be sure, mostly indirect, through the work of Vatican Council II, but the emphasis he gave to human freedom in his 1963 encyclical, *Pacem in Terris,* inspired a rethinking of the kind of discipline then prevailing in Catholic colleges. "Only in freedom can man do good," the pope wrote, so deans and presidents began to wonder if their students had enough freedom to learn how to make responsible choices. The sixties and seventies would see a totally new life-style on Catholic college campuses, one based on a heightened awareness of the psychological and sociological atmosphere in American society and supported by the strong commitment to respect for individual freedom.[95] An interesting letter from the president of the College of the Holy Cross to the bishop of Worcester shows that this kind of question had already occurred to superiors in Rome. Father Swords wrote to the bishop that Father General wished the Jesuits at Holy Cross to stop using disciplinary sanctions in connection with compulsory Mass attendance lest the students have the wrong motive for attending. Holy Cross wishes to do this, he told the bishop, but they would also like permission to have evening masses, so that the students will have choice about daily mass.[96] College leaders hoped that the new liturgical rites and the wider scope for lay participation would engender not only a positive student response to the abolition of required attendance, but also a high degree of attendance at the newly-permitted evening masses.

Freedom was also the underlying value preached by those who urged curriculum revision in order to minimize required courses and maximize student choice. This movement was another indication of dissatisfaction with the old ways. By the mid-sixties there was already a call for less structure in classes, fewer requirements, and individually-designed interdisciplinary majors. All of these academic "reforms" were in place within the next decade.

On many Catholic campuses the debate about a new core of requirements focused on the role of religion and philosophy courses, a topic explored further in chapter 4. The study of religion was being developed in other private and public colleges, and faculty in those non-Catholic institutions were seeking public recognition for the study of religion as a viable academic discipline. In 1963 the American Academy of Religion was organized primarily by Protestant religion teachers to justify their courses in secular universities. Catholic institutions utilized the same argument, i.e., that it was a true academic discipline and not apologetic, in their attempt to justify their programs as worthy of degree credit. In 1954 the teachers of religion in Catholic colleges had founded the Society of Catholic College Teachers of Sacred Doctrine. By the late sixties it had evolved into the College Theology Society, the change of name being indicative of the change in methodology in college classrooms, and had decided that the purpose of religious education in colleges was not "confessional" but rather to understand "an important human concern."[97]

On some Catholic campuses the religion program was named theology; in other cases the term "religious studies" was used. What was clear was that the old seminary-inspired texts and the apologetics approach were no longer acceptable. Some colleges introduced a course based on the *Summa* of St. Thomas Aquinas; others followed the lead of John Courtney Murray, S.J., Bernard Cooke, S.J., and Gerard Sloyan in emphasizing the use of Scripture and the history of Christianity. According to Patrick Carey, in all of these attempts, "Historical consciousness provided the integrating core of the discipline and the curriculum."[98] But in whatever direction they moved, religion departments no longer saw their mission as fulfilling a pastoral function. Rather, it was a rigorously academic, "non-confessional" study of religion as a universal human phenomenon.

Struggles of the Sixties

As presidents defended the independence and autonomy of their institutions, faculty began to insist on more recognition of their role in the governance of the universities. Not only did they fight for the freedom to express their opinions without fear of recrimination from those in authority, but they also pressed for control over hiring, tenure, salaries, and firing. Settlement of grievances behind closed doors, so common, as we saw, in earlier times, was no longer acceptable.

The link between individual academic freedom and faculty involvement in institutional governance became especially clear in the faculty strike at St. John's University, New York, in 1965. Indeed, this strike became a defining moment in Catholic higher education. It is helpful to recall the understanding of academic freedom that had characterized Catholic colleges and universities in the United States and to test it against the criteria established by the American Association of University Professors as enunciated in their Statement of Principles of 1940.[99]

Academic freedom in European universities had traditionally referred to a teacher's right to express his or her opinions without fear of recrimination from those in authority. It also pertained to the right of the university student to explore various fields of knowledge and come to conclusions different from the teacher's. Since most American colleges were founded by religious denominations, the difficulties over academic freedom often related to the strictures placed on faculty by church bodies rather than governments.

In the twentieth century, the self-appointed guardians of academic freedom in America have been two major professional groups: the American Association of University Professors and the regional accrediting agencies that determine standards and evaluate performance. Among the areas the accrediting agencies examine is the extent to which institutions comply with AAUP principles and the commitment they show to an environment of freedom on their campuses.[100]

There was little attention paid to academic freedom at the annual gatherings of the National Catholic Education Association (College and University Department) prior to 1965. Until then most treatments of the topic on the part of Catholic leaders were limited to proclaiming the freedom of faculty to "teach what is true." In 1936 a resolution had been passed at an NCEA meeting favoring academic freedom "rightly understood," which meant that it was the freedom to "teach what is true."[101] In the fifties and sixties faculty handbooks of several Catholic universities state that "Faculty are free to teach provided their statements are not contrary to the teaching of the Catholic church or the Constitution of the United States." This concept was challenged by Professor Gerald F. Kreyche of DePaul University in a talk at NCEA in 1965.[102] He urged the members to embrace the normal academic guidelines regarding academic freedom. At a major symposium held at the University of Notre Dame the following year, the presenters argued strongly for an end to specific "Catholic" restrictions on freedom.[103]

Another troublesome area in the sixties regarding academic freedom concerned invitations to persons outside the college community to speak on campus. An illustration of the furor caused by anyone suspected of socialist or communist leanings was the case of Roger Garaudy, a French philosopher who was invited to speak at Saint Louis University by the philosophy department in November 1966. Loud protests came from irate alumni who opposed having such a "socialist" as a guest of the university. President Reinert handled the situation by closing the lecture to the public and at the same time defending the right of the philosophy department to bring Garaudy to speak to faculty and students as a matter of academic freedom.[104] In a similar case at Santa Clara University in 1967, President Patrick A. Donohoe defended a Christian/Marxist dialogue despite pressure from outside the campus walls.[105]

A different reason was given for the "speakers ban" imposed by the rector of The Catholic University of America on four distinguished participants in Vatican Council II. In 1963 the graduate student council had listed Godfrey Diekman, O.S.B., John Courtney Murray, S.J., Hans Küng, and Gustave Weigel, S.J., as potential invitees. The rector struck their names from the list on the grounds that "they all represented a particular point of view on issues still under study and unresolved by the Fathers of the Second Vatican Council, and that until these issues were officially settled, the University wanted to be impartial." Despite strong opposition to the rector's decision by some members of the board of trustees (Ritter, Hallinan, Alter, and Shehan), his authority was upheld. The rector, Bishop McDonald, had already embarrassed the university when he had been vice rector by his insistence that he give prior approval to all speakers; now as rector he was intensifying his control, and some trustees found his actions indefensible.[106]

Several cases alleging violation of academic freedom emerged in the sixties.[107] But the major event that served to highlight the new role that the defense of academic freedom would play in Catholic higher education was the faculty strike at St. John's University in December 1965. The significant intervention of the AAUP and the Middle States Association of Colleges and Secondary Schools in this dispute served as a wake-up call to the administrators of other Catholic universities.[108] Now that they were moving into mainstream American higher education they would have to accept the rules that prevailed there.

The issues which caused the strike at St. John's were not directly related to the freedom of individual teachers but rather to internal administrative matters: grievances about the lack of faculty participation in decision making, inadequate faculty salaries and benefits, and overall dissatisfaction with the governance and administration of the university. The fact that faculty at a Catholic university would go public with their grievances and resort to a strike, however, was indeed revolutionary.

Frustrated and angry, over two hundred (out of 522) faculty had walked out of a faculty meeting with the president in March 1965. Some of the problems were similar to those on all American campuses; inability of the administration to cope with the consequences of rapid growth was clearly one of them.[109] Another was that the university was not considering changes in the board of trustees that would bring laypersons into governance.

Rev. Edward J. Burke, C.M., had been serving as president since 1961, and there was great dissatisfaction with his lack of communication and generally negative attitude toward faculty participation. A month after the walkout from the faculty meeting, the trustees, all Vincentians, appointed Father Joseph T. Tinnelly as the Coordinator of Planning with the task of studying ways to improve the administration. Dr. John J. Meng, president of Hunter College, was named special consultant. Between April and August some steps were taken by the administration to involve faculty in the planning and the study of salaries and benefits. In July 1965 the board of trustees was reorganized to include Vincentians from other institutions, but it still excluded laypersons. On July 17, 1965, the Provincial Visitor announced the appointment of Rev. Joseph T. Cahill, C.M., as the new college president. A Faculty Planning Council, democratically elected, now prepared to work with him, but cooperative relations soon evaporated.[110] On December 15, 1965, thirty-three members of the faculty were notified that their contracts were terminated as of June 1967 and twenty-two of them were told to leave campus immediately. What had caused this precipitous action?

On December 22 Father Cahill issued a statement to explain the trustees' reasons for the terminations. It listed eight factors that entered into the decisions, most of which dealt with the authority of the trustees and the faculty's attempt to undermine it by advertisements, demonstrations, and distribution of propaganda that confused the general public. One factor that is of special note is "A continuing effort to impugn the credibility of the Vincentian community." This named the underlying tension which AAUP could not solve. Specific charges against individuals would not be made by Cahill, for he found it contrary to the "basic rules of confidence."

Part of the problem was that the board of trustees had resolved in October 1965 to adopt the AAUP Statement of Principles "in principle." Hence, the AAUP saw itself as the appropriate group to assist the faculty in this situation. To the AAUP committee the administration's case was not persuasive, partly because the other administrative officers, three deans, had not recommended the suspensions that had occurred. By mid-March of 1966 the Deputy General Secretary of the

AAUP, Dr. Bertram Davis, could write that the basic problem at St. John's was the denial of any voice to the faculty. He referred to the "stifling system whereby the Board of Trustees consisted of the administrative officers and seven faculty members, and the administration appointed the department chairmen."[111]

The situation at St. John's was also studied by the Commission on Institutions of Higher Education of the Middle States Association of Colleges and Secondary Schools and on April 29, 1966, it referred to the action taken as "reprehensible" and went on to examine the locus of responsibility for the decision. The board of trustees had stated that "the actions taken by it, [were] on its own responsibility, freely and without coercion by the administrative officers or by the Vincentian Order." Since this statement was made by the university trustees, it was accepted by the Middle States commission as locating responsibility in the legal board, not beyond it in some form of religious government.[112] The commission did not approve of the actions but agreed that "it was an act of responsible men who were convinced they were taking their responsibility seriously."

Consequently, Middle States did not revoke the accreditation of St. John's, but it did call for the correction of the serious institutional weakness in the administrative structure. The commission also expressed the opinion that the AAUP censure was "richly deserved." It mandated St. John's to show cause by December 31, 1967, why its accreditation should not be withdrawn; in other words, St. John's must reform itself so that its educational mission could go forward.[113]

The AAUP censure of St. John's occurred at the annual meeting in June 1966. This followed, as is customary with AAUP, the publication of the report of Committee A on Academic Freedom and Tenure in the spring 1966 *Academe*. AAUP's concern had spread from the initial termination notices of December 1965 to the whole structure of governance and its impact on the relationship of faculty to administration. New statutes and bylaws were formulated by St. John's board in the summer of 1966, and an ad hoc committee of AAUP visited the campus on March 21 and 22, 1967. A final report was issued in the AAUP *Bulletin* for fall 1968.[114] The report contained an analysis and criticism of the earlier statutes of St. John's (the Statutes of 1960) on the grounds that the objectives of the university "were stated in broad *theological* terms" and *a priori* approval had to be given to faculty publication by the college's committee on publications. The report noted the contrast between these older statutes, still in effect in 1966, and the new ones officially adopted in 1968. The general objectives of St. John's—in 1966—were stated as "... the offering such opportunities to achieve traditionally classical and professional education as will enable men and women to develop in learning and culture according to the philosophical and theological principles and traditions of the Roman Catholic Church." In 1968 we read, "The fundamental purpose is to offer men and women, in a Catholic atmosphere, the opportunity to achieve for themselves a higher education in the liberal arts and sciences and to prepare for certain professions. . . . [The university] is dedicated to the intellectual growth of its students. . . . [It] is committed to a Christian vision of reality," and it hopes to be "a locus where the Church is able to reflect upon itself and its mission."[115] St. John's had learned the hard way that membership in the community of American higher education had its own price. Having agreed to the AAUP guidelines "in principle," the trustees found themselves unable to justify decisions which clearly violated them. Even at St. John's, despite its opposition to seeking Bundy money, the independent denominational tone of the mission statement gave way to a generic statement of objectives.

The St. John's case had an impact that went far beyond the perimeters of Catholic institutions. Although at the time, the Middle States Association was not willing to link accreditation specifically with academic freedom, such a link was accepted operationally in subsequent years. Moreover, a proposal initiated by a faculty member from St. John's at the AAUP annual meeting in 1965 led to a full reconsideration of the "limitations clause" of the 1940 AAUP Statement of Principles.[116]

The 1940 Statement of Principles on Academic Freedom and Tenure had included recognition of the fact that church-related institutions might wish to place some restrictions on their faculty because of special objectives of the institution; AAUP insisted only that such restrictions be made clear at the time of hiring. But at the AAUP meeting in July 1965 a faculty member from St. John's introduced a motion: "Whereas it may be that the 1940 statement implies an ambiguous status for the faculties of church-related college and universities with respect to their rights to academic freedom; therefore be it resolved that the AAUP form a special committee composed predominantly of members from church-related institutions to study and make more explicit the meaning of the 1940 Statement of Principles on Academic Freedom and Tenure vis-à-vis church-related institutions."

Such a committee was formed, but before it could begin its work several other academic freedom cases arose in the Catholic sector: the

Cody affair in Chicago, the University of Dayton problem, and the decision concerning tenure for the Rev. Charles Curran, an assistant professor of moral theology at The Catholic University of America. The first two involved conflicts with the local bishop over institutional autonomy rather than academic freedom as such. We will deal with them below.

On the other hand, the case of Charles Curran was an internal institutional decision and concerned a tenure decision in a department that awarded pontifical degrees. In 1966, despite the recommendation of the theology department that Curran be promoted to the rank of associate professor, the board of trustees voted to inform him that his appointment would be terminated August 31, 1967. Perhaps emboldened by the success of the strike at St. John's, the faculty declared that, in protest against this arbitrary decision, they would not teach. A week later the chancellor, having polled the trustees, reported that the action of the board had been nullified and Curran was reinstated. This, of course, was not the end of Curran's problems at Catholic University, but the action of the board and chancellor indicated a new climate on campus and a willingness to bow to faculty demands in a way never envisioned before.[117]

Meanwhile, a subcommittee of Committee A of AAUP was attempting to clarify the meaning of the "limitations clause." However, it soon found itself involved in a more significant question: should there be a limitations clause at all? Richard H. Sullivan, president of the Association of American Colleges, reported to the AAUP committee that the Commission on Religion in Higher Education (of AAC) had adopted a resolution on April 1, 1968, which read: "the Commission is strongly opposed to having church-related colleges (or any other colleges) singled out as requiring special exemption from the principles of academic freedom, solely because of their religious aims."[118] The Council for Protestant Colleges and the College and University Department of NCEA took the position that such a clause seemed to identify church-related institutions as second-class citizens. Friedman, the Executive Secretary of the College and University Department, responded to the consultation initiated by the AAUP committee: "Unless there is at this time a significant increase in problems related to academic freedom in church-related colleges, I fail to see any need to single out these institutions. The impression might easily be left, even if unwittingly, that these are the only ones that have problems relative to academic freedom."[119]

In 1969 a series of meetings was held by a joint committee of AAC and AAUP on the question of the limitations clause. AAC had been an original cosponsor with AAUP in 1940 of the Statement of Principles, and so it was thought that the interpretation of the clause should include consultation with them. After such discussion had taken place and many responses to the published draft had been received, Committee A of AAUP reported as its conclusion that "most church-related institutions no longer need or desire the departure from the principle of academic freedom implied in the 1940 Statement and it does not endorse such a departure."[120]

The reason given in the committee report for this "interpretation" was the overwhelming response to its draft urging the abolition of the limitations clause. The committee report cited the changed atmosphere in church-related institutions:

> The attitude towards the limitations clause which these responses reflect is, in the experience of the Association, becoming increasingly widespread and emphatic. As regulations become subject to revision, particular admonitions which could serve to restrict academic freedom are being abandoned, often being replaced by assurances of full academic freedom as a requisite to genuine pursuit of the institution's broad religious aims. In recent years, issues of academic freedom in a religious context have been frequently and vigorously raised, tested, and resolved: in no case known to the Association have such resolutions embodied a limitation on academic freedom as set forth in the 1940 Statement because of an institution's religious aims.

The subcommittee had, however, gone further in its recommendations. It wished to have Committee A assert that the invocation of the limitations clause "exempts an institution from the universe of higher education." Committee A declined to adopt this recommendation, preferring instead the rather ambiguous concluding sentence of its statement: "the invocation of the clause does not relieve an institution of its obligation to afford academic freedom as called for in the 1940 Statement."[121]

AAUP dealt with academic freedom with specific attention to faculty rights. The relationship of academic freedom to institutional autonomy was also raised with regard to speaker policies, organized demonstrations for civil rights or against the Vietnam War, the free speech movement, student rights, and general campus disorders. It was not just the freedom of individual faculty or students but the right of the university to govern itself—institutional autonomy—that was threatened by both federal and state policies. The loyalty oaths of the fifties had been dropped, but by the end of the sixties, state governments were questioning the ability and the will of universities to prevent disorders on their campuses. The issue of controlling demonstrations and other forms of protest was taken up by the various state legislatures in the early seventies, and demands for stringent university policies raised questions of just how "autonomous" were private universities and colleges.[122]

Catholic universities also had their autonomy threatened in the name of religious orthodoxy.[123] The case at the University of Dayton in 1966 has gone down in history as "The Heresy Affair." Here the conflict was initiated by a member of the philosophy department, Dennis Bonnette, and had as its target other members of the philosophy department (Baltazar, Chrisman, and Ulrich). Not surprisingly, it came about because of the shift away from Thomism as an "official" philosophical system. Bonnette leveled his charges in a letter to Archbishop Karl J. Alter of Cincinnati, urging him to fulfill his duties as required by canon law. He sent a copy of his letter to the apostolic delegate, Egidio Vagnozzi. The archbishop carefully avoided interfering in the university but asked the president, Rev. Raymond A. Roesch, S.M., to investigate. Roesch had Bonnette prepare a statement substantiating the charges. It was submitted to the president under date of October 28, 1966, and charged the faculty members with "deviating from Catholic doctrine." The accused then responded to the particular charges. Father Roesch consulted Rev. James I. O'Connor, S.J., a well-known canon lawyer, and in November met with a committee set up for the purpose of reviewing the charges. Those accused were cleared and this was reported to Alter, who was satisfied. However, when the announcement was made concerning the results of the investigation on December 3, 1966, Bonnette and eight of his supporters termed the report a "whitewash" and publicized their view on Phil Donahue's radio program. Support for the president came from the Faculty Forum, which censured the eight members who had signed the Bonnette statement. Meanwhile, some local pastors expressed dissatisfaction with the religious atmosphere at the University of Dayton, and this prompted the archbishop to form a fact-finding commission. This commission found that there may have been some teaching which showed a lack of respect for the magisterium, but none of it was contrary to defined doctrines. All agreed that it would be well to have some guidelines drawn up for future use.[124]

It is important to note in this case, as in the earlier one at New Rochelle described in chapter 1, that the ecclesiastical authority did not intrude into the working of the structures within the university. In both cases, the charges came from colleagues, and proper procedures were followed to resolve the crisis, with the accused being vindicated.

On the other hand, a local situation that illustrates the kind of episcopal interference with higher education that aroused opposition from university administrators, as well as from AAUP chapters, was the so-called Cody Affair in Chicago in 1966. On September 21 Archbishop Cody gave notice that "before extending an invitation, or honoring a request, by which an extern priest takes up residence or accepts any other commitment (pastoral, executive, academic, fund-raising, etc.) in the Archdiocese of Chicago, . . . deans of university faculties [among others] must obtain certification of credentials" from the archbishop.

A public statement protesting the archbishop's decree was immediately issued by faculty from the various Catholic colleges and universities in the Chicago area. Prior certification of credentials for a person invited to a campus "constitutes . . . an intrusion" into the life of the university. The committee formed to lead the opposition stated, "Recent experiences (for example, in the organizing of symposia and lecture series) have shown that those upon whom the effect of such a decree is most likely to fall are the more creative members of the academic community whose pioneering work has brought them into controversy."[125] This time, unlike many other AAUP-supported protests, the faculty committee was supported by the administrators of the institutions. One of the objections cited by the AAUP chapter at Loyola was that the archbishop referred to the colleges as "ecclesiastical entities."[126] Although a series of three letters were sent to the archbishop, no reply was received.[127]

In the discussion carried on during this controversy, reference is made to the St. John's case, the documents of Vatican II and the role of the laity, the *Horace Mann* case regarding "sectarian" institutions, and the basic question of the role of faculty, both lay and religious, in Catholic colleges. Position papers were written and circulated among the Chicago colleges for discussion in the hope of stimulating faculty to examine their situation. In November 1966 the committee (now calling itself the Interfaculty Committee on Academic Freedom) undertook a survey of ecclesiastical control in the local Catholic colleges and universities.[128]

From the survey it is apparent that faculty concerns were broader than the Cody decree, since the questions deal with the whole question of the role of faculty in governance. In a letter to Professor Philip Denenfeld, Staff Associate for Committee A of AAUP, dated February 25, 1967, the interfaculty committee reported that it had been unable to establish communication with the archbishop, but in the meantime had stimulated discussion on committee members' campuses about the deeper question of the relation of religious commitment to the search for truth in a university setting.[129] In a position paper drawn up by some faculty at St. Xavier College, the initial sentence reads: "The fundamental proposition underlying the continued viability of the church-related institution of higher learning must be that academic values and religious commitment are not incompatible.[130] Finally, on May 30, 1967, the interfaculty committee met with Cardinal Cody and subsequently, on September 22 and October 17, with the assistant chancellor of the archdiocese, Father Richard Keating. By the end of the year attempts to negotiate a compromise had failed, and the matter was evidently dropped.

The following year Pope Paul VI issued his encyclical *Humanae vitae*, in which artificial birth control was condemned. A major protest in the form of a dissenting statement was drawn up by theologians at The Catholic University of America. Father Charles Curran was the spokesman for the group and was allied with twenty other faculty members; over six hundred scholars in the country signed the declaration.[131] The board of trustees then instructed the acting rector of the university to convene a committee that would investigate whether the dissenters had failed in their responsibilities toward the university. In March 1969 the committee gave its report, finding that the dissenters had acted responsibly, and the board accepted this decision, although making it clear that they were not implying approval of the theological position taken by the theologians.[132] By their actions, the trustees had given approval to the principle of due process and recognized the importance of academic freedom. While they still did not adopt the AAUP Principles, they acted according to them.[133]

By 1970, then, it would seem that the general thinking among administrators was to work with the AAUP Principles as much as possible, to oppose episcopal efforts to override decisions made by faculty and administrators at Catholic colleges, and to insist that they were committed to the principle of academic freedom and did not regard it as incompatible with religious commitment. During the decade ahead, faculty handbooks and policies were revised to include AAUP documents dealing with governance, student rights, and the 1970 interpretation of the 1940 Principles.

Many of these developments concerning freedom and autonomy can be related to the teaching found in *Gaudium et Spes* (*The Church in the*

Modern World). Relations with government, with foundations, with the church itself, and with other institutions of higher learning were all colored by a new appreciation of the modern world and a new understanding of the role of the Catholic university in mediating faith to secular cultures. A new generation of laity, by now well represented among the faculties, administrators, and trustees of the Catholic colleges, was attuned to the implications of Vatican II teaching and the ways it should be implemented in American culture. A similar commitment to *aggiornamento* was evident among the religious sisters, brothers, and priests who administered and taught in these institutions. Together they were ready to recognize the values in the secular world and assist their students to integrate these values with their faith traditions. To balance this recognition of secular values, equal attention might have been given to the document on the church, *Lumen Gentium,* which emphasizes some slightly different aspects of ecclesiology, but such attention seems to have been lacking.

In an address at a convocation at Fordham University in 1966, Father John Courtney Murray, S.J., summed up the distinctive relationship between the Catholic university and secular reality:

> A work of differentiation between the sacral and the secular has been effected in history. But differentiation is not the highest stage in human growth. The movement toward it, now that it has come to term, must be followed by a further movement toward a new synthesis, within which the differentiation will at once subsist, integral and unconfused, and also be transcended in a higher unity. Here, I suggest, is a task for the university that bears the name Catholic.

"The task," Murray concluded, "is to be the bearer of the new movement that will transcend the present dichotomy of sacral and secular, and it is to be the artisan of their new unity."[134] In a 1966 speech Rev. Michael Walsh, S.J., president of Boston College, linked the role of the contemporary Catholic university explicitly to Vatican Council II in a way that reinforced the commitment voiced by Murray: "The Second Vatican Council has given Catholics a new understanding and appreciation of the strengths, the values, and the proper integrity of the secular order. With this new understanding the Catholic University is in a strategic position to fashion a unity of the two orders, to point to a new synthesis of sacred and secular."[135] Jesuits on the East Coast were not the only ones to articulate this new task. The same Vatican II language is found in the responses to a survey done by the College and University Department of NCEA in the spring of 1967. Examining areas such as college theology programs, student rights and responsibilities, ecumenical activities, and liturgical and other spiritual life questions, the survey found extensive changes since Vatican II and attributed the changes to the fact that the Council had established a "climate of change—the spirit of *aggiornamento* is in the air." In conclusion, the authors point out that "Catholic Higher Education is in a state of ferment, in the excitement of an uncharted course, and is learning to live with uncertainty and ambiguity—both characteristics of the modern world."[136]

THREE

Uncertainty
and Ambiguity

The words quoted from the NCEA study at the end of the preceding chapter serve well as a title for a discussion of events in the 1970s. Gifted with an exciting vision of the future of Catholic universities in the United States, the presidents of these institutions struggled to achieve their goals within a climate of uncertainty and ambiguity that, at times, tended to overwhelm them. Many of their anxieties were shared by other institutions of higher learning, and the causes lay in the social, political, and economic context within which they all had to function. But Catholic universities found an additional source of ambiguity in trying to work out the appropriate expression of their relationship to the church.

Financing the Enterprise

The major uncertainty was the question of financial viability in an era that had lost confidence in the very nature of higher education. It arose from the issues in society which seemed to have no solution: the Civil Rights movement, the recognition of poverty and its consequences in American society, and the war in Vietnam. Beneath the surface there was a widespread suspicion that the universities were not places where solutions would be found but were indeed part of the problem. Clark Kerr observed that the fundamental issue "came to be the relationship of the mission of higher education to a pluralistic society when access to a college education became an 'entitlement' and response to the needs of society superceded the vision of 'pure research' or 'classical education.' As the convictions of the academic community were challenged by this philosophy of entitlement, there was a simultaneous breakdown in many other institutions of civil society."[1] There was also serious uncertainty about the financial future of a system which tried to provide access to all.

The Ford-Roy study in 1964–65 had identified finances as the top concern of Catholic colleges. In 1968 in a paper delivered at Kinshasa to the IFCU Assembly, Father Robert Henle, S.J., named the three major problems facing Catholic universities in the United States and again, the first one was "increasing financial difficulties." It took precedence over the other two problems which Henle noted, namely:

In the new climate, will Catholic colleges and universities have a distinctive contribution to make?
Will the restructuring destroy the Catholic character or strengthen it?[2]

Henle's questions indicated the link between securing sufficient financial support and being able to continue the distinctively Catholic life of the institution. The impact of the recent separation of the colleges from the religious communities, especially the financial consequences, was not yet clear.

Why was the financial picture so bleak? The unprecedented growth in the college-going population in the sixties had mandated enlarging faculties and making extensive additions to facilities on the campuses. Expenses soared, loans were secured, properties mortgaged, and significant deficits were incurred between 1968 and 1972. Despite the obvious financial needs, opinion in the private higher education community was divided as to the wisdom of looking to the federal government for funds other than research grants or construction loans, lest it lead to an unhealthy dependence of private education on public funds.[3]

At the same time, violent reactions on campuses to societal issues caused disillusionment among those from whom contributions were expected, both in the state legislatures and in private foundations. At the annual American Council on Education meeting in 1971, President Theodore M. Hesburgh, chair of ACE, summed up the situation: "After a century when the society at large could not do enough for universities and colleges, when these institutions represented the epitome of just about everyone's hope, a degree being the closest earthly replica of the badge of salvation, suddenly the American public, our patron and faithful supporter, is rather completely disillusioned about the whole enterprise. . . . at the same time that the universities are being expected to solve more problems than ever before . . . they are being misunderstood, abused, and abandoned by government and foundation."[4]

Part of this disillusionment can be traced to the internal intellectual disarray that the universities were experiencing. Curriculum revisions were made to respond to student interests, grading systems were undone by those who considered grades an obstacle to the learning process, and in many institutions evaluation of faculty began to focus more on research and publication and less on the quality of teaching and the contribution to the broad formation of students. Having accepted the AAUP guidelines on academic freedom, governance, and student rights,[5] the administrations were now bound to make decisions according to certain new processes that had been developed. It was a time of multiple faculty committees and of experimentation with ways of involving both faculty and students in governmental structure. The political climate in the late sixties had led to a hands-off attitude where student behavior was concerned and this, in turn, led to campus confrontations previously alien to that environment.[6] All of this created an image of a house that was unable to put its internal life in order and therefore was unworthy of financial support.

For the Catholic colleges and universities the financial problem was compounded. Historically dependent on tuition from middle-class families, their only other source of significant income was that coming from the "contributed services" of the religious faculty and administration. This term referred to the custom by which the members of the religious community that founded the college were awarded salaries, but the community used only what was absolutely necessary for maintenance of the sisters, brothers, or priests, and returned the rest to the college at the end of each fiscal year. Depending on the number of religious on staff, this contribution was a significant part of the operating budget of most Catholic institutions, often running into millions of dollars. With the departure of so many religious from their communities during the sixties and the shift in commitment away from institutional apostolates, this sum decreased sharply and in some cases disappeared altogether within the decade.[7]

Once a college was separated from the sponsoring religious community, it was necessary to pay salaries and give benefits to the religious on a par with the lay faculty, with no assurance of a return gift from the community. At the same time, colleges were making efforts to enroll students from disadvantaged families (hence, more scholarship dollars were needed) and were increasing the number of lay faculty (requiring more and better salaries). Accumulated dollar endowments were almost nonexistent; the concept of the religious as a "living endowment" had been used as needed by accrediting agencies and foundations when they required a certain level of endowment.

It was now clear that to minimize the dependence on tuition and fees and still balance the budget would require an infusion of funds from another source. In the 1964–65 fiscal year the dependence on tuition and fees was about 80 percent in the Catholic colleges for lay men and 65 percent in those for lay women.[8] In the following decade, as religious left faculties or requested full salaries, this dependence had no way of decreasing unless another source of support could be found. Where else might the colleges look for help?

As we have already noted, until 1956 Catholic universities and colleges were normally excluded from foundations' lists of grant recipients.[9] Apart from federal construction grants or program support of a very specific kind (in science or languages), these institutions were receiving no support from Washington. Although about $23.4 billion was being allocated to higher education by the federal government in 1970, most of it, apart from the G.I. Bill, was going to the major Ivy-League and large state universities for research and development.[10] From the individual states there was little or no aid for private higher education, beyond some scholarships for students. As we have seen, New York's Bundy grants, begun in 1968, aided only "nonsectarian" colleges, thus raising an identity problem for colleges with a religious affiliation. Fortunately three of the states that did have programs of general aid, Illinois, New York, and Pennsylvania, included 41 percent of the Catholic colleges in the nation.

There is ample evidence that the leaders of the Catholic colleges and universities were worried about the viability of their institutions. Proud of their history of overcoming obstacles, the colleges wondered if they could surmount this one. Circumstances had changed so much that it was hard to predict. There was a need for creative initiatives and, once again, Father Reinert, president of Saint Louis University, proved himself a leader.

He spoke with remarkable frankness to his newly established independent board of trustees on January 20, 1970, about the financial crisis of the university. The report of an ad hoc committee set up to study the fiscal health of the university had projected an accumulated deficit over the next five-year period of $11,620,000. The university had an unrestricted endowment of only $5,000,000. Consequently, the board mandated a balanced budget for 1970–71. The cuts which would have to be made in order to achieve this ran deep into every area of university life.

The salaries of full professors at Saint Louis were already 22 percent below the average for professors in the United States. Yet, the trustees found it difficult to identify areas where cuts could be made other than that of faculty salaries. What could not be denied, however, was that the anticipated deficit might mean the end of the university.

At the meeting Father Reinert presented several options for dealing with the crisis. After lengthy discussion the board agreed to address parts of each option: (1)separate Parks College (a school focused on aeronautics) from the university and make it available to McDonnell Douglas or Southern Illinois University; (2) assert that SLU's primary concern would be a strong undergraduate and graduate program "characterized by its innovative, dynamic character, and by the principles of a liberal education imbued with Christian motivation and inspiration . . . entrusting the area of applied technology, important as it is, to other agencies and institutions," a choice that called for redesign of the curriculum and would therefore need thorough discussion with deans and faculty; and (3) consider the pros and cons of the medical school, from a financial point of view.

The trustees voted to approve the first two proposals, severing connections with Parks College and redesigning the curriculum for the College of Arts and Sciences, Commerce and Finance, and the Graduate School, with a view to giving priority to these schools in the allocation of university income. On the other hand, they deferred a decision regarding the professional schools (Medicine, and also Divinity, Law, and Social Service) and considered a proposal that each of these schools assume fiscal responsibility for its own budget. Some trustees urged total disinvestment in the medical school because it needed extensive renovations.[11]

Despite these steps, the financial situation worsened. The board of trustees at its meeting in July 1970 heard another disheartening report from its ad hoc committee on financial status. The projected operating deficit for 1970–71 was now over a million dollars, despite the board's mandate for a balanced budget, and the proposed ways of dealing with the crisis had not solved it. Reinert now addressed three alternative proposals for the future:

1. In addition to Parks College and the Engineering School, completely phase out other schools such as Medicine, Law, and Social Service. But while this would solve the short-term problems, it would not have an effect on the long-term operating expenses of the university.

2. Rather than outright disinvestment, rank the present schools in two priority groupings. The first would include the College of Arts and Sciences, the School of Commerce and Finance, and the Graduate School. The programs of these schools would be reorganized in line with the philosophy of education articulated and approved at the January meeting and in harmony with the work currently being done within the university known as Project 21; major sources of revenue would be allocated to them. The second group would include the professional schools, making them semiautonomous, each one responsible for its own financial well-being.

3. Seek a public sponsor for the university or for one of its schools, for example, the medical school. Total public sponsorship would mean persuading the state of Missouri to take over the entire university.

President Reinert found himself unable to support any of these options. He told the trustees that he could not bring himself to "sell out" the university after twenty-six years of intimate involvement with it. He insisted to the board that adopting any of these options would be a tragedy; it would mean that "an excellent educational institution with a unique past contribution to this country and, more important, an institution whose unique contribution is desperately needed in the future is about to be dismantled, dismembered, and allowed to disintegrate." He also feared that it would have a domino effect on other Jesuit and Catholic universities and ultimately on all of private higher education. At the climax of his dramatic presentation, Reinert asked the board for a leave from the university for the coming year to give him full time to seek a solution, so as to "satisfy my conscience" that nothing further can be proposed.[12]

The board approved his proposal on July 26, 1970, and he began his study and travel in the fall. Funded by the Danforth Foundation, Reinert went on a fact-finding tour of higher education and a campaign to educate the public to the likely prospect that private higher education would fail unless more support was forthcoming.[13] It was a bold plan; the process as well as the successful outcome is described in Reinert's *To Turn the Tide*.

Although Reinert was the only president of a major Catholic university to acknowledge the problem publicly, others were similarly threatened by bankruptcy. At Fordham, for example, President Leo Mc-Laughlin, S.J., had communicated his worries over the financial picture as early as 1968 to Rev. James Hennesey, S.J., the current rector.[14] In the histories that have been written of individual Catholic universities the early 1970s are clearly times of extreme financial troubles. The dependence on tuition meant that when enrollments dropped (as they did in the early seventies), revenue was unable to keep up with operating expenses.

Particularly difficult was the situation of the smaller liberal arts colleges that were limited in resources and lacked a public image that might attract donors. Their alumni/ae were not yet in positions of wealth and power, and although they were personally loyal and generous to their alma maters, they could not set up sufficient endowments. On average, these colleges were 58.3 percent dependent on tuition and fees.

In 1972 Alexander W. Astin and Calvin B. T. Lee published *The Invisible Colleges* as one of the series commissioned by the Carnegie Commission on Higher Education.[15] Although names are not given, the authors indicate that in the group profiled there were many Roman Catholic colleges. One can assume they were not atypical. Unbalanced budgets, ever-increasing debts, decreasing enrollment, and serious inflation left faculty salaries far behind the cost of living and threatened the very viability of the institutions.

One example of the situation on the smaller campus was that at the College of New Rochelle. When the new president, Joseph McMurray, came to campus in February 1971, the current budget projected an operating deficit of $380,000 and the cumulative deficit was approaching $700,000. At an open faculty meeting, Dr. McMurray explained that tuition covered less than two-thirds of the cost of educating a student and, having been denied Bundy aid from New York State, new sources of income were absolutely necessary if the college were to survive the next five years. The director of alumnae relations added that gifts had dropped, due in part to the student strike the preceding spring and the more permissive attitude toward student discipline on campus.[16] Similar financial distress was reported at other Catholic colleges, to which they responded with increasingly sophisticated development and fundraising efforts, reductions in staff, and promotion campaigns by admissions offices. But none of this sufficed.

On both large and small campuses the economic crisis was related to the sociopolitical landscape. At the same board meeting at which President Reinert gave the bleak financial outlook, he covered in some detail the situation of the black community; protests against ROTC recruitment; disciplinary procedures against students and faculty; and the need for a contingency plan to handle anticipated political activity regarding the Vietnam War. Campus disruptions of the preceding spring were related, in part, to Kent State and Cambodia and were part of a world-wide situation. Reinert himself had several personal confrontations with black students and students opposed to ROTC.

As President Hesburgh pointed out at the ACE meeting the following January, these events were leading to disillusionment and despair on the part of former supporters. On his own campus, Hesburgh had faced similar confrontations from students, leading to his letter of February 1969, later cited by many of his colleagues, in which he outlined his policy toward disruptions of university life. (He would give a fifteen-minute ultimatum to students, or non-students, who did not follow the proper mode for dissent.)[17] In his letter Hesburgh referred to the fact that he had been bombarded by both hawks and doves among alumni and friends since the preceding November, when a confrontation had occurred. He expressed his fear that legislators, benefactors, parents, and others would react to disruptive behavior in a way that would threaten the autonomy and liberty essential to the life of the university unless the university community itself took steps to keep necessary order. He was also, no doubt, concerned that their financial support would diminish.

Despite the loss of public confidence in the institutions of higher education, President Reinert remained convinced that private higher education was absolutely necessary for a healthy democracy and argued that public higher education would benefit from whatever was done to assist private universities. Using his position of leadership in both the Association of American Colleges and the NCEA College and University Department, Reinert criss-crossed the country explaining his views and attempting to persuade participants in the Danforth-sponsored process called *Search*.[18] In the end, he rallied others around the legislation that was pending in Congress, a higher education bill sponsored by Claibourne Pell in the Senate and Edith Green in the House. Eventually this alliance led to the Higher Education Act of 1972, a law which did much to dispel the uncertainty about both enrollment and finances. It provided for "Basic Education Opportunity Grants" and various other forms of student aid available to students in all post-secondary ac-credited institutions. This would be the savior that colleges had all been looking for.

The desperate financial situation of the early seventies also called forth some very creative innovations within Catholic colleges. They tapped new "markets" for students and developed new educational methods for meeting some of the criticism that came from the students of the sixties. New programs began to receive foundation grants; they were listed in each issue of *College Newsletter* and were thus shared with colleagues. Many of these programs were geared toward previously underserved students; others proposed new methods of teaching. As a way of increasing enrollment, almost all the Catholic men's colleges and some women's colleges went coed in the seventies. Other women's colleges sought new students among older women whose education had been interrupted by marriage and family responsibilities. Collaborative programs between colleges and universities were seen as a way to reduce administrative overhead. Joint proposals to build libraries or science facilities often received favorable response from NEH or NSF. A few Catholic institutions actually merged; perhaps the most successful mergers were those between San Diego College for Women and San Diego College for Men (1971), and between Loyola and Marymount in Los Angeles (1973). In the mid-seventies, when large debt had been accumulated in the smaller women's colleges, there were acquisitions such as Boston College's absorption of Newton College and the University of San Francisco's of Lone Mountain. In 1971 a merger of the University of Notre Dame and Saint Mary's College was announced, but as they worked toward final plans the deal fell apart.[19] Master plans, development offices, and extensive fund-raising efforts, especially among alumnae/i, were the order of the day. About twenty-two Catholic colleges closed their doors during this decade. By 1974 the board at Mundelein College was considering going coed or joining Loyola University as two options which might help alleviate the financial situation. Mundelein did neither and continued to try to attract women students of various backgrounds. It developed its weekend college, which had started in 1964. Ultimately, in 1991, it became Mundelein College of Loyola University.

Although there were repeated calls at NCEA meetings for a master plan for Catholic higher education, no grand scheme of inter-institutional planning ever emerged. Some blamed this inability to develop a plan on the traditional competitive spirit among the religious orders that had founded the colleges. However, "merger" was not a popular or successful model among non-Catholic private institutions, either. The lack of a grand plan may be as much related to academic mind-set as to the character of religious communities.

Several women's colleges encouraged enrollment of older women who had begun but not finished college; they were known as "special students" and joined in the regular classes, meeting all the requirements for the degrees offered. Greater flexibility was sought in a program initiated at the College of New Rochelle in 1972. Known as the School of New Resources, this form of adult education was built around the students' own work experience and was developed at locations within already existing communities so that the resources of the community would play an important role. One highly innovative campus was that at the headquarters of the AFL-CIO Municipal and State Workers in Manhattan. The mode of education was suited to the adult learner and included independent study, small seminars, and the development of a portfolio based on the individual's life experience. This same approach would later be taken by Carlow College and DePaul University.

Alverno College in Milwaukee focused its attention on curriculum reform. Capitalizing on one of its existing strengths, attention to values, Alverno became a model for the country and attracted many adult students. Other women's colleges such as St. Mary-of-the-Woods and Marymount established weekend degree programs aimed at students with full-time responsibilities who could only manage classes on weekends. Outreach to minority women led to the establishment of the Doheny campus of Mt. St. Mary's in Los Angeles, an extremely successful program later copied by others. With the coming of distance-learning capabilities, these colleges have been able to move forward with many innovative programs. The evolution of Barry College in Miami to university status is a good example of such creativity.

In contrast, institutions such as the College of the Holy Cross, Saint Benedict's, St. John's (Minnesota), Santa Clara, and Saint Mary's in Notre Dame, Indiana, reaffirmed their exclusive concern for undergraduate liberal arts education for the traditional age group and focused on academic excellence and greater selectivity in admissions policies. Many of the men's colleges had become or were becoming coeducational. In the early sixties the Father General of the Jesuits, Rev. John B. Janssens, S.J., who had been unalterably opposed to the move to accept women students, finally gave halfhearted approval but stated that the Jesuit college presidents should discuss the issue with local ordinaries before moving to coeducation, since he did not want to antagonize the women's colleges. Despite this advice, very few Jesuit presidents seem to have engaged the women's colleges in the conversation. In 1961 Santa Clara won approval from the bishop and began accepting women in all departments. In the next decade its enrollment grew from 1,500 to 5,000.[20] Holy Cross decided on coeducation in 1972 in order to increase the number of students and, at the same time, secure young women with high SAT scores.[21] Gradually all the men's colleges and about half of the women's colleges became coeducational; forty-three other women's colleges remained single-sex institutions until the nineties.[22]

The year 1974 was the low point for enrollment in women's colleges. The worst for men's colleges was two or three years earlier, primarily because of the draft and the war in Vietnam. Interestingly, the decision to become coed seems to have been made by many colleges with little discussion of the shift in educational philosophy implicit in the decision. For the lifetime of Catholic colleges in the United States, coeducation had been a practice forbidden by church authorities, except in extenuating circumstances. Religious communities, for the most part, taught in schools that were either for men or for women. Yet, almost overnight and without philosophical or theological consideration, their colleges became coeducational. The economic factor seems to have won the day, although *ex post facto* some fine rationalizations have appeared.

Disillusionment in Higher Education

The financial crunch in higher education was aggravated by society's widespread disillusionment with all social and political institutions. The protests against the war in Vietnam were succeeded by the crisis of Watergate and the forced resignation of President Nixon. Added to the humiliation of the withdrawal from Vietnam, Watergate marked a low point in national morale. The effect on higher education was dramatic.[23] Faculty and student behavior reflected the anti-authority climate, and a mood of cynicism replaced the idealism that characterized the protests of the sixties. According to Clark Kerr, by 1969 there were already those on campus who "see dissent as the central function of the university; others see the academy, as a collectivity, helping to change society; while still others see the university as a 'partisan camp,' a 'base for guerrilla activity against the surrounding society.'"[24] From Berkeley these attitudes had traveled across the country, although the rhetoric was less violent and the partisans fewer on Catholic campuses. Indeed some, like Villanova, were marked by conservative countermovements.[25]

In an article written in 1975, Kerr noted the loss of public confidence in higher education. "Seldom has so great an American institution passed so quickly from its Golden Age to its Age of Survival."[26] Within this context, some asked, Should they survive? Several authors indicated a lack of certainty about the answer. The student was now assuming the role of consumer, according to David Riesman,[27] and former faculty dominance in the university had given way to student power: "The swing in the mood of many faculty over the past fifteen years [1965–1980] from euphoria to paranoia has been sharper than the actual changes in institutional boom and bust warrant." If we recall some of the faculty-inspired curriculum changes and grading practices that began in the sixties for the sake of "relevance," we understand Riesman's disillusionment. He regretted the move to put students on committees and boards, as if their very "willfulness and impetuousness and indeed self-rightousness were the qualities most needed in university governance."[28] He was critical of independent study when the faculty did not understand the amount of supervision needed. He pointed out that the overall counterculture which rejected the constraints of campus life was also visible in the various "liberating" movements which did not always work to the benefit of the group identified: women, African-American, Hispanic, and so on.

Riesman expressed disappointment that Catholic colleges and universities had themselves become "secularized" as a result of their new drive for academic excellence. "Only a few years after the Catholic colleges and universities had been attacked for their anti-intellectualism and their backwardness when compared with their secular counterparts by John Courtney Murray S.J., Thomas O'Dea, Monsignor John Tracy Ellis, Philip Gleason, Robert Hassenger, James Trent and many other Catholic intellectuals, a number of the Catholic colleges moved into the very forefront of what was then the academic avant-garde."[29]

This linking of the struggle for academic excellence and the capitulation to "secularization" would be repeated many times by critics both inside and outside the Catholic community, but it is difficult to find a causal connection. There was certainly an increase in faculty encouragement of students to pursue Woodrow Wilson, Danforth, and Rhodes Scholarships, as well as in seeking both faculty and student grants under the Fulbright program. At many Catholic colleges and universities the lecture series and course titles of the sixties and seventies testified to a lively appreciation of the intellectual life among students and faculty of the period. The growing number of Ph.D.'s on faculties and the increasing applications for chapters of Phi Beta Kappa signified a livelier interest in academic rank. But to what extent should this desire to compete with the academic standards of secular colleges be considered "secularization"? The complexity of the period is demonstrated by the fact that these same students and faculty were engaged in altruistic projects leading to later service in such groups as Peace Corps, Vista, and Teachers Corps. Such altruism was countercultural to the mood of cynicism which accompanied the revelations about Vietnam and Watergate, and it often had religious roots rather than merely secular inspiration.

Defining the Enterprise

The "uncertainty and ambiguity" experienced by all of higher education was intensified for Catholic universities and colleges because of their perplexing relationship with the Roman Catholic Church. In 1970 the College and University Department of NCEA set up a special task force to consider, in the light of Vatican II, the "Purpose and Identity" of Catholic colleges and universities.[30] This committee was also asked to consider (in a spirit of ecumenism) whether some of the goals could be better achieved in conjunction with other church-related institutions. Simultaneously, another task force of the Department was meeting with the president of the Association of American Colleges regarding a possible merger of the two organizations.[31] This idea was turned down because the Executive Committee saw the need for a forum for specific Catholic issues.

Why, at this particular moment, did Catholic colleges and universities determine to reflect on their "purpose and identity" and to do it as a national organization?[32] One reason, no doubt, was the less visible link to religious orders brought about by the new governance structures introduced in the late sixties. No longer under the authority of local or provincial authorities acting as trustees, but now governed by independent boards of trustees composed of both lay and religious members, the colleges and universities were, in the eyes of some, less "Catholic." The document prepared at Land O'Lakes in 1967, with its emphasis on autonomy and freedom, sounded to some like disaffiliation from the church.[33] And yet to others it was a necessary expression of the role of the Catholic university in the larger world of American higher education, an environment which prided itself on its independence and academic freedom.

The fact that the new independent boards of trustees were composed of lay and religious members meant that the institution was no longer clearly "Jesuit," "Mercy," "Franciscan," and so on. The transfer of authority over the legal and fiscal affairs of the college to independent boards had indeed created an ambiguous role for the religious community regarding the assets they had previously controlled. As religious orders, they had treated their property as church property regulated by the canon law of the Roman Catholic Church.[34] But now this understanding was questioned. Had not the donors given their gifts to the college and not to the order? Were not government funds given for the support of research or construction of buildings for classrooms or dormitories and, in fact, could not be given to a religious community? Under this reasoning, the theory gained credence that the "trustees" were accountable only to the state which gave the institution its corporate charter, and not to officials of the Catholic church. As discussed in chapter 2, this view was put forth by Rev. John McGrath, a canon and civil lawyer from The Catholic University of America, and gained widespread acceptance in a remarkably short time.[35]

McGrath's opinion was challenged in a letter from the Sacred Congregation for Catholic Education in Rome in 1974. Alarmed at what it perceived to be a give-away of church property without any prior authorization from the Holy See, the Congregation notified the American bishops of its concern. The National Conference of Catholic Bishops (NCCB) was asked to form a committee with representatives of the leadership conferences of men and women religious and prepare a report on the current situation. What, the Congregation inquired, is happening with the properties of the colleges and universities? Once transferred to independent boards of trustees, do these colleges still consider themselves "Catholic"? To whom are they accountable?[36]

A Joint Commission on Ownership of Catholic Institutions was set up in response to this request and met on January 25, 1975. This was the only meeting of the commission since it, in turn, recommended to NCCB that a comprehensive study of the question be made and that some tentative guidelines be given to the bishops. In the meantime, a work newly completed by Rev. Adam Maida was distributed by the Pennsylvania Catholic Conference to the hierarchy for guidance.[37]

The situation was complicated by the fact that in April 1974 the same Roman Congregation had urged the Episcopal Conferences to set up a special committee to discuss the implementation of the 1972 document, "The Catholic University in the Modern World," and to handle "Catholic University problems." The American bishops, under the leadership of Bishop William Borders, had created a committee jointly with the NCEA College and University Department; the first meeting of the committee had taken place in December 1974. It was known as the Bishops and Presidents' Committee. The question was now asked: What relationship did Rome see between these two committees?[38] The answer was that the Bishops and Presidents' Committee had a broader scope and, since the NCCB commission on ownership had no more meetings, the issue was moot. The Bishops and Presidents' Committee retained its role as liaison between NCCB and NCEA/ACCU. This committee was a symbol of growing collaboration between American bishops and the Catholic universities and colleges, which nurtured a pastoral view of the relationship that should characterize their interaction. From its beginning in 1974 it provided a forum for discussion of issues and a helpful channel of communication for both constituencies. Lacking any legislative or executive authority, the committee promoted an exchange of views on both national and church issues.

In January 1976 a conference of fifteen bishops and a hundred academicians met at Notre Dame to reflect on the documents of Vatican II and continue the IFCU discussion at Salamanca in 1973. The goal of the conference was to promote collaboration between bishops and the scholarly community as they went about the task of evangelization in the modern world.[39] With careful analysis and patient discourse, the participants identified the ambiguities which would continue to plague the relations of Catholic universities and the hierarchy, indicating the difficulties to be met in implementing the 1972 document "The Catholic University in the Modern World" in the way expected by Cardinal Garrone. It is clear that the bishops present at this Conference on Evangelization were in tune with "the American context" and evaluated proposals for achieving the purposes of Catholic universities within that framework.

A positive experience of the relationship between the universities and the hierarchy was the bicentennial celebration sponsored by the NCCB in 1976. The preparation of position papers on various social issues brought university faculty and bishops together in a constructive way, and the culminating conference in Detroit in October 1976, designated the "Call to Action," was a high point in the experience of being the church for many academic leaders who had had little prior contact with hierarchy.[40] The influence of this meeting on the research agenda of the universities will be dealt with in the next chapter.

One of the internal factors in colleges and universities that made discussions about their Catholic or even their Christian character increasingly difficult, despite the many collaborative efforts, was the new role of faculty. The emphasis on faculty rights, and the sheer numbers of lay faculty, many of whom had degrees from secular universities, often conflicted with the responsibility of the trustees and administrators to promote the mission of the college or university insofar as it identified itself as Catholic. In a talk given December 6, 1974, Msgr. John Murphy, the new Executive Director of the NCEA College and University Department, quoting Earl McGrath on the value of Catholic higher education and the lack of nerve on the part of some of its leaders, insisted that identity was the major issue facing Catholic colleges. "Unfortunately," Murphy continued, "there is considerable evidence that Catholic colleges and universities have many academically credentialed persons on their faculties who are ignorant of, indifferent to, and, yes, even hostile to the Catholic dimension of these institutions."[41]

The minutes of the NCEA department's Purpose and Identity Committee from 1970 to 1978 witness to difficulties which surfaced within the committee as soon as the question of hiring faculty who would support the institution's Catholic mission was raised. There was sharp disagreement about the extent to which the Catholic character of the institution should be emphasized in public statements. On the one hand was the strong desire to retain a clear relationship with the church, and on the other the fear that, despite the *Tilton* decision and the subsequent *Roemer* case, government funding might easily be lost if "sectarianism" were detected. What kind of language could pass between this Scylla and Charybdis?

The general position of the colleges, following the *Horace Mann* decision in 1966, had been one of great caution in expressing their church relationship. In a confidential memo of April 20, 1967, President Maguire of Loyola University Chicago wrote: "Catholic higher education in the United States has with considerable struggle achieved substantial respect in our pluralistic society. However, should an authority apart from the Board of Trustees exclude non-Catholic theologians the integrity and the very existence of our academic institutions would be imperiled."[42] And in an address to the annual meeting of AAC in 1973, Rev. Charles Whelan, S.J., of the Fordham Law School pointed to the "tug-of-war" going on between the government and the churches and suggested that the solution would be found in observing three principles: voluntarism, pluralism, and academic freedom.

In 1977 a subcommittee was appointed by the Purpose and Identity Committee to produce a statement on identity that could be used by institutions in their own self-studies. A draft was developed by Rev. James Burtchaell, C.S.C., and debated within the subcommittee for over a year. While there was unanimity among the members regarding their desire to retain their Catholic identity, they were strongly averse to saying anything in a public statement that could be used against them. The chair of the subcommittee, Dorothy Ann Kelly, O.S.U., president of the College of New Rochelle, had serious reservations about preferential hiring, and the attorney for her college, Charles Horgan, argued that the dissent in *Tilton* by Justice Brennan was something that should be kept in mind. Horgan was of the opinion that "All other things being equal, a determined effort to hire Catholics for the faculty is a violation of the Federal and State anti-discrimination statutes."[43] An opinion submitted to the committee by Jordan Kurland of AAUP was less definite on this point, but he did think that the language used in the Purpose and Identity Committee draft, i.e., that Catholics "must predominate" on the faculty, was too strong. Although later research would modify the opinion of an absolute ban on preferential hiring,[44] it probably represents the view of many presidents and their lawyers in the seventies. Concern was expressed in the NCEA College and University Department newsletter, *Update* (January 24, 1975), about the potential harm from the presidential Executive Order 11246, which dealt with discriminatory hiring practices. If the institution claimed exemption to this executive order on the grounds of being a religious organization, it then might become ineligible for federal grants to higher education.

The first draft of the revised Code of Canon Law appeared in 1977 with its provision that all theology teachers must have a canonical mission, thereby renewing fears about loss of government funding. Possibly this fact led the subcommittee to abandon the effort to create a public statement on identity. In 1978 and 1979 ACCU was busy working with other church-related colleges in preparing for their National Congress, and it was hoped that this assembly might reach a broad agreement on the Christian character they all claimed. In this way they would avoid the label of sectarianism. In any case, the effort of the Purpose and Identity Committee to define the American Catholic university or college came to an end in 1978.[45]

During the next decade, however, there would be continued conversations on the topic and in some instances a renewed emphasis on the sponsorship of a particular religious community as a way of avoiding the title of Catholic. Universities often referred to themselves not as Catholic but as Franciscan, Jesuit, Dominican, Mercy, and so on. One author, writing in the nineties, entitled his article: "Jesuit, Si! Catholic, Not so sure."[46]

In 1978, the same year that the Purpose and Identity Committee ceased to exist, the ten Jesuit provincials of the United States wrote a letter to all the Jesuits who were involved in the twenty-eight universities which they had founded. Clearly recognizing the fact that they no longer controlled or governed the institutions, the provincials nevertheless reaffirmed their commitment to the apostolic mission of the university or college and promised to continue to prepare young Jesuits for service in them. The 32nd Congregation of the Society of Jesus had issued a call to the "service of faith and the work of Justice," and the provincials were determined that the response of the Jesuits in the universities would be an essential component of the response of the order as a whole. The separate incorporation of the communities and the colleges which had occurred in the previous decade was not to be seen as putting an end to their Jesuit apostolate but rather as opening up a new possibility of collaboration with the laity in the service of the Kingdom.[47]

Changes had been dramatic. The Jesuit provincials pointed out that "In the past decade, the social, cultural, and educational context in which we exercise our mission has changed irrevocably." However, "this changed world is the only one in which we are called to work out our mission." This positive stance may not have been universally appreciated, but it was crucial to the argument in favor of continuing to support the work of the colleges and universities after relinquishing control of them. By now, lay leaders with administrative expertise were taking hold of the reins in many of the smaller institutions, fund-raising activities were showing results, and government aid to students had brightened the enrollment picture. The tremendous uncertainty about finances that characterized the early seventies was beginning to dissipate. However, the ambiguity about the distinctive Catholic identity of the institutions and how it could be maintained would continue.

FOUR

New Horizons

While defining the "Catholic" side of the coin of institutional identity was problematic, the "American" side was flourishing. Not only did individual universities build collaborative arrangements with other institutions not under Catholic auspices, but as a group they began to play a role on the national scene. In the seventies and eighties, presidents of Catholic colleges and universities moved into leadership positions in national higher education organizations, gradually being recognized as colleagues who could contribute something out of their particular tradition to debate over public policy in higher education. Consortia among institutions in particular regions generally now included Catholic colleges and universities. Common concerns, discussed in the preceding chapter, outweighed distinctive missions.

Consortia in Higher Education

In addition to the College and University Department of the National Catholic Educational Association (after 1978 to resume its original name of the Association of Catholic Colleges and Universities),[1] many Catholic institutions already held membership in other associations: Association of American Colleges, American Council on Education, Association of Governing Boards, American Association for Higher Education, and the Council of Independent Colleges, among others. The presidents of Catholic institutions, following the path of Reinert, Hesburgh, and Gannon, began to recruit new members and to hold elected office in such groups.[2]

Association of American Colleges

A long-standing relationship of Catholic colleges with the Association of American Colleges has been noted. Similarities among private colleges, particularly the church-related ones, had made this association the point of reference for matters dealing with liberal arts, religion in higher education, rank and tenure for faculty, good administrative practice, and financial management. In the sixties, AAC provided consultants on administration, one of whom was Rev. Edward V. Stanford, O.S.A., president of Villanova University from 1932 to 1944.[3] Father Stanford and two colleagues in the AAC consulting service visited over 300 campuses, 140 of which were Catholic, advising the presidents on management and governance. In 1965 Stanford wrote *A Guide to Catholic College Administration*.[4]

Because AAC had endorsed the AAUP 1940 Statement of Principles, it was consulted by the AAUP Committee A on the interpretation of "the limitations clause" that was proposed in 1970.[5] Through AAC, Father Friedman, Executive Secretary of the NCEA College and University Department, was able to make his voice heard in that matter. Although AAUP wanted to confine the discussion to the interpretation of the limitations clause, AAC and the other associations thought that issues such as campus unrest and faculty tenure should also be brought into the conversation. At a meeting on October 6, 1970, the AAC board of directors decided to defer formal endorsement of the interpretive statement until other related issues were dealt with. AAC invited AAUP to join with others in reviewing academic tenure, stating that AAC itself planned to develop a statement on academic responsibility. The door was left open to further cooperation.

In the seventies there was increased leadership within AAC from among the presidents and deans of Catholic institutions. Ann Ida Gannon, Bishop James Shannon,[6] and Theodore Hesburgh had already served as chairs of AAC; the next decade saw others, including Paul Reinert, following in their footsteps. Among the active members were representatives from a cross section of Catholic higher education: Alverno College, Providence College, College of New Rochelle, Saint Louis University, St. Mary-of-the-Woods College, Rosary College, Xavier University of Louisiana, Lone Mountain College, and St. Xavier University, Illinois. The interest in "liberal education" served as the element which attracted many Catholic colleges to this particular association. Interdenominational friendships were forged successfully, leading to the suggestion that the major Catholic and Protestant organizations of higher education be subsumed into AAC. Although the Council for Protestant Colleges accepted that proposal, NCEA did not.[7]

National Association of Independent Colleges and Universities

In the mid-seventies a group within AAC, dissatisfied with the lack of energy in dealing with federal funding issues, decided to spin off a new organization and let AAC concentrate on the educational issues. With the development of a federal program of assistance to higher education, especially the Higher Education Act of 1973, private universities saw a great need for representation "on the hill." Individual large universities already had staff members in Washington, and the public sector had their organizations (AASCU, or American Association of State Colleges and Universities, and NASULGC, or National Association of State Universities and Land Grant Colleges), so it was important that private higher education also organize.

In 1976 the National Association of Independent Colleges and Universities was founded with two components, one for research (called the National Institute for Independent Colleges and Universities, or NIICU) and one to lobby on behalf of independent higher education (NAICU proper). From the beginning, the special concerns of church-related institutions were recognized by the formation of a Secretariat within NAICU composed of executives of denominational associations with higher education departments. Over the years this group monitored federal issues from the point of view of the church-related colleges and often influenced the direction of NAICU policies. Presidents of Catholic universities and colleges exerted strong leadership within NAICU, since their constituency was a large one; of 1,600 private colleges in the United States, 800 were church-related and over 200 were Catholic. As of February 1977 there were 128 Catholic college members out of a total membership of 573.

The lists of officers and directors of NAICU over the years, as well as the membership in the Secretariat, reveal the importance that Catholic universities attached to participation in this particular organization. To have a voice "on the hill" required highly qualified staff, and most of the Catholic cohort found it more economical and more effective to work through NAICU than to attempt individual lobbying.[8] The diversity among private or independent institutions often caused tension within NAICU; decisions were made regarding federal policies which did not affect all of them in the same way. The large research-oriented universities and the small liberal arts colleges often had different perspectives on federal aid. However, in the two decades of its existence NAICU has, on the whole, been of great help to Catholic colleges and universities.

Women's College Coalition

Another offshoot of AAC was an organization created by the colleges that remained single-sex for women. It began as a subgroup dependent on AAC but found the largely male leadership unsympathetic to the particular concerns of the relatively small women's colleges. In 1976 it became a separate organization and engaged in various projects to promote the image and success of this special group of colleges. Today there is a membership of sixty-six, of which twenty-six are Catholic colleges.

Association of Jesuit Colleges and Universities

Although the Jesuit universities quickly became significant participants in NAICU, they did not limit their activity to the issues on that association's agenda. As early as 1958 the Jesuit presidents had established the Jesuit Research Council of America to promote and oversee applications for grants of various kinds. It had a full-time director who served twenty-two member institutions. The need for a representative in Washington to alert members of federal grant opportunities led them to open a Washington office in 1962.[9] In 1970, when the Association of Jesuit Colleges and Universities was founded, the Research Council and its executive director, Joseph Kane, were subsumed into it. Mr. Kane and his colleagues in other church-related groups worked hard on Capitol Hill for the interests of the non–Ivy League private colleges throughout the seventies and eighties, and strongly urged church-related priorities within the NAICU Secretariat.[10]

Prior to the founding of the Association of Jesuit Colleges and Universities (AJCU),[11] a "Commission of Presidents" existed under the umbrella of the Jesuit Conference, but in 1970 it opted for a free-standing association directed by the presidents rather than by the provincials who governed the Conference. It was one more sign of the complexity of American Catholic higher education and witnessed to the importance of the independent boards of trustees which by now governed several of the leading Jesuit universities.[12] If decisions in the internal administration of the colleges were being removed from the purview of religious authorities, should not the corporate stance of Jesuit universities also be free from provincial oversight? This new organizational structure would allow the presidents more freedom in planning and in collaborating with other higher education leaders and, it was hoped, would bring about a stronger Jesuit influence in the world of higher education. From time to time there were suggestions that the Jesuit university presidents cooperate more with one another on long-range planning, but AJCU was never able to achieve that goal. Nevertheless, the fellowship shared in the association no doubt eased contacts among the presidents and enabled them to act in concert when necessary.[13] In the AJCU the Jesuits had a base of operations which gave them significance in the eyes of the

other associations and thus kept the concerns of Catholic higher education from being forgotten by those on the Washington scene.[14]

Other Associations

Even for smaller colleges, the multiplicity of new organizations testifies to the increasing complexity of life in academia. The Council of Independent Colleges (CIC) paid special attention to the needs of colleges
with enrollment under 2,000 (later, 4,000). The American Association
for Higher Education (AAHE) developed networks among administrators and faculty dealing with curriculum and teaching innovations.

In addition there were specialized groups: Association of Governing Boards (AGB), American Association of Colleges for Teacher
Education (AACTE), the Council for the Advancement and Support
of Education (CASE), the Council of Graduate Schools (CGS), and
the Association of American Universities (AAU), each with a Dupont
Circle address, a mission, and membership dues. State associations
were also being formed to assist with state and federal relations and to
encourage participation of trustees in fund-raising and political activities.[15] Colleges and universities, because of financial constraints, were
often forced to choose among the multiple organizations, even though
they saw the importance of being present in all of them. Unlike the
others listed above, the Association of American Universities chose its
members according to highly selective academic criteria. As Catholic
universities began to move into research and doctoral programs, they
sought admission to this elite group. The Catholic University of America was a charter member in 1900 and has remained the only Catholic
institution on the list to the present day.

NCEA College and University Department/
Association of Catholic Colleges and Universities

The unique concerns that united the Catholic institutions within
the ACCU—referred to as the College and University Department of
NCEA between 1904 and 1978—kept its membership roll steady, normally at 95 percent of the potential members. During the seventies, its
members constantly addressed the question of identity, the unfortunate
multiplication of small colleges, financial constraints, and the need for
research capability which would serve the needs of the church, particularly in the area of peace and justice issues. Information about grants
received by different members and new programs initiated on various
campuses was shared through *College Newsletter* and later on through
Update and *Occasional Papers.*[16] At annual meetings, held in conjunction

with the NCEA convention until 1974 and usually reported in *College Newsletter*, the presidents considered questions of governance, sponsorship, relations with Rome, academic freedom, legislative and judicial matters, and faculty rank and tenure. In 1974 the election of a new Executive Director, Msgr. John F. Murphy, brought strong leadership that would address many of these matters. A decision was also made not to hold its annual meeting at the time of the general NCEA convention but rather at the time of the AAC annual meeting, later changed to the NAICU meeting, thus signifying the concerns that Catholic colleges shared with the rest of higher education. Father Murphy reorganized the board and committee structure and became a significant player in the affairs at One Dupont Circle as well as in church circles. He worked tirelessly to achieve understanding of Catholic higher education by the bishops and the Congregation for Catholic Education. In the six years of his tenure, two of his goals were realized: the 1980 document of the American bishops, "Catholic Higher Education and the Pastoral Mission of the Church,"[17] and the creation of ecumenical fellowship among the leaders of other church-related colleges. The latter was highlighted in the National Congress of Church-Related Colleges and Universities, 1979–80, discussed later. In 1978 Father Murphy initiated action to restore the original name, Association of Catholic Colleges and Universities. While this did not change the relationship to the parent organization, NCEA, it did provide an independent public image and enabled the association to take different positions from NCEA on matters regarding public policy.[18]

Neylan Colleges

One of the committees organized under Msgr. Murphy dealt with the question of "sponsorship." The transfer of governance and property to boards predominantly lay had created a new challenge: "How did the colleges now relate to the sponsoring religious community?" And, indeed, what did sponsorship mean? This was particularly significant for the women religious, many of whom had never thought of ministries other than teaching in the college which their community ran. Their mission was often stated with a narrow focus: the education of young women. With the shift to coeducation by men's colleges and a developing trend in that direction among about half of the women's colleges, the sister-presidents found themselves in need of clarifying the mission of their colleges.[19] They felt a common bond, based on their heritage as women who had founded colleges for women. In 1978 Sister Jeanne Knoerle, S.P., president of Saint Mary-of-the-Woods, convened a group of fifteen of these presidents to "blue-sky" about the future of their kind of college.[20] Their very "invisibility" among the higher education institutions made it difficult to attract foundation support or major alumnae donors, yet they saw value in what they had built and were now struggling to maintain and strengthen. Changes in religious life had reduced commitment on the part of some communities to the college which they had founded; a certain anti-institutional mentality among community members made it difficult for these sister-presidents to see teachers and administrators coming along behind them, and they wondered if there were any future for their colleges.

While the sister-presidents' questions were similar to those of men religious, their experience as members of religious communities was quite different. Their link to their own colleges was defined by historical particularities rather than by centralized authority. In many cases, the community had only one college, and even in communities which sponsored several institutions (Mercy, Carondolet, and Sacred Heart), each college stood alone. These colleges had moved to independent governing boards of trustees, and the religious communities were unsure about their future role in the life of the colleges. The presidents were also puzzled by the lack of interest shown by the Leadership Conference of Women Religious in the ministry of higher education.

After a few days together, with spirits invigorated, the presidents laid plans for an organization that would serve "colleges founded by women religious and still maintaining some relationship with that community." Funded by a grant originally given to NCEA for Sisters in higher education, this group took the name of the donors, the Neylan sisters. After some administrative details were worked out, the Neylan colleges, as a subgroup within ACCU, hired an executive director to manage the organization, then held triennial conferences, commissioned a study on minorities in their institutions, held annual meetings, and offered workshops for sister-trustees. What began in 1978 continues into the 1990s, as these often "invisible" colleges have adapted in remarkable ways to changing demographics, lessening control by religious communities, and pressures to strengthen financial management and increase financial resources.[21]

Graduate Education

As mentioned above, membership in the Association of American Universities, founded in 1900, was open only to those institutions that met AAU criteria for advanced study and research activities. Within

AAU the graduate deans constituted a subgroup, widened by regional organizations of deans. In 1960 the various groups of deans formed the Council of Graduate Schools (CGS), an organization not limited to AAU members. On its list of founding institutions we find The Catholic University of America, Fordham, Georgetown, Loyola in Chicago, St. John's in New York, Saint Louis University, and the University of Notre Dame. The distinction between AAU and CGS, not only in membership but also in purposes and agenda, serves to illuminate two distinct perceptions that existed among leaders in American higher education about the function of graduate education.

The first group (AAU) sought to develop replicas of the major research universities in Germany. For the founders of AAU at the turn of the century, this was partly because they resented the fact that large numbers of American graduate students studied in Germany instead of at American universities, but also because they themselves had benefited from the rigorous training available in Berlin, Munich, Heidelberg, and other German universities.[22] The goal of such education was to learn from the great teachers by listening to lectures and participating in the seminars, called by Friedrich Paulsen the "nurseries of research."[23] The second group (including the founders of CGS) insisted that the American experience must be grafted on to the German model. They tended to emphasize the importance of graduate education in building on the undergraduate studies and training teachers for both high schools and colleges, as well as preparing students for research and for the professions.

A significant American model for the first group was Johns Hopkins University, founded in 1876, with its declaration that "graduate and advanced education was its most important mission." A few years later The Catholic University of America was founded on the same principle. In 1900 the presidents of Harvard, Columbia, Johns Hopkins, the University of Chicago, and the University of California invited their counterparts at nine other universities, including Catholic University, to form an association that would try to raise both the image and the reality of American graduate education. They became the charter members of AAU.

The rapid growth of graduate education between 1900 and 1940 was more along the lines desired by the second group, those who were concerned about training teachers and other professionals. Total graduate school enrollments grew from 5,831 in 1900 to 106,119 in 1940; however, the earned doctoral degrees per year only increased from 382 to 3,290,

while master's degrees increased from 1,583 to 26,731. The questions repeatedly raised at AAU meetings were, Is the Ph.D. a degree for college
teachers or for researchers? Or, could it serve both?[24] And what was the
role of the master's degree?

A significant change occurred in American graduate education in the
post–World War II period as many "newcomers" challenged the well-
established research universities. Hugh Davis Graham and Nancy Diamond maintain in *The Rise of American Research Universities: Elites and
Challengers in the Postwar Era* that the traditional ways of ranking universities obscure the success of newly competitive universities. Among
these we can identify some of the Catholic universities, although they
are still working hard to achieve full recognition as research universities.[25]

Graduate education had existed in Catholic universities since the
twenties, but it was generally weak in research and catered to part-time
students interested in masters' degrees.[26] According to Gleason, "some
Catholics regarded American-style graduate work itself as an insidious
form of secularization."[27]

Prior to World War II, Catholic universities were more likely to target secondary-school teachers and potential college faculty than to support the development of outstanding researchers. As earlier chapters
show, their horizon was expanded and considerably altered by the government funding which became available for basic scientific research
during and after World War II and by the foundation support that developed.[28] Both of these sources—government and foundations—also
offered support for faculty and graduate students in the form of fellow-
ships and loans. Since some of these programs, particularly the Woodrow Wilson National Fellowship program and the Danforth Foundation grants, were aimed at increasing the number and quality of college
teachers for the impending surge in college-going youth, the objectives
of the CGS group were also being addressed. At least temporarily, funding for research activities and for the education of future college teachers created partners rather than adversaries in the debate about graduate
education.

Such a reconciliation matched the goals of Catholic universities.
Although the influx of European scholars to their campuses in the thirties contributed somewhat to the esteem for the German model, the
lack of financial resources made that model difficult to emulate. There
were some outstanding scholars in the forties and fifties on Catholic
campuses. However, they were so unusual that the criticism voiced by

John Tracy Ellis in 1955 was heard with open ears.[29] Even The Catholic University of America, founded for graduate education, had lost ground academically.[30] In 1966 one writer identified several well-known professors at Catholic universities: Walter Ong, S.J., and George Klubertanz, S.J., at Saint Louis; Morris Pollard, Timothy O'Meara, and John Noonan at the University of Notre Dame.[31] We could add to the list names of scholars at Fordham, Catholic University, Loyola of Chicago, and Boston College. But the rise in research activities in Catholic universities did not so much witness to Ellis's concerns about handing on the Catholic tradition of scholarship and learning as to the new opportunities for government research grants. Science and engineering were the major fields in which funded research became a possibility, while scholars in classics, history, or philosophy did not fare so well. Nevertheless, there began to be a change in the mind-set of administrators and faculty across the board: they started to envision their own campuses as housing "great" Catholic universities. Perhaps Father Hesburgh articulated this vision most clearly, but many of the Jesuit presidents echoed his call.

As one author put it: "Just as the way for the academic man to get ahead was to earn the doctorate, the way for an institution to get ahead was to offer it. There is no man who does not need to climb. Neither, apparently, are there many institutions. And, in our educational system, climbing means getting into the big league of graduate, and especially, doctoral study."[32] By 1974 the author of a small pamphlet, "Jesuit Education at Boston College," could write: "In short, intellectual development was taken as the principal goal of the college's curriculum and *the research-oriented graduate school as the standard of institutional excellence.*"[33]

Throughout the history of graduate schools at Catholic universities, one notes the conflict between the theoretical advisability of collaborative planning when expanding master's and doctoral programs (often voiced at national meetings as well as in private correspondence) and the drive to make one's own university the best in every field. William Leahy, in *Adapting to America*, regards the duplication of doctoral programs in particular as a great weakness. He cites the growth in graduate programs between 1940 and 1980 from eighty-two to at least 160, and the increase in the number of Catholic universities giving doctoral degrees from nine to twenty-one.[34] He also gives several instances of neighboring Catholic universities competing with one another by offering doctorates in the same areas of study.[35] Several of these competitors were Jesuit institutions, but despite the efforts of leaders in the Society as well as leaders within the universities, such as Paul Reinert and Robert Henle, to marshall their resources and focus their programs in specific areas, no collaboration was achieved.[36]

One of the obstacles to such joint planning was, no doubt, the way that American universities were organized internally, each school or department seeking prestige and support for its own priorities. In addition there were several external pressures on the universities. The development of graduate education, like that of undergraduate programs, was monitored by the regional accrediting agencies, the state education departments, and the specialized professional accrediting groups. Nathan Hatch in *The Professions in American History*[37] describes the way in which the offerings of graduate schools were affected by the new professional degrees in such areas as business, counseling, journalism, and public service. The sixties and seventies saw increased pressure to respond to students who sought professional training in these fields as well as in the more traditional ones of law, education, and social service. A career-oriented direction was part of the temper of the times to make studies "relevant" and to demonstrate "the usefulness of learning."[38] Consequently, the report of statistical growth in graduate enrollments does not necessarily reflect an interest in research and scholarship, especially in the arts and sciences.

Many of the Catholic colleges and universities, serving a population still very interested in upward mobility, tended to see a local market for a kind of graduate education that would function primarily as a support for career goals.[39] For this kind of education there were numerous candidates, and many of the smaller colleges began to offer master's degrees in education, social work, business, and nursing. By 1980, according to ACCU, there were approximately 89,000 graduate students in Catholic colleges and universities; 111 institutions were offering some graduate programs, while twenty-three were offering doctoral degrees.[40] The three granting the largest number of doctoral degrees were The Catholic University of America, the University of Notre Dame, and Saint Louis University. But, according to Timothy O'Meara, former provost at Notre Dame, the task now was to "transform solid programs into preeminent ones."[41]

In spite of its past leadership in the granting of doctoral degrees, the role of The Catholic University of America was being severely challenged. The mission of the founders, carried on through several generations, was to be the sole American Catholic university offering doctoral education. The colleges established by so many religious orders would be "feeder schools" for the university until such point as there was a demonstrated need for other Catholic graduate schools.[42] The immediate post-war increase in potential graduate students created, in the mind of the Jesuits, such a "point." From here on, each college would determine its own growth and would find irrelevant the plight of The Catholic University of America, as its enrollment base of seminarians, sisters, brothers, and priests began to evaporate. The challenges to the claims of academic freedom at the university in the sixties and seventies tarnished its image even more. Despite this, some leading scholars, such as Johannes Quasten, Joseph Komonchak, John Tracy Ellis, Avery Dulles, John Zeender, James Provost, Elizabeth Keenan, and Robert Kennedy made their home at Catholic University and attracted good students. The university presidents after 1967, Clarence Walton and Edmund Pellegrino, were themselves known as scholars in their own fields, respectively, business and medicine. The influence of CUA was probably felt more through the work of these individual scholars than through national leadership in the university world. The influence CUA had exerted through programs of affiliation for small beginning colleges came to an end in 1969, and its workshops for administrators in Catholic colleges, common in the fifties, were no longer offered.[43] Both of these programs had constituted a vehicle for leadership among the Catholic faculties at other institutions.

Economics dictated that the undergraduate population at CUA be increased so as to support the scholarly activities of the faculty and graduate students. This need had often been discussed at the university but, until the seventies, the forces which opposed changing the university's graduate focus had won. Gradually, attention shifted to recruitment of undergraduates. Consequently, a crisis arose in regard to the university's identity. Priority was given to residences, more recreational and athletics facilities, student services, and so forth, and CUA, the natural leader in Catholic graduate education, lost ground in its doctoral programs. It also had new competitors; Boston College, Saint Louis, Loyola of Chicago, Notre Dame, and Fordham all began to seek recognition as successful American universities. A blow to the prestige of all these universities had been the American Council on Education survey in 1966, which rated only seven departments at Notre Dame and three at CUA as "adequate or better in the quality of their doctoral offerings."[44] The others were not even in the running. The task ahead was envisioned as one of securing the needed endowments and personnel to move up the ladder to success in doctoral programs and research activities. We shall see that, to some degree, this task is being accomplished.[45]

Research in the Service of the Church

The inclination of Catholic universities to seek excellence in their graduate programs and to compete with major secular universities was welcomed by the American bishops. Indeed, the expansion of Catholic research activities was often justified by reference to the necessary role of the university in "service to the church." It was frequently said that the university "is the place where the church does its thinking." As the bishops became more visible in their attention to public policy, the universities saw themselves as being able to offer the bishops data and interpretations based on knowledge of the social sciences as well as theological and ethical perspectives for use in preparing their pastoral letters.

One such opportunity was presented in 1974, when the bishops began to plan for the bicentennial celebration two years hence. Addressing an audience at The Catholic University of America on March 5, 1974, the General Secretary of the Bishops' Conference, Bishop James S. Rausch, described the plans for the "Call to Action" Conference, also called the Conference on Justice, to be held in October 1976. He invited full participation by scholars in the planning process, stressing the importance of their contribution to the study of the issues and the development of blueprints for "changing the orientation of the society in which we live." He noted that, in his opinion, the relationship between the bishops and scholars was the single issue most requiring attention at that time.[46]

As noted in the previous chapter, the University of Notre Dame hosted an invitational meeting on January 11–13, 1976, entitled "Vatican Council: Ten Years Later." Over a hundred participants discussed the various ways in which the universities could help "the church" do its "thinking." When the report on the meeting was published,[47] an appendix listed five pages of "research needs" that had been identified. These had been gathered from the regional and parish consultations done in connection with the bicentennial "Call to Action" project, the IFCU agenda, the USCC/NCCB, an inter-university Committee on Research and Policy Studies, set up in 1975, and the Joint Committee of Catholic Learned Societies and Scholars.

The Call to Action Conference in October 1976 recommended that Catholic universities undertake research useful to bishops and other groups within the church working on social policies. Interest was expressed by several university presidents and was encouraged by the bishops in regional meetings, such as that held at Loyola-Marymount and at The Catholic University of America. The inter-university Committee on Research and Policy Studies had worked on the production of a directory of scholars who were competent and available to collaborate.[48] Lack of funding for research posed the main obstacle to success in this endeavor.

One successful research effort was an ecumenical project. Interest in legal issues which impinged on church-related institutions led to the foundation of the Center for Constitutional Studies in 1977 at the University of Notre Dame. Sponsored by the chief executives of the various associations of church-related colleges and universities, the Center was founded by the provost of the university, Rev. James Burtchaell, C.S.C., and directed by two lawyers with exceptional competence in church-state issues, Philip R. Moots and Edward McGlynn Gaffney. The Center produced several important studies: among them, Philip R. Moots and Edward McGlynn Gaffney, Jr., *Church and Campus* (1979) and *Government and Campus* (1982). Seminars in conjunction with these studies brought many bishops and presidents together. The Center later relocated to Mercer University in Macon, Georgia, and then to Baylor University, where it continues to serve an important purpose.

The discouraging part of the story is that after all the effort to bring bishops and universities together on research needs, there was no comparable agreement on funding. The same disappointment followed attempts to pursue the aims of the pastoral letters on peace and on the economy,[49] each of which added items to the research agenda.

The quest continued into the eighties with the initiation of the Institute for Inter-university Cooperative Research.[50] With leadership from Dr. Edmund D. Pellegrino, president of The Catholic University of America, nine research universities (CUA, Georgetown, Notre Dame, Dayton, Boston College, College of St. Thomas [Minnesota], Loyola University Chicago, Fordham University, and Villanova) formed a consortium to undertake research projects collaboratively. Presenting the idea behind the IICR to some Catholic foundations [FADICA] at a meeting in 1980, Dr. Pellegrino gave voice to his confidence in the role Catholic universities should play in the scholarly world: "I believe unequivocally that research and graduate education are indispensable to the unique intellectual ministry of Catholic universities, that this ministry is crucial to the future of a democratic society and that without it our culture will be impoverished and secularized. I believe, therefore, that some limited number of Catholic universities must expand the number and quality of their graduate endeavors and take their place with the foremost research universities of the world."[51] The institute hired an executive director, Mr. Frederick Brigham, and Catholic University offered him an office on campus. Affiliated with ACCU, the institute worked hard to achieve its goals. Researchers at the nine universities used satellite communication to develop projects and assign pieces of the research to different institutions. Unfortunately, after a few successful projects were completed, the IICR died for lack of funding. It failed despite the many protestations of support from the bishops and the universities for significant research projects related to the interests of the church community.

In the early seventies most of the Catholic universities were too insecure financially to make a sufficient investment in research. As their financial position improved in the late seventies and early eighties, the universities began to seek endowed chairs for recognized scholars, to broaden the opportunities for faculty to engage in writing and publishing, and to create a more friendly attitude toward research. In 1980 the bishops wrote in their pastoral letter on Catholic higher education: "In these efforts (scholarly research) the Church would be materially assisted if cooperative efforts could be organized to mobilize the combined research capabilities of the Catholic universities of this country. We shall work with the universities to find the resources necessary for research of high quality and utility." Quoting John Paul II in his address to the university presidents in October 1979, the bishops said: "Catholic scholars should examine all the fundamental questions in human culture with the highest degree of intellectual rigor."[52] Encouragement was continually offered by Pope John Paul II to universities around the world concerning their responsibility for critical research. However, the many other concerns of the American church in the years since 1970 have resulted in a lack of the episcopal energy envisioned in the pastoral letter urging cooperation in "finding the resources" needed for research "of high quality and utility."

This search for resources had intensified at several of the universities, notably the University of Dayton, the University of Notre Dame, Georgetown University, and Boston College. The success of their efforts to receive government grants and to raise substantial private funds was gratifying. However, the importance of building a sizable endow-ment became the first priority, since the overwhelming dependence on tuition could only be offset by a sufficient income from endowment. As indicated earlier, the attainment of this goal had an urgency about it because of the declining number of religious on faculty and in ad-ministration, a decline accompanied by the gradual abolition of the con-cept of "contributed services" as a "living endowment." The issue of episcopal help in financing the research efforts of the universities was frequently raised at the meetings of the Bishops and Presidents' Com-mittee during the decade of the eighties, but even the suggestion that NCCB merely share in the expenses of the IICR met no positive re-sponse.

An additional problem surfaced in the discussion about episcopal support of IICR; if the bishops had a "share" in it, would they also seek to control the research agenda? This, of course, tied in with the larger question of academic freedom. Hence, as often happens, the necessary collaboration failed from lack of trust as well as lack of resources. The reaffirmation of the importance of the Catholic university's function as a center of research in *Ex Corde Ecclesiae* in 1990 served to renew pro-posals for some kind of research institute that would serve the church in its mission to society. The quest for funds for such an endeavor has been renewed by a group of scholars who are seeking to establish a free-standing Catholic Institute for Advanced Studies.

Curriculum Revision: The Impact on Philosophy and Theology

As we have indicated, there were many external pressures on Ameri-can higher education in the seventies. Political agenda such as the anti-war demonstrations were accompanied by a wave of demands for more "relevant" curricula and were part of a general anti-institutional envi-ronment. Transported onto the campus, such pressures were sometimes welcomed and utilized by the internal constituency (faculty and stu-dents). Like other institutions, Catholic colleges and universities re-vised curricula to meet the demands of the "consumer," a new name for the student, and the administration gave way before faculty insistence on their rights in the determination of course content and grading prac-tices. Interdisciplinary seminars on topics of current interest dotted the landscape and more traditional courses in Western civilization and En-glish literature often became objects of scorn. By the eighties the move-ment was toward Black (or, later, African-American) studies, Women's

studies, Native American studies, and so on. The groups that had previously been ignored in the traditional liberal arts courses now sought
identification and recognition. Although the rhetoric used by Catholic
college presidents and other administrators continued to focus on the
liberal arts tradition, the requirements for the degree, negotiated by faculty and students on curriculum committees, gradually minimized the
importance of that tradition in the student's education.

Perhaps the greatest change in curriculum in the Catholic colleges
and universities occurred in the areas of religion and philosophy. What
had previously been seen as two essential components of a unified search
for truth now became simply two different academic disciplines taught
according to the specialties of the professors. No longer was philosophy seen as the necessary foundation for theological studies. Furthermore, there was no agreement as to what kind of philosophical system
might serve to integrate a liberal arts curriculum in the way that neo-
scholasticism once did.[53]

We have already discussed some of the work done by scholars in
the forties and fifties. These new insights had a profound effect on the
curriculum of Catholic higher education.[54] By the late seventies the re-
duction in credit hours and the shift to electives in philosophy and theology altered dramatically the role of these two disciplines in the general
education given to all students. The traditional names for philosophy
courses—metaphysics, epistomology, ethics—gave way to "relevant"
titles ("The Experience of Being," "Christian Perspectives on Marxism," etc.), while the field of religion underwent a radical restructuring.[55]

The ambiguity about the terms "religion," "religious studies," and
"theology" as descriptors for departments and programs created enormous confusion that inevitably surfaced not only in faculty discussions
about curriculum but in many subsequent discussions about the Catholic identity of institutions. If the students were not receiving competent
and convincing presentations of Catholic teaching in their religion
classes, could the college claim the name of "Catholic"? Patrick Carey,
in his study of the situation at Marquette University, reminds us that
until the mid-fifties courses in religion were basically courses in apologetics, lacked scriptural foundation, and were inadequate in the light of
theological advances. Theology, properly so-called, had been assumed
to be proper study only in seminaries and theologates; the task of college teachers of religion was assumed to be one of basic instruction in
Catholic faith and practice.

This idea had been challenged in 1943 when Sister Madeleva Wulff, C.S.C., initiated a doctoral program in theology at Saint Mary's College in Notre Dame, Indiana, for Sisters and lay people unable to gain admittance to theological schools.[56] Many of them were college teachers who lacked the opportunity to study for advanced degrees. Following Vatican Council II, the emphasis in the documents of the Council on the role of the laity in church ministries and the need for education encouraged increasing numbers of persons to pursue higher degrees in the fields of Scripture and theology. In turn, this led to college faculties whose education had not been in seminaries and theologates; often, indeed, they had theological degrees from non-Catholic institutions where lay people were accepted as students.

Added to this was the new spirit of ecumenism, which inspired Catholic colleges to offer a broader selection of course offerings including studies of religions and theologies other than Roman Catholic. Consequently, some departments began to use the terminology of "religious studies" to cover a very broad field of offerings. Professional associations also tended more and more toward using that descriptive. The breadth of the course offerings made them more palatable to non-Catholic students who were now being required to take religion courses, a situation which had only recently developed in some colleges. In some instances this new requirement was due to state education departments that accepted the college's claim that religion was intrinsic to the liberal arts degree only if religion was required of all who received the degree. Courses required of Catholic students *only* were regarded as "confessional" and therefore not compatible with government criteria for being legally "nonsectarian."[57]

In the spring of 1967 the College and University Department of NCEA surveyed changes occurring on Catholic college campuses.[58] So soon after Vatican Council II, there were already eighty-two institutions that had developed programs, including chairs of ecumenical studies, to promote ecumenical dialogue. At the same time, ninety-eight schools reported that in the past three years the number of required hours in theology/religion had been reduced. Elective courses in theology had been introduced and were seen by some critics as implying that there was no longer a set pattern by which to achieve the objectives of teaching theology in colleges. Lay faculty were now present in the theology departments at 122 colleges. Very few, either clerical or lay teachers, had doctorates. A hopeful sign was that seminary-type lectures were being replaced by newer methods of teaching.

There was no uniform pattern discernible in the changes made by the Catholic higher education community in this regard. What is obvious is that the teaching of theology suffered in the process, and a generation of students may have graduated from Catholic colleges innocent of knowledge of the Catholic roots of their education. Apparent in discussion among faculty at national meetings of the College Theology Society and the Catholic Theological Society of America is the ambiguity and discomfort they experienced as they reflected together on their task as educators.[59] Yet there was strong resistance to suggestions that while it was a fact that Roman Catholic theology (i.e., theology based on the Roman Catholic tradition) was an academic discipline, those teaching it in Catholic colleges needed to be in harmony with or, at least, respectful of the teaching of the Catholic Church. Fearing ecclesiastical oversight of "theology" courses, some faculty retreated to the term "religious studies" to describe their course offerings; in some instances they did not change what they were doing but simply had a new name for it.

An attempt to clarify the academic purpose of the study of religion or theology was made by Rev. William J. Sullivan, S.J., then an assistant professor of theology at Marquette, in an address to a joint meeting of the College Theology Society and the College and University Department of NCEA on April 14, 1971.[60] Pointing to the traditional courses in religion at Catholic colleges, Sullivan argued that the purpose they served, i.e., an apologetic or custodial purpose, was no longer functional. He argued that the purpose of theology is knowledge, whereas the object of religion is a certain form of conduct. Theology should not be confused with religious education even though it is taught within a specific religious tradition. Roman Catholic institutions have a tradition that recognizes the role of the intellect in exploring the content of faith. While a theology department must operate within the framework of academic procedures, it need not be neutral. The college can indeed, quite legitimately, require all students to take courses in theology or religious studies, since the basic ideal that the Catholic university professes includes a curriculum that deals with all aspects of human life.

Such discussions regarding the kind of theological education that should be given to undergraduates occupied the agenda of several national and regional NCEA meetings. At the same time, changes continued to be made in individual institutions, based not so much on theoretical positions regarding theology/religious studies as on secondary school curricula and graduate school programs. In the secondary schools a constant series of new textbooks indicated dissatisfaction with things as they had been prior to Vatican Council II, combined with confusion about some of the new teachings after the Council. To this was added the weakness of doctoral programs in the Catholic research universities, which left the colleges without leadership in their attempt to update curricula.[61]

At The Catholic University of America, where so many clerical teachers of religion on the high school and college level had been trained over the years, the relation of religious education to theology was the source of a major conflict in the middle seventies. A department of religious education had evolved within the School of Education and, under the leadership of Rev. John Cooper and later Rev. Gerard Sloyan, it had become known for its openness to new trends and for its willingness to educate sisters and laypersons, a need not yet met by the school of theology. The overlapping of this program with that of the department of theology (one of the ecclesiastically erected departments) was obvious and created internal tension.

In July 1971 a newly formed ad hoc committee held its first meeting under the chairmanship of John K. Zeender of the history department. This committee had a mandate from President Clarence Walton "to work toward the unification of the Schools of Theology and Canon Law and the Department of Religion and Religious Education." The diligence of the committee in seeking to accomplish this task is shown by the fact that it held its tenth meeting on December 2 of the same year. Lengthy discussions on the distinction between theology and religious studies are recorded in the minutes of this committee. Perhaps most significant is the new understanding of the role of the social sciences in the study of religion, an insight not present in traditional theological studies. New scholarship in Scripture, now recognized as valid by Pius XII, required knowledge of anthropology, archaeology, and languages, fields which were taught in the Graduate School of Arts and Sciences.

Finally, in its report of April 1972, the committee recommended the creation of an academic entity to be called "The Graduate School of Religious Studies" within which there would be five departments: theology, canon law, church history, sacred scripture, and religion and religious education. The process by which they reached this recommendation is extremely enlightening with respect to the interests which surfaced at any suggestion of unification of the various departments. The arguments put forth pro and con make it clear that the ambiguity about appropriate terminology in high schools and colleges was present at the top level of Catholic higher education as well.[62]

A rather disheartening picture of the situation in Catholic colleges and universities in 1975 is given by J. Patrick Gaffney, S.M.M.:

> The problem is that "theology" as taught today on the undergraduate level is elusive; it is difficult if not impossible to squeeze it into the boundaries of any one formula or definition. So many pressures have been exerted on it that it does, at times, take on novel if not strange forms. On the practical level, hardly two institutions treat the discipline in the identical way. The increase of non-Catholics into our colleges, the tight university and departmental budget with its concomitant difficulties, the trend away from core requirements, the development, not to speak of the upheavals, within the discipline itself, its divorce from campus ministry and its struggle to be counted—having been for all practical purposes dethroned—as an equal partner among the humanities, its attempt to appeal to a dynamic, ever-changing "new breed" of students and speak to their experiences and needs, all these have shaped a "different" type of theology on the undergraduate scene.[63]

Obviously, in the light of such ambiguity concerning programs in theology, there was little or no argument for retaining heavy philosophy requirements as necessary support for theology, particularly as the philosophers now moved toward methodologies other than that of neoscholasticism. In addition to providing the foundation for the teaching of Thomistic theology, scholastic philosophy had also served to facilitate the integration of knowledge deemed essential for the development of a true Catholic intellectual life.[64] Many authors have pondered the causes for the quick demise of scholastic philosophy, but the fact that it disappeared is incontestable. As a result, the link between philosophy and theology was severed, causing significant damage to the handing on of the values of Western civilization, particularly the Catholic intellectual tradition developed in Europe.[65]

A questionnaire answered by twenty-two Jesuit colleges (excluding those in New York State, which were set aside for a separate study, possibly because of the impact of Bundy money) contains evidence of radical change by 1972. In addition to the new laypersons and non-Catholics on the board of trustees, most of the colleges had added non-Catholics to the faculty, including the theology department, and reported that the percentage of Catholics in the student body had declined from 89 percent to 79 percent. Theology and philosophy requirements had been drastically reduced. Non-Catholic students were usually required to take some theology courses; these are taught as an academic discipline.[66]

That theology was no longer to be taught as "confessional" is attested to in the minutes of the annual meeting of the College Theology Society in 1967.[67] When the representatives of Jesuit colleges and universities met in Denver in 1970 they agreed that all undergraduates must take at least two courses in the theology department, but that no one can be required to take a "confessional course, that is, one that assumes commitment to a particular tradition."[68]

Thus, the discipline of theology evolved during the years under study in this work and, as is usual with such changes, there were both good and bad results. By the late eighties many colleges would give serious consideration to upgrading the role of theology in the curriculum, not as the criterion for judging other disciplines, but as an essential component of an education given at a Catholic college and as an important player in interdisciplinary studies.

The "new horizons" described in this chapter were vital to the viability of institutions of higher education at the end of the twentieth century. Many, though not all, of the changes Catholic universities underwent were in response to the external pressures experienced by other American universities at the time. Derek Bok has summed them up under two main headings: (1) pressure from government enforcing a multitude of regulations to achieve social goals such as affirmative action for minorities and women; and (2) pressure from students whose idealism of the sixties took on an anti-institutional complexion in the seventies with the long drawn-out conflict in Vietnam.[69] To become players on the field of American higher education and to deal with these pressures, the Catholic colleges and universities strained resources to meet accreditation requirements, to increase enrollment from a more diversified pool of students, to subsidize graduate education and research activities, and to collaborate with leaders in the very institutions competing with them. They had come a long way from the "ghetto" mentality, and they were regarded by many of their non-Catholic colleagues as worthy of respectful attention, even if they were still ignored by others. To achieve this status they may also have shut out, at least temporarily, some of the wisdom resident in their own rich tradition. In the process they also engaged in a lengthy dialogue with the Roman authorities concerning the impact of these changes on their identity as Catholic universities and colleges.[70]

FIVE

Partnership
with Laity

In February 1963 a new model of Catholic higher education
appeared with the founding of Sacred Heart College in Bridgeport,
Connecticut. Following the inspiration of Vatican Council II, Bishop
Walter W. Curtis, bishop of Bridgeport, decided to open an institution
that would best meet the needs of his people and that would be "entrusted" to laymen. It would be coed and commuter, thereby focusing
on providing maximum opportunity for the local men and women seeking a bachelor's or associate's degree. Begun with nine full-time faculty
and 173 students, it grew to approximately 100 faculty and over 1,700
full-time students by 1967–68 with a total enrollment of 2,276. Bishop
Curtis determined that, unlike existing Catholic colleges, it would be
administered and staffed exclusively by laymen. By clear intent, it would
foster an atmosphere of ecumenism. Both of these characteristics have
marked its evolution over the years, although it has become partially a
residential college and added master's degrees in certain areas as well as
various programs for adult learners.[1] It has remained in the hands of
laypersons.

This venture of Bishop Curtis was unique,[2] but its spirit and purpose surfaced during the late sixties and early seventies in many other
institutions. Indeed, if one wants to find a single aspect of Catholic higher education that changed most in the years under study, one
must consider the startling rise of the laity within the ranks of faculty,
administrators, and trustees. In 1960 there was still a great predominance of members of the founding religious community at every level of
Catholic institutions. By 1990 they constituted a small minority of the
teaching faculty, research scholars, and administrators in Catholic colleges and universities.[3] After 1967 almost all institutions had a significant number, often a majority, of lay trustees. As time went on, even in

institutions where the president was still a member of the religious community, most of the vice presidents and deans were not. As in other matters, this was not a uniform development, but movement toward greater presence and real partnership with laity was obvious on almost all Catholic campuses.

It was a movement that impacted on the ever-present question of Catholic identity. For while "laicization" should never be confused with "secularization" (used pejoratively), the predominance of lay men and women in the college's internal constituency meant that the relationship of the college to the church no longer had a clear canonical character as an apostolic work of a religious community. Roman Congregations had been accustomed to deal with problems in Catholic universities through the Superior General of the particular religious community that sponsored and governed the institution. Even in cases where bishops had been involved in the early days of the college and had invited the religious community to take charge of it, the authority of the bishop over its affairs had been minimal. Bishop Curtis, having founded Sacred Heart University with its all-lay administration, wanted the administration to make all necessary decisions even though he still influenced selection of trustees and had a role in the appointment and dismissal of presidents. Religious communities continued to serve on the boards of trustees and in faculty and administrative posts in the colleges they had founded, but the governance of the institution was no longer exclusively in their hands.

There are few, if any, histories of Catholic higher education in the United States which attend adequately to the tremendous contribution of Catholic laity to the strength of the enterprise. Not only the support of tuition-paying parents but also the contribution of dedicated lay faculty and administrators (whose low salaries subsidized the operation) made it possible to maintain and develop approximately 250 colleges and universities. In addition to the financial basis they supplied, the competence and talent among the laity made them an important factor in the life of Catholic higher education.[4]

The quality of the education given in these institutions is a tribute to the thousands of lay faculty who enriched the curriculum with their own scholarship and dedicated teaching. The attainment of a Phi Beta Kappa chapter often depended on lay faculty to provide the five members needed for the application. Since many bishops before Vatican Council II prohibited religious from studying in "secular" universities, lay faculty and administrators were often the ones who provided contact with the larger world of American higher education and who, by their participation in Phi Beta Kappa and other scholarly associations, brought recognition to the institutions they represented.[5]

In chapter 1 we touched briefly on the theological and practical literature of the fifties which focused on the evolving role of the laity in the Roman Catholic Church. Although the lay men and women who contributed to Catholic higher education were not all Catholics, a high percentage were, and this meant that the way the role of the laity was understood within the Catholic tradition was important. The work of Yves Congar was perhaps the most significant from a theological point of view, while works like that of Donald Thorman and Thomas O'Dea dealt with some of the practical questions that needed to be answered. John Henry Newman had once pointed out that without the laity there would be no church, but the strong hierarchical and clerical emphasis of the nineteenth century and the dependence of American immigrants on their local pastors for not only spiritual but also educational counseling had obscured Newman's vision. In the mid-twentieth century, movements such as the Catholic Evidence Guild, the Grail, the Catholic Rural Life Conference, Catholic Worker, and various units of Catholic Action flourished under lay direction. But they were generally regarded as somewhat marginal by church authorities until the point when they sought ecclesial recognition—a "mandate"—for their organizations.[6]

John Courtney Murray, S.J., in explicating the essential role of the laity within the church, continued the interpretation given by Leo XIII, Pius XI, and Pius XII to the various forms of Catholic action. Recognizing the importance of lay action in matters of civic decision, and seeing the layperson as mediating spiritual values to the temporal order, Murray wrote: "The ministerial and hierarchical priesthood mediates grace and the Holy Spirit to human beings, which is the divinizing mission of the church. The laity mediate the Christian spirit to institutions of civil society, which is the humanizing mission of the church."[7]

The lay-directed movements under the general umbrella of Catholic Action in the forties and fifties were well known on Catholic campuses by way of the lecture circuit and through publications such as *Commonweal*, *Jubilee*, and *Integrity*. By the late fifties there were programs of lay volunteers for overseas missions, many under the auspices of the religious communities. Nevertheless, until the mid-sixties, Catholic higher education itself was directed by religious communities or bishops with little or no consultation with laypersons.[8] There are three distinct levels of university life where radical change subsequently occurred: the administration, the trustees, and the faculty. We will look at each of these levels in turn, noting the growth in numbers and in power of the laity that characterized the decades after 1960 and created a true partnership between them and the founding religious group.

Administration

In the early history of colleges and universities sponsored by religious communities, administrators were named by the duly appointed religious superiors. Presidents often recall the circumstances of their appointment by provincials as a cause for amazement at the naiveté with which it was accomplished. Sister Ann Ida Gannon, B.V.M., president of Mundelein, confesses that although she was "installed" as religious superior of the community in 1957, she had no induction as president, since it simply went with the office of superior. Father Hesburgh recounts that the president of the university handed him the keys to the office while walking across the campus and that was it! The provincial had simply made the appointment. Deans were similarly given "obediences" on the day appointed, often with little or no training in administration.

The first breakthrough came in the late fifties and early sixties when the simultaneous appointment as president and religious superior ended for most communities. The main reason for this change was to enable the president to remain in office beyond the canonical six-year limitation on the incumbency of the superior. Although provincials continued to select persons for presidencies and deanships until the late sixties, the technical appointment gradually was made by election by the board of trustees. Until 1967, however, these boards were generally made up of members of the Council of the religious communities. Even after the trustees became predominantly lay, the choice of president was usually made in accord with the wishes of the provincial. Often the board "election" was a rubber stamp of the Council's choice. Other administrative appointments such as deans and vice presidents were soon left to the wisdom of the president and/or boards of trustees.

Deans of business, engineering, law, and medical schools had often been laypersons. In the expanding years after World War II, it also became common to seek vice presidents for business offices and development work from among lay candidates with expertise in those areas. The school of liberal arts and the office of student life, however, were headed by religious as long as possible. Jesuit universities were very clear about policy in this regard, as were many of the other men's colleges. By the seventies several of the colleges founded by women religious had turned to lay presidents, but these still sought to keep nuns in the office of academic dean in order to influence curriculum, and in the office of the dean of students in order to keep alive the general religious and social culture of the campus. These early lay presidents faced difficult financial situations but speak eloquently of the support they received from the sisters, some of whom became mentors for them.[9] Lay presidents were also to be found in diocesan colleges, and they report a high level of trust from the local Ordinary as a pleasant aspect of their job. Trustees of the colleges sponsored by men religious generally did not hire lay presidents.

Continued increasing enrollments in the sixties led to more faculty and this, in turn, resulted in a search for administrators with expertise beyond that of the sponsoring religious community. Customarily, top administrators had worn many hats: members of the religious community governing councils, trustees of the college or university, part-time faculty, and proctors in the residence halls. In the larger colleges and universities it was clear that the hiring process followed in American higher education, the declining numbers of religious interested in serving in academic circles, and the desire to add faculty of outstanding educational degrees made it necessary to have highly-placed lay academic administrators with contacts and experience outside the walls of the campus.

Despite the desire of the Jesuits to keep control of curriculum and faculty hiring in the hands of Jesuit administrators, the increase in laypersons holding the position of academic vice president at Jesuit institutions by the late sixties and early seventies was significant. This had not happened without due consideration. As early as 1958, Father General Janssens had indicated to the American provincials that they should address the question of the status of laymen in Jesuit universities. Janssens did not have a problem with the presence of laypersons on faculties, but he expressed concern about their "level of ascendancy on the administrative ladder, their involvement in the policy making process . . . and their academic jurisdiction over Jesuit members of the faculty."[10] Yet, as was pointed out by the presidents, one could not increase lay faculty to the point required by the expansion of their universities and not allow them the opportunity of rising in the ranks to deanships and academic vice-presidencies, offices most concerned with faculty issues. It was also important that the administrators have credibility in the eyes of the new members of the faculty, and degrees from major universities affirmed the status of lay deans and vice presidents. It is interesting to note that at the same time that Jesuit presidents were recognizing these facts, they nevertheless declared that "As administrators of Jesuit colleges and Jesuit universities, we readily recognize our responsibility to clearly establish and to spell out in our structural organization the lines of Jesuit leadership and control, particularly in each key spot. *We recognize that legal authority must be clearly and exclusively invested in Jesuit hands.*"[11] This attitude would change rapidly in the late sixties. By 1970, for example, there were no Jesuit deans at Loyola University in Chicago.

Different reasoning characterized the position of women religious in their institutions. When Ann Ida Gannon, B.V.M., became president of Mundelein College in Chicago in 1957, there were only seven lay faculty. Within a few years, according to data of a self-study carried out in 1962–64 under the direction of the lay academic vice president, there were 118 full- and part-time faculty, of whom 69 were sisters, 2 priests, and 47 lay. In terms of full-time faculty, by 1965 there were 28 sisters out of 62; by 1967, 31 out of 83. This growth led Sister Gannon to continue increasing the number of lay administrators, so that by 1967 there were two lay vice presidents, an assistant dean, registrar, director of public relations, director of financial aid, and many staff persons.[12]

A study by Karen Kennelly, C.S.J., details the growth in lay presence among administrators and faculty in the colleges sponsored by women religious.[13] In many cases, the sisters originally constituted the majority of administrators with the same duplicative roles that we found among the men's religious communities, for example, sister superior/president. Kennelly notes that the majority of lay faculty in these colleges were women;[14] she does not say whether the same was true of administrators, but it is probably safe to assume that in areas such as finance and development men may have been more widely represented, while in academic affairs and student life sisters and lay women predominated. If the college became coeducational in the seventies, the proportion of lay men may have increased. I have not discovered statistics on the cumulative number of lay men/women or lay/religious among administrators in Catholic colleges. A search through individual catalogues may be the only way to study the trend, but common experience is that from 1960 on, the increase was very significant and the list of appointments reported in *College Newsletter* bears that out. However, it was not the case everywhere. At Villanova University, for example, despite enormous growth in lay faculty, the first lay vice president was appointed only in 1968.

The administrative post still reserved for a member of the religious community was that of the president. Some institutions mandated in their statutes that the president be a member of the religious order that sponsored the institution, but many others did not.[15] As mentioned above, by the seventies, a group of some twenty or thirty lay men (and a very few lay women) had assumed the presidency in colleges sponsored by women religious or by dioceses; the larger universities sponsored by men religious (Jesuits, Holy Cross, Augustinian) have continued to select presidents from among their own ranks.[16] If it is true that the exception proves the rule, then the University of Detroit Mercy, a merger of the Jesuit University of Detroit and the Sisters of Mercy's Mercy College, is that exception. After the merger, the presidency was held by a Dominican sister, Maureen Fay, who had been president of Mercy College. By 1980 there were lay presidents in approximately thirty-five Catholic colleges and universities; in 1990 this number had increased to ninety-nine. While the trend is a clear one, several institutions present us with an alternation between lay and religious presidents based on availability and credentials.[17]

The Catholic University of America, which always had a number of distinguished lay faculty, had its first lay president in the election of Clarence Walton in 1969. However, several of its administrators had been outstanding laymen, and the leadership of Roy J. Deferrari and Martin McGuire, among others, was crucial to the academic development of the university. Colleges related to dioceses, rather than to religious communities, also had a higher percentage of laity among their administrators.[18]

Lay administrators in the sixties were still conscious of the tight link between the institution and the religious community or the diocese that had founded it and still governed it. They knew that the president, as a member of the religious community, was not free to make changes without consulting local or provincial superiors and that financial matters often required permissions from headquarters in Rome. The presidents also began to feel the tension between their religious superiors' educational philosophy and understanding of religious authority, on the one hand, and the bewilderment of the increasingly lay faculty and administrators at some of the presidential decisions which were made in "council" and communicated without supporting reasons. They knew that basic change was needed. It was also obvious to them that the goal of moving the college up in the ranks of American higher education was hindered when actions to change curricula, modify rules of student life, award tenure, and approve budgets and investments required prior approval from the religious community's leadership. The presidents began to dream about independent boards of trustees to whom alone they would be accountable, and lay administrators and faculty had reason to support this vision.

Trustees

We have already discussed the expansion of boards of trustees to include laymen that occurred in the late sixties and early seventies. Webster College, under the direction of the Sisters of Loretto, was the earliest Catholic college to declare for an independent board (in 1966), but its president, Sister Jacqueline Grennan, S.L., also announced that this meant that it was no longer to be a "Catholic" college, since she regarded such an identity as a contradiction in terms. Her stance made it necessary for Hesburgh at Notre Dame, Reinert at Saint Louis, and those who followed their lead to emphasize that there was no contradiction between being "Catholic" and being governed by independent boards. The only college to follow Webster's path was Manhattanville College in Purchase, New York.[19]

Among the diocesan colleges, the number of lay trustees also increased significantly. Seton Hall had a board composed of thirteen laypersons and seven clergy in 1967, and the College of St. Thomas in St. Paul reported fourteen lay and five clergy. In 1972 a report on Jesuit institutions (other than those in New York) for the period 1961–71 pointed out that boards had been expanded and diversified to include laymen and non-Catholics and that fewer university administrators were now included among the trustees. The number of faculty had doubled, with most of the new faculty being lay people, including a growing number of non-Catholics. In the area of student personnel, a startling change had occurred; in 1961 eighteen of twenty directors had been priests or religious, while in 1971 none of them were. A similar but less drastic change is reported in the faculty of the theology department: in 1961 there were no lay members but in 1971 they constituted over one-fourth of the faculty and included non-Catholics.[20]

One of the questions that surfaced during the gradual transition at Boston College, described in some detail in chapter 2, was the requirement in the bylaws that the president must be a Jesuit. Rev. Charles M.

Whelan, S.J., a professor at Fordham Law School, recommended drop-ping this requirement because of the weak 5 to 4 decision in the *Tilton* case. He also favored a new preamble to the bylaws which spoke only of the "Jesuit tradition" and the "Judeo-Christian heritage," rather than its "Catholic" character. However, the search committee had already been directed to select a Jesuit for the presidency and had found J. Donald Monan, S.J., who would lead Boston College through the next two decades as it grew in both enrollment and quality of students and fac-ulty. The new independent board of trustees would give significant support to the president in various internal struggles with faculty and in creating an endowment that would permit the college to become one of the leading Catholic research universities.[21]

We could multiply stories of individual colleges and their shift to independent governing boards, but what is unquestionably true is that, no matter what the structure devised or the length of time it took to create it, the contribution of the new class of "real" lay trustees was enormously important to the growth and strengthening of the Catholic colleges and universities. The trustees, men and women, Catholic and non-Catholic, brought to their task not only expertise in a variety of fields but a dedication to the institution that they now held "in trust." In the beginning, quite naturally, they took their cues from the presi-dent and members of the religious community who served with them on the board, but gradually they became more confident and independent. Many of them were alumnae/i of the college and had a deep respect for its traditions and educational purposes. Presidents saw to it that these new trustees joined the Association of Governing Boards. Many of them participated in various workshops on trusteeship sponsored by the Association of Catholic Colleges and Universities. The names of these pioneer lay trustees are not known to most students of higher education or church history, but they deserve recognition. By 1979 some 77 percent of the Catholic colleges and universities had adopted the new format and expressed satisfaction with the mixed composition of the board. The "new guardians" of Catholic higher education, as Martin Stamm called them,[22] were essential players in the continued advancement of the institutions to a higher level of scholarship and teaching during the eighties. And their phenomenal success as fund-raisers made much of the advancement possible. It is arguable that more significant than gov-ernment funding in the eyes of the presidents was the entrée into the corporate world and the foundations which they acquired by electing lay trustees. The stories of these pioneer lay men and women are ones that remain to be written, but the biographies of Daniel Schlafly and

Edmund Stephan, the first lay chairs of the boards at Saint Louis and Notre Dame, respectively, in 1967, would be a good beginning.[23]

The initial group of lay trustees were generally friends of the president and of the religious community that had founded and governed the institution. They were clearly committed to continuing the tradition of the founders and had no interest in lessening its Catholic character. They presumed that there would continue to be members of the religious community who were competent and interested in faculty and administrative posts and that, as trustees, they would be primarily involved in the financial and legal matters of the institution. Deference to the sister-president or father-president is obvious in board minutes. For that reason, little formal attention was paid to orienting the lay trustees to the mission of the institutions for which they were increasingly responsible. The trustees assumed that the "mission" was the province of the Jesuits, the Religious of the Sacred Heart, the Sisters of St. Joseph, the Holy Cross priests, and so forth. As non-academics, they also respected the role of the faculty in determining curriculum, even though they found some of their attitudes difficult to understand. Agenda for meetings of the board's academic affairs committee in the seventies and eighties were often dominated by faculty and student representatives seeking to provide new curricula, usually at the expense of such traditional areas as philosophy and religion. In the context of student and faculty unrest, the trustees, so new to the issues of higher education and deprived of the academic wisdom of administrators and faculty belonging to the religious community (no longer eligible for election as trustees), may have failed to question some of the changes that were made during the seventies, changes that affected the Catholic character of the institution. They focused on the external constituencies—the funding agents, the local civic community, the legal questions—and on improving the image of the university or college as a significant contributor to American life. All of that was very much needed if the institutions were to survive the difficult financial situation in the seventies, but by the time they reached the next decade, they were conscious of some deep questions about the specific mission of Catholic colleges and universities.

Faculty

It can be surmised that behind the move to lay participation in trusteeship and in the administrative offices of the universities was the pressure brought by the dramatic post-war increase in enrollment which forced the rapid hiring of a considerable number of new, usually lay, faculty.[24] According to the 1967 McGrath-Dupont survey cited earlier, in the 160 institutions reporting, 69 percent of the faculty were laymen.[25] While the presence of lay faculty was not an innovation on some campuses, the addition of new fields and the desire for academic excellence meant that wider searches had to be conducted for potential teachers and more lay candidates had to be considered. According to the Ford-Roy study, the presence of full-time lay faculty was considerably greater at the men's colleges; the median for those reporting for 1964–65 was 69 percent lay, and in one-fourth of the group more than three out of four full-time faculty were lay.[26] The women's colleges numerically constituted the largest cohort within Catholic higher education (55 percent of those serving lay students) but were generally much smaller in size of student body than the men's colleges. Among them there was a wide range with regard to lay full-time faculty; about one-fourth reported fewer than 25 percent lay faculty and another fourth well over 60 percent. The study found significant differences between those colleges founded before 1950 (more lay faculty and larger student bodies) and those founded after 1950, mostly for sisters. But the trend was clear; those colleges that depended almost exclusively on members of their own religious communities to staff the institutions would not survive the seventies.

An example of a dramatic shift in the proportion of lay faculty to religious was that which occurred at Villanova. In the two decades following World War II the faculty grew from 78 in 1944–45 (65 percent Augustinian) to 331 in 1963–64 (14 percent Augustinian).[27] In cases like this it was obvious that issues regarding salaries and benefits would engender calls for faculty senates and administrative attention to the needs of the lay faculty. It became clear that there must be new procedures, new policies, and new attitudes. The faculty strike at St. John's in 1965, due largely to the absence of structures by which faculty could share in decision making, reverberated on many Catholic campuses.[28] In censuring St. John's, the AAUP gave notice to many other institutions that they needed faculty handbooks, committees on promotion and tenure, and faculty senates with recognized authority over curriculum. While many colleagues from among the clerical and religious faculty joined in the effort for recognition, the impetus came from laypersons for whom the issue of salaries and benefits had a greater urgency.[29]

Handbooks began to appear and faculty organization charts showing faculty senates or academic councils became a normal part of the scene. Internal battles were often waged over the proportion of elected to appointed members in such councils. Tenure already existed in some institutions, although it was granted by the presidents without much consultation or official process and usually was given only to lay teachers. Now, in line with AAUP policies, faculties at Catholic colleges began to insist on peer evaluation of colleagues and recognition of committees on rank, salary, and tenure with a decisive role to play in the process. In a letter of October 24, 1968, the Executive Secretary of the NCEA College and University Department urged all members to incorporate the AAUP Statement of Principles of 1940 into their own documents.[30] Within the next decade chapters of AAUP were established on many campuses and individual membership in AAUP increased.[31]

A contemporary comment on the new "faculty freedom" at La Salle College in 1967 pointed out that the general mood in American higher education was intensified in Catholic colleges because of the importance given by Vatican Council II to the role of the layman. At schools like La Salle College in Philadelphia, the change had been dramatic, with laymen now exceeding religious by five-fold.[32] La Salle actually was one of the few Catholic colleges that had always had laymen on its board of trustees (since 1869), but the administration had remained in the hands of the Christian Brothers. Now, in 1967, the major issue was involvement of laity in administration and faculty; two vice presidents (public relations and financial affairs) were lay and a faculty senate was functioning. According to the president of the senate, "faculty recommendations on salaries, core curriculum, teaching load, tenure, and college objectives have—in the past seven or eight years—been accepted with little or no modification." The establishment of the senate simply "formalizes what the faculty has been doing for many years through *ad hoc* committees."[33]

La Salle was proud of its record in this regard, and attributed it to enlightened leadership and the fact that lay and religious faculty worked closely together. The fact that it was governed by brothers rather than by priests may have reduced the image of "clericalism," although it is true that many laypersons do not avert to such distinctions. Nevertheless, the tremendous increase in numbers of students, and therefore of lay faculty, made formal structures necessary. When the president, Brother Bernian, was asked about the emerging role of laymen at La Salle, he said: "It's something we had to do, not because others were doing it, but because it was the only right way to conduct the College. La Salle needs the dedicated layman today more than ever before."

The important contributions of the lay faculty in both teaching and research accentuated the need for university officials to defend the principle of academic freedom. When faculties were composed mainly of religious personnel, any seeming aberrations from Catholic orthodoxy were handled behind the scenes by religious superiors. The advent of laymen with more critical approaches to learning and with diverse backgrounds that included study at secular universities required new processes for handling cases of complaint from chancery offices or indignant parents and alumni/ae. Hence, the role of the AAUP took on great significance. The 1970 "interpretation" of the "limitations clause" in the 1940 Principles, noted in chapter 2, was seen as a victory for academic freedom on Catholic campuses, but its very ambiguity presaged continuing trouble.[34]

By 1970 it could be said that the Catholic higher education community in the United States had adopted the general American principles regarding academic freedom.[35] Symbolically, the AAUP conferred its Alexander Meiklejohn Award for an outstanding contribution to academic freedom on Rev. Theodore Hesburgh, C.S.C., in April 1970. His orchestration of the Land O'Lakes document in 1967 and his consistent defense of American Catholic higher education in all the dialogues with the church authorities in Rome provided sufficient reason for the award.

This award to Hesburgh raises an interesting question: how much did true academic freedom depend on the involvement of the faculty in decision making? Five years earlier it had been the crucial issue in the AAUP censure of St. John's University. But at Notre Dame and other Catholic universities, faculty handbooks with provision for senates or academic councils were just coming to birth. At Loyola in Chicago, there was a faculty complaint when the Jesuit trustees reversed a previous policy of electing half of the Faculty Council and moved to appoint them all, and in 1966–67 there was faculty protest about some non-renewal decisions. As the seventies progressed, the demand for a defined role for faculty in the formulation of university policies was intense in all American universities. Respect for the judgment of one's peers in determination of promotions and tenure was now extended to demands for legislative authority of faculty committees over changes in curriculum and student life. The financial crises in the early seventies provided the occasion for faculty to insist on a role in developing budget priorities. But in many Catholic colleges and universities such faculty demands were only slowly implemented.

The internal struggle for power on many campuses often pitted the administration against faculty and students. Protests against the war in Vietnam led to general anti-institutional rhetoric, and what might have been a gradual development in the structures of faculty governance was interrupted and gave way to radical demands. At the same time, the "professionalization" of the faculties, begun in the late fifties in most Catholic colleges, intensified loyalty to one's discipline and one's scholarly associations above that owed to one's institution, and thus the old familial type of governance would no longer work.

Many faculty rejoiced that the old familial type was dying. In his study, *The Academic Man in the Catholic College*, based on data collected in 1960, John D. Donovan was quite negative about the previous situation. To him, "the ultimate authority for major academic policies and practices resides outside the college, in the office of the ecclesiastically-defined superior." Many of those interviewed did not see much chance of a change in the way things were decided: they saw themselves as "objects" of decisions rather than as actively participating "subjects."[36] The image of family which seemed so appropriate to the Catholic identity of the college had its dark side; it failed to include everyone and it also kept power within a paternalistic mode. Faculty found this increasingly unacceptable and successfully pressed for change. They envisioned a family composed of adults, not children and parents.

They were aided by the revolutions occurring in both the church and American society regarding participative decision making. As we have seen, a separation of the university governance structure from ecclesiastical superiors was gradually coming about, and independent boards of trustees were being established. This meant that laymen, as trustees, would now have legal authority over the university, thus ending the dependence on religious superiors. Ironically, many of these laypersons had less understanding of the claims of faculty for participation in governance than some of the old-time superiors. The internal constituencies have thus continued to struggle for power, most notably at times when the issues under consideration result from political or economic forces. Budget priorities, enrollment trends, racial and gender diversity, professional training vs. liberal arts—these are areas where the positions taken by trustees depend less on the lay/religious distinction than on basic ideologies. When concrete decisions need to be made and concrete votes are taken, these ideologies become apparent. And unfortunately, the commitment to the "mission" of the Catholic university, which should be the determining factor, is often circumvented.

When we reflect on the revolution in the role of laypersons on the campuses, we need to take into account the tremendous changes going on at the same time within religious life. Vatican Council II had called for a renewal that would put religious more in touch with the needs of the modern world. Religious faculty who worked in Catholic colleges and universities had always learned much about the modern world from their lay colleagues and they now welcomed a deeper partnership with them. In many instances they began to vote with them when divisive issues arose, regarding themselves primarily as faculty rather than as members of a religious community expected to vote as a bloc. What was going on here? In a legal challenge concerning the right of the Franciscan religious faculty to vote in elections concerning unionization at St. Francis College (they had been excluded by the National Labor Relations Board), the Court of Appeals found that to exclude them on the basis of their vows was unreasonable and arbitrary.[37] Thus, in the legal arena, the distinction between lay and religious faculty was erased.

Religious faculty joined their lay colleagues in the pursuit of academic excellence, gradually focusing less on their "apostolic goal" of character formation and moral development of young people, and more on competitive achievement in the various disciplines of study. The shift in perspective is evident in the catalogues of the colleges and in reflective essays written by faculty of the period on the purposes of Catholic higher education. Paul Reiss, a professor of sociology and vice president at Fordham, later president of St. Michael's College, wrote of the potential role conflict experienced by some religious of the period inherent in this shift in goals. He described a solution that seemed to be emerging as "role specialization," the decision of religious on college campuses to be either religious-religious or academic-religious. Reiss claimed that integration of the academic career and the religious role is difficult to achieve, if not impossible, for "one cannot be writing an article in physics while hearing confessions, counselling students, or providing religious instruction in a parish."[38] For this reason, many religious at this time opted out of higher education in favor of more "direct" apostolic service. Those who remained did not universally accept Reiss's position. Undoubtedly, they experienced tension, but those with a strong commitment to scholarship and teaching viewed it as inevitable but not determining.[39]

It is interesting to speculate on what "might have been" if the proportion of religious faculty to lay men and women had remained as it was in the 1950s. What if the number of religious had continued to climb? What if there had been continued control of administration by members of religious communities? And where would the colleges be had they not established independent boards with dedicated laymen as members? Obviously, such speculation is outside the realm of history, but what seems obvious from history is that the gradual inclusion of lay men and women in the governance of the institutions as faculty, administrators, and trustees has been a source of growth and strength in Catholic higher education in the latter part of the twentieth century. It has contributed enormously to an improved public image, thereby securing support from non-Catholic as well as Catholic sources.

As with so much in the history of these institutions, a practical need, that of increasing faculty and administrators as rapidly as possible to deal with the post–World War II enrollment boom, led to the changed internal constituency of Catholic colleges and universities after 1960. Actions taken to meet this need were simultaneously justified by the new ecclesial recognition of the role of the laity in Catholic enterprises. Theological reflection followed the decisions that were made rather than preceding them. Lay men and women who taught in Catholic colleges were now conscious of living out their own unique vocation; they were no longer simply helping the religious founding group carry out its mission. Their commitment to the values of the founders created a forceful model for the students and gave the colleges themselves something of a new identity. The Catholicity of the institution could no longer depend on the presence of members of the religious community. It would have to be cultivated and strengthened by a partnership of men and women, both lay and religious, who understood and believed in it. The promotion and safeguarding of the mission and heritage of the college had become a shared responsibility.

SIX

Are They
Still Catholic?

Like a refrain, the question about the Catholic identity of the colleges and universities was heard at the end of every verse in which the colleges and universities celebrated their improved place in mainstream higher education. As they moved into the eighties, dealing with government regulations about equal opportunity in hiring, changes in family structures, and diversity in the background of students, they were often put on the defensive about their basic mission as institutions within the church. How had the adaptation to American higher education changed their relationship with the church? How had the loss of so many religious community members and the consequent shift to predominantly lay faculty, administrators, and trustees affected that relationship? How significant was government funding in their inability to define their Catholic identity? Were all the changes made in curriculum and student life justifiable in terms of the *aggiornamento?*

Having been born, in John Paul II's words, "from the heart of the church,"[1] universities in every era have engaged in a process of acculturation. They gradually changed their identity from the original model of medieval corporations of scholars or of students to the complex and diversified creatures of their own place and time. In the attempt to redefine themselves and carry out their missions more effectively in the modern world, the Catholic colleges and universities in the United States, as we have seen, were constantly interacting with several diverse constituencies. To one author, they should be described as coming "from the heart of the *American* Church."[2] Their identity was constantly being negotiated with government, American higher education, the church, and the internal constituency. What was the result?

We have traced the relationship of Catholic colleges and universities with federal and state governments as it developed through judicial and legislative interpretations of the First Amendment. By 1975 they were fairly certain that their eligibility for federal funds would be upheld by the courts, unless they displayed "legal sectarianism" in their curriculum and in hiring practices. However, their freedom of action was now being limited by new regulations intended to bring about greater equity in society. We have noted the increased dependence of private colleges on funding from public resources, state as well as federal. In addition, we have examined the influence of fund-raising from private donors, both individual and corporate, as well as from major foundations. To present one's institution to these various "publics" required careful use of language about one's mission and purposes. Leaders of Catholic higher education were warned that in making such presentations they should avoid being "sectarian" in the way that the courts defined it,[3] and yet alumni/ae, donors, and parents often sought a clear "Catholic" image. Another constituency with whom the institutions were engaged in discussions about their identity was an internal one, that of trustees, administration, faculty, and students. By the end of the seventies this conversation was taking place within a community largely composed of laypersons rather than members of a religious order. But, whether faculty were lay or religious, they were now in tune with colleagues in other sectors of American higher education and shared in the values of the professions and the secular associations, such as AAUP.

Finally, and foundationally, the colleges were engaged in an ongoing effort to negotiate their identity in dialogue with the Roman Catholic Church. Prior to the sixties, their Catholic character was seldom disputed. However, following Vatican Council II it seemed important to the academic leaders to articulate the character of the Catholic university in terms such as openness, ecumenism, and collegiality, rather than in phrases such as "education for service to family and church" or "formation in Christian values." This shift in descriptive language required explanations and reassurances for those who counted on the colleges to transmit the faith tradition to a new generation. The dialogue regarding Catholic identity led to engagement with different ecclesial partners: the religious orders, the local bishops, the National Conference of Catholic Bishops (NCCB), the Roman Congregation for Catholic Education (under various titles),[4] and the popes. In the preceding chapters we have indicated points at which serious tension with Roman officials arose: IFCU elections, honorary degrees, questions regarding ownership of property by the religious community, attempts to control hiring and tenure decisions on grounds of orthodoxy, and widespread criticism of the teaching of theology or religious studies. During the years after

Vatican Council II, Catholic higher education (as well as other Catholic institutions) was busy "redefining its Catholicism,"[5] and such a task required of the partners to the dialogue a mutual understanding of the language being used as well as of the accommodations being made to American culture. Between 1965 and 1990 there is an extraordinary paper trail which enables us to follow the dialogue, primarily through the documents that were developed by the International Federation of Catholic Universities and the Congregation for Catholic Education in Rome. We see in them the diverse points of view brought to the discussion by university presidents, American bishops, and Roman Curial officials. When they are studied side by side with all the changes occurring in American higher education during these same years, it becomes obvious that the experiences and therefore the opinions of those involved in the dialogue are radically different from one another.[6] The efforts noted earlier in the work of the Purpose and Identity Committee of NCEA College and University Department (1970) and the Bishops and Presidents' Committee (1974)[7] to define a Catholic university were complemented by the international attempts of the IFCU at its various regional meetings.

Beginning with the IFCU Assembly in Tokyo in 1965, the Catholic universities attempted to claim the autonomy and freedom characteristic of the modern university, while at the same time identifying themselves as "Catholic."[8] Following Tokyo, as we have seen, the American leadership met at Land O'Lakes and drew up a document which became their chief declaration of independence from authorities outside the university. They also insisted, however, that "the Catholic university must be an institution, a community of learners or a community of scholars, in which Catholicism is perceptibly present and effectively operative."[9]

When the next IFCU Congress was held in 1968 at Lovanium University in Kinshasa, the Congo, the American delegates attempted to include language from Land O'Lakes and were only partially successful. The American experience was not universal, and the vocabulary of "autonomy" and "academic freedom" proved to be unacceptable to many delegates from other continents. The document drawn up at the meeting in Kinshasa stressed the role of theology and the creation of a Christian community of learning that would promote ecumenism and social justice. Nothing was said of autonomy or academic freedom.[10]

However, Cardinal Garrone, now the Prefect of the Congregation for Catholic Education and a participant in the Kinshasa meeting, recognized the importance of continuing the discussion. On January 10,

1969, he sent out a questionnaire to all Catholic universities asking them to reflect on and report about the way in which they were implementing Vatican Council II. At the same time he invited them to elect delegates to a meeting to be held with representatives of the Congregation. As a result, thirty-nine delegates arrived in Rome in April 1969.[11] The debate focused mainly on the meaning of "autonomy" and its relation to the dependence of the universities on the magisterium of the church. Eventually, the delegates agreed on a text which drew from both Land O'Lakes and Kinshasa.[12] Of particular note was the development of the four characteristics to be looked for in any Catholic university:

1. A Christian inspiration not only of individuals but of the community as well;
2. A continuing reflection in the light of Christian faith upon the growing treasure of human knowledge;
3. Fidelity to the Christian message as it comes to us through the Church;
4. An institutional commitment to the service of Christian thought and education.

Agreement on these principles, although not always on their meaning, would become evident by their subsequent appearance in all the various documents leading up to and including the 1990 apostolic constitution, *Ex Corde Ecclesiae*. Furthermore, assent was given to the fact that not all Catholic universities had the same canonical status, but they were all nevertheless "Catholic." The text reads:

> All universities that realize these conditions [the above four principles] are Catholic universities whether canonically erected or not. The purposes of the Catholic university can be pursued by different means and modalities according to diverse situations of time and place, and taking seriously into account the different natures of the disciplines taught in the university. . . .
>
> Two basic categories can immediately be discerned: those institutions which have a juridical bond to Church authority in one form or another and those which do not.

This acknowledgment of non-canonical Catholic universities was welcomed by the Americans, since the 250 or so colleges and universities in the United States at that time were all lacking in "canonical erection," with the exception of specific faculties at The Catholic University of America. It also made room for the smaller colleges that were "Catholic" but did not seem to be included in the various descriptions of the "Catholic university."

In addition, the 1969 Rome document included the statement from Land O'Lakes: "To perform its teaching and research functions effectively the Catholic university must have a true autonomy and academic freedom." This was followed by a lengthy analysis of the philosophical and theological principles relating to the autonomy of the university. Boldly, it states that the freedom of research and teaching is "limited by no other factor than the truth it pursues. Every limitation imposed on the university which would clash with this unconditioned attitude for pursuing truth would be intolerable and contrary to the very nature of the university."

This clear recognition of academic freedom was slightly modified when the document addressed the teaching of theology. It pointed to the role of revelation in the research of the theologian and granted that the magisterium can intervene, but "only in a situation where the truth of the revealed message is at stake." However, "in every case the intervention of the competent ecclesiastical authority should respect the statutes of the institution as well as the academic procedures and customs of the particular country."

In the light of later actions by the Holy See, it is interesting to note the understanding expressed here for the freedom of the theologian:

> He must be allowed to question, to develop new hypotheses, to work toward new understandings and formulations, to publish and defend his views, and to approach the theological sources, including pronouncements of the teaching Church, with the free and full play of modern scholarship. His work should normally be reviewed and evaluated by his scholarly peers as is the case in other disciplines.

On the other hand, caution is urged upon those teaching theology. The teacher must "present the authentic teaching of the Church . . . but may and should form his students to an intelligent and critical understanding of the faith, prudent account being taken of the maturity and previous preparation of the students."

Finally, there is an acknowledgment that "In a university without statutory relationships with ecclesiastical or religious superiors, these authorities may deal with the theologian as an individual member of the Church. If they can make representation to the institutional authorities, any juridical intervention in university affairs must be excluded."

Underneath all of these statements we can almost hear the American delegates trying to explain the independence of their institutions, newly reflected in the transfer of governance to boards of trustees no longer directly linked to the authority of the religious community. The ongoing efforts of these institutions to upgrade their theological faculties in a way that would win recognition from peers in the wider American higher education community and their desire to strengthen their distinctive character as Catholic were clearly in tension, but the post–Vatican II climate gave hope of a resolution, and the Rome document of 1969 reflected that hope. The recommendation that the bishops should be advised by "men trained in universities and experienced in the university ministry" no doubt contributed to their optimism.

The delegates left Rome with a sense of achievement, having submitted the text to the Congregation for its October 1969 meeting. It was sent to the colleges and universities for their review, and in a cover letter inviting their comments, Garrone said, "The present document which ensued as a result of this work by the delegates constitutes the *first part* of a dialogue between the Congregation and Catholic Universities." When the document was reviewed by the Congregation some problems with it were identified. Cardinal Garrone then asked for further review and response from the universities.[13]

Complying with this request for further dialogue, Father Hesburgh convened a group in Chicago on February 12, 1970, including Paul Reinert, Robert Henle, Neil McCluskey, John McGrath, Gregory Nugent, Clarence Friedman, Michael Walsh, Clarence Walton, and Daniel Schlafly. In their response to Cardinal Garrone, the importance of their new structures of government is stressed. The "norms" in the latest draft, as contained in the Congregation's response, were unacceptable and seen as "outside interference." "Perhaps," the group wrote, "most of all, the members of the laity who, as members of the governing board of a Catholic institution, assume the immediate and gravest responsibility for the life of the university or college, would find outside interference intolerable and be unable to serve."[14] Father Hesburgh added, "The divergence between the two positions (delegates and Plenarium of the Congregation) seems almost total and absolute."

Cardinal Garrone now moved the process forward by initiating further meetings with the IFCU Council in January 1971, a broad-based symposium in May 1971, and regional meetings at Land O'Lakes, Caracas, and Grottaferrata. At this point, Garrone impressed the delegates favorably, listening to their concerns and trying to incorporate them in the document. In a report to the NCEA Executive Committee, Father Henle expressed the gratitude of the delegates to the Cardinal "for his patience, his warm receptivity and his understanding."[15] A final meeting of Garrone with the IFCU Council was held at Grottaferrata in February 1972, which resulted in proposing further revisions for the Congregation. The next step would be the Second International Congress of Delegates from the universities in November 1972 to discuss the Grottaferrata text.

An interesting comment is that of Neil McCluskey, S.J., who had participated in most of the meetings. He noted that "The responses given in the Results of the plenary session [of the Congregation] are friendly and sincere, tactful and intelligent, pastoral and paternal. Happily gone is the old tone of condemnation, reproof, and threat. Unhappily, on the critical issues of autonomy and academic freedom, the responses are in direct opposition to the position paper unanimously adopted by the delegates to the Rome Congress"[1969].[16]

Indeed, the Congregation had submitted five pages of "observations" on the Grottaferrata/Rome text which dealt with the critical points of disagreement and provided the agenda for future meetings.[17] In presenting their observations on the document submitted to them, the members of the Congregation meeting in Plenary Session on October 3, 1969, had based their discussions on the mandate given to the universities by Vatican Council II to make the Catholic university "a sort of public, stable, and universal presence of Christian thought in the entirety of human higher culture, so that by its study and institutions it might form its students into men of outstanding learning who are able to undertake the more serious obligations of human society as well as preparing them to be witnesses to the faith before the world" (quoting *Gravissimum educationis*, no. 10). Their observations focused on the role of the Catholic university in "ordering, according to a very precise hierarchy of values, . . . the whole of human culture, with respect to the message of salvation." The Congregation sought greater specificity about the ways in which the autonomy of the university and the magisterium would be harmonized. They had strong reservations about the treatment of theology as an academic discipline with the same freedom in teaching and research as that enjoyed in other disciplines. They wanted more concrete norms regarding the levels of intervention by church authorities.

In his report to the Executive Committee of the NCEA College and University Department after the meeting on May 4–6, 1971, of IFCU

representatives with Cardinal Garrone and his staff, Father Henle observed that the continuing theme about which there was a difference
of opinion was the relationship that should exist between the Catholic
university and the Sacred Congregation. The Congregation insisted on
a juridical dependence on ecclesiastical authority and disagreed with
the universities on the academic freedom that should be granted to philosophy and theology.

While all these discussions were going on, significant concerns
about the American scene were being expressed by Father Friedman of
the NCEA College and University Department. The *Tilton v Richardson* case in Connecticut was in litigation, and he feared that if the decision were unfavorable for the four colleges involved, the Catholic colleges would lose federal aid.[18] In a letter to Most Rev. Joseph Schroeffer,
Secretary of the Sacred Congregation,[19] he called attention to this problem and stressed the fact that federal aid to Catholic universities in 1967
amounted to more than 125 million dollars.[20] Friedman also wrote to
McCluskey that while he was favorably impressed by the draft from
Grottaferrata, he was disappointed that he was not invited to the May
meeting with the staff of the Congregation, because he was "deeply disturbed by the ban issued by the Doctrinal Congregation prohibiting
the appointment to college and university positions of laicized and ex-
priests. That amounts to a religious test for priests."[21] The previous
month he had written in the same vein to Henle, arguing that this ban
on hiring laicized priests (issued January 13, 1971) posed a potential
conflict "with the policies and procedures of the American professorial
community."[22] In another communication to McCluskey he expressed
his concern about the "harassment of theologians at Catholic institutions," warning that if it doesn't stop, "they will transfer to independent
or public institutions."[23] Finally in July 1972 he put the issue squarely to
Henle, stating that in his opinion, "the time has arrived for a decision as
to whose document it will be, the universities or the Congregation."[24]

Friedman's pent-up anger exploded when the Holy See entrusted the
selection of the delegates for the November 1972 Second Congress of
Delegates to a committee of three under the direction of President
Clarence Walton of The Catholic University of America, whereas the
selection of delegates to the First Congress had been done under the
aegis of NCEA.[25] Evidently Friedman's reaction was reported to Rome,
because Msgr. Marchisano of the Congregation soon instructed Walton to ask Friedman to be one of the three persons to help in the selection of the delegates and to invite him to participate in the meeting next
November.[26] Friedman thought that the slight of NCEA was a "devas-

tating vote of no confidence" and was pleased that the chair of the College and University Department's Executive Committee, Msgr. Terrence Murphy, intended to follow up in the effort to discover the reason for it. Friedman pointed out that Father Hesburgh was also dismayed by the fact that the selection of delegates had been shifted away from NCEA. Friedman wrote: "I continue to be hurt, disturbed and puzzled by the decision of the Congregation to take the selection of delegates away from the College and University Department. I consider it a repudiation of myself and the Department."[27] The revised text of the Grottaferrata document, one prepared by Garrone after the Congregation's plenary session and intended to be used as the basis for the November 1972 meeting, further angered Friedman. He was very upset that the "Introduction" had been removed, and he referred to the new text as "a butchered copy of the Grottaferrata document."[28]

Friedman's reaction was shared by some of the other participants in the Grottaferrata meeting. It is not hard to understand their dismay at the excision of the introduction. It was in that section of the document that the Catholic university, precisely as university, was discussed in great detail. One is struck by how clearly it built on the documents of Vatican Council II and how the perceptions expressed in it would continue to be defended by the universities right up to the apostolic constitution *Ex Corde Ecclesiae*. Indeed, some of the principles enunciated in the introduction to the 1969 draft are included in the 1990 document, especially in its articulation of the role of the Catholic university vis-à-vis the various cultures and institutions of contemporary society. Several statements in the discarded introduction regarding the nature of the Catholic university are worth noting:

1. It should be characterized by its universality, i.e. openness to all knowledge and all values;
2. It is characterized by its respect for the free human person;
3. It must be a truly human community;
4. It should promote the unity and progress of all mankind;
5. It must be a dynamic agent for social change, change which looks toward the future;
6. It must strive toward a synthesis of order and freedom, of tradition and renewal;
7. It must not align itself with any single political party or ideology.

Fathers Friedman, Hesburgh, and Henle had all been involved in the development of the many documents and revisions since the first IFCU

Assembly in Tokyo. To them, the elimination of the contextual introduction meant that the document would lack balance and would deal only with the ecclesial aspects of the life of the Catholic university. They had hoped that the concepts of autonomy and academic freedom would be linked to the nature of the university as such. By deleting the opening reflection on the role of the university vis-à-vis the world around it, the Congregation, in their opinion, had repudiated the work of the delegates. When the group convened by Hesburgh in Chicago on February 12, 1970, wrote to Cardinal Garrone, they expressed their dismay at what the Congregation had done to the original Grottaferrata text: ". . . in all frankness it must be stated that a number of the Responses (from the Congregation) are based on assumptions and principles which are no longer operative, tenable, or even relevant to American higher education."[29]

Cardinal Garrone, in a letter of June 22, 1970, to Hesburgh, disagreed with the observation that the Plenarium had repudiated the statement of the delegates and urged that the Congregation's desire for further dialogue and work on the document was not unreasonable. The Americans state unequivocally that their universities are Catholic; it is because of this, Garrone argued, that Rome is seeking to define "autonomy" more precisely so as to understand the role of the magisterium and how its responsibilities are to be exercised. He suggested that concrete examples be given of "usurpation" of the universities' freedom or autonomy by the magisterium. He also asked for examples of what lay trustees, government agencies, and accrediting agencies regarded as "unjust interference" with university operations.[30]

After the responses to the draft were received by Garrone, he and his entire staff met with the Executive Council and the Steering Committee of IFCU in Rome during the first week of May 1971. It was decided to widen the consultation by regional meetings of IFCU. Following this meeting, Hesburgh wrote a very frank letter to Cardinal Garrone on May 17, 1971. He expressed regret that an adversarial relationship often developed but thought it was inevitable when the staff were at a central location and the others came in "from the realities of living on the frontiers of action." Hesburgh said that more important than such tension was the common purpose of creating a Catholic university, "perhaps the most difficult and most important institution to create in the Church today." He pointed out that there had been a decrease in the number of universities that consider themselves Catholic (for example, Montreal, Laval, and Lovanium in Kinshasa) and that others who were members of IFCU had dropped membership (Fordham and three other Jesuit universities). Latin American universities are in great difficulty because of political upheavals.[31] He pleaded therefore for encouragement rather than constant criticism by the church officials. He then dealt with the control of theology and insisted that "after all, for three-fourths of the Church's history orthodoxy was somehow maintained by bishops, theologians, and even laymen without the existence of a Congregation." Since control has not worked in the past, "we must find new methods of leadership and inspiration that will make for theological growth that will assure orthodoxy and faith in some manner different than the control of the past which was deadening and regressive."[32] He ended his letter with a deep personal appreciation for the attitude of listening which the Cardinal projected at the meeting and assured him of their continued hope in his leadership.

Hesburgh followed up on the May 1971 meeting in Rome by inviting a group of thirty participants to Land O'Lakes in September for a regional meeting, so that further refinements in the text might be developed.[33] In his letter of invitation, Hesburgh wrote: "If I may be permitted a personal note, Catholic higher education has never had a tranquil existence in Rome. Historically, Rome has been uncomfortable and sometimes uneasy with 'Catholic' institutions of higher learning. Perhaps for the first time in history we are facing a Pope and a group of curial administrators who are willing to listen and to learn and are most sympathetic to our endeavors. It seems to me that this opportunity is worth the sacrifice of a few days to respond to their sincere interest and to work to make something important happen in Catholic higher education in our time." By this time, Hesburgh had been succeeded by Rev. Hervé Carrier, S.J., in the presidency of the IFCU, but he was still close to Pope Paul VI and was the acknowledged leader of American Catholic higher education. His spirit of reconciliation as the meeting of November 1972 approached was an important factor in the final agreement.

During 1971 there were also IFCU meetings in Kyoto, Grottaferrata, and Caracas, and a final one was held at Grottaferrata on February 3–5, 1972. Under date of May 10, 1972, Cardinal Garrone sent a new text to all the presidents, based primarily on the text that emerged from the February meeting of the IFCU Council at Grottaferrata. He recalled the history of the document from the first meeting in Rome of April 1969 up to the present. The text was being studied by the Congregation, "making use of the opinions of various experts and proposing certain observations, especially about the serious and delicate problem of the relationship of freedom of teaching and research on the one hand and of the responsible role of the magisterium of the Church on the other." Garrone announced that a general Congress would be held in Rome on November 20–30, 1972, to which delegates would be elected by the universities. In addition to studying the draft document, the delegates would discuss the theme: "the possibility and means of collaboration between the universities in the area of research in the Church—exchange of viewpoints."

The Cardinal pointed out that the goal of the universities and the Congregation is the same: "the progress of the truth of the faith and the reign of Christ," but they emphasize different aspects of achieving it. "Each must understand and accept the point of view of the other and not be amazed or irritated at certain matters. A compromise is not what is treated of here, but a collaboration that is trusting and generous from which will come a complementary relationship." He attempted to set the stage for a discussion that would be symbolic of this trust: "there must be an effort to obtain a text in which there is eliminated every trace of polemics and every appearance of mutual lack of trust in pursuing the common goal."[34]

During the summer of 1972 the delegates were selected: Joseph Cahill, C.M. (St. John's), Margaret Claydon, S.N.D. (Trinity),[35] Robert Henle, S.J. (Georgetown), Theodore Hesburgh, C.S.C. (Notre Dame), Terrence Murphy (St. Thomas), Gregory Nugent, F.S.C. (Manhattan), John Padberg, S.J. (Saint Louis), John Raynor, S.J. (Marquette), and Clarence Walton (Catholic University). All except Cahill had been involved in the work of the College and University Department of NCEA and had lived through many of the previous meetings together. There was strong agreement among them that the autonomy characteristic of all true universities must be protected, and that the value of doing so was that it would, in the long run, promote the reputation and therefore the influence of Catholic universities in the various cultures in which they existed. It must be noted that the delegates were not very specific about how this influence would reflect the Catholicity of their institutions.

Once again in Rome in November 1972 the delegates labored over the language to be used in the document. Basic to the discussion was the text known as Grottaferrata/Rome, already reviewed by the delegates after the Congregation's plenary session had attached its "observations." Ten days of position papers and interventions did little to change minds, but at last they had an agreed-upon text: "The Catholic University in the Modern World."[36] Henle later remarked on the changed atmosphere: ". . . remarkable for its candor and frankness, for the sincerity and determination of its discussants, and for its complete openness and freedom."[37] Before leaving Rome, the delegates asked that the document be distributed as approved by the Congress, without further emendation by the Congregation. This was done by Cardinal Garrone's office, and the text was published in the *College Newsletter* of March 1973. This was certainly a gesture of confidence on the part of the Congregation, or at least of Cardinal Garrone, but, unfortunately, this was not the end of the matter.

On April 25, 1973, a letter from Garrone to all the presidents informed them that "The Catholic University in the Modern World" had been approved by the Plenary Assembly of the Congregation (composed of thirty-seven cardinals and bishops) and by Pope Paul VI on April 6, 1973. Nevertheless, along with praise from the Plenary Assembly for the work of the delegates came word of the necessity for attending to two lacunae: (1) each institution must set out formally its character and commitment as "Catholic," and (2) each one must create within itself "appropriate and efficacious instruments for self-regulation in matters of faith, morality and discipline."[38] A further puzzling comment was that while recognition was given to institutions "with no statutory bonds to ecclesiastical authority," they were not removed from "those relationships with the ecclesiastical authority which must characterize all Catholic institutions." The meaning of this distinction would be debated for years to come and would never be satisfactorily resolved.

A decade earlier the conflict over the awarding of honorary degrees had raised a red flag about Roman desire to control American Catholic institutions.[39] Now, when the end product of the IFCU meetings at Tokyo (1965), Land O'Lakes (1967), Kinshasa (1968), and Rome (1969, 1970, and 1972) did not win the whole-hearted support of the Congregation, there was anger and frustration among the university presidents. It was disheartening to be told that Rome was still not satisfied with a statement of non-juridical relationship.[40] Garrone directed that his 1973 letter should be affixed to the document whenever it was disseminated, and NCEA complied.

While the Americans and the IFCU were attempting to deal with Garrone's letter, another action by Rome complicated matters further. A questionnaire was sent to all Catholic universities from Rome asking for input on a document to be prepared on ecclesiastical faculties. Upon receipt of this by several "non-ecclesiastical" universities, their presidents, through NCEA, sought an explanation as to why they had been included. They suspected that it might be a foreshadowing of Vatican control over non-ecclesiastical universities.

In April 1975 Rev. John F. Murphy, Executive Secretary of the College and University Department of NCEA, visited Rome and attempted to convey to Cardinal Garrone the concerns of the American Catholic universities and to inform him of various positive developments: meetings of presidents with bishops, peace and justice programs, discussions about Catholic identity. After his return to Washington, he wrote to Garrone, summarizing the items discussed during their visit and calling attention to "the troubling issue of the resigned priest teacher. We are most anxious that some favorable consideration be given to the requests made by the International Federation of Catholic Universities. I would leave aside for the moment the question of whether justice forbids action against these men who have received permission from the proper Church authorities to withdraw from active ministry."[41]

In his response, Cardinal Garrone expressed his appreciation of the effort being made to work more closely with the bishops. However, he insisted, "The name 'Catholic' is more than an adjoined adjective that externally adorns an institution. Much less can it be merely something autodetermined by the institution itself. To be 'Catholic' means to have a living relationship with the Church and this, of course, is impossible apart from the Bishops of the Church." It was a reasonable statement, and the presidents probably agreed that the name "Catholic" must indeed mean something recognizable, but it gave rise to a fear: would there now be an attempt to develop a mechanism for recognizing "Catholicity" in a university, based on its relationship to the bishop? The crux of the issue was identified: what were the criteria for such recognition?

Garrone outlined the matters which concerned him about the American Catholic colleges and universities: the "tenure" of professors who attack the doctrines and morals of the Catholic Church, campus and dormitory morality, the invalid alienation of ecclesiastical property, confusion between theology and religion, religious science, religious sociology, religious education, etc., and the difficulties that come from the confrontation between academic freedom "as it is understood in your country and exigences of the Catholic faith and of Catholic theology, deriving as they do from authoritative revelation that is guaranteed by the Pope and the Bishops, constituting the Magisterium of the Church."[42]

As to the treatment of laicized priest-teachers, Garrone stated that the regulation about them was from the Congregation for the Doctrine of the Faith, not from the Congregation for Universities and Seminaries, but that the universities should certainly arrange contracts in line with the norms. He retorted to the comment about injustice by maintaining that forbidding them to teach seminarians "is not a sanction or punishment, but derives from the nature of the case. No implication of injustice can be involved."

At the IFCU meeting in New Delhi in September 1975, an informal meeting of the American delegates with Cardinal Garrone seemed to clarify the matter: the document in preparation was intended to apply only to ecclesiastical faculties, but the Congregation thought input from others would be helpful. If the presidents wished to make a corporate reply through NCEA, that would be acceptable, but individuals were also free to submit their own responses.

Upon his return from New Delhi, Msgr. Murphy reported to the Bishops and Presidents' Committee about both the formal and informal meetings with Cardinal Garrone.[43] In addition to the question about the addressees for the intended document, i.e., was it only for ecclesiastical universities, the delegates had raised the question of laicized priests on theology faculties. Garrone had agreed that there was a concern about the faculty members who were teaching future priests, but indicated that he understood the difference for those in typical colleges where the prohibition need not apply. The American delegates thought that this opened the way for the typical (non-seminary) colleges to hire laicized priests.[44]

On September 10, Murphy sent a letter to all the presidents informing them about the communication with Garrone at New Delhi.[45] However, on October 6, 1975, Murphy was informed by Cardinal Garrone that in his letter he may not have made it clear that although NCEA could collect and send responses to the questionnaire from Rome, individual universities were also free to send their own responses. Garrone noted that Murphy's letter might be misunderstood; he was uneasy about some of the points made in it and thought that some institutions had a point of view different from NCEA and might react adversely to the conversation as reported. Garrone wanted to send out his own explanation and he enclosed a copy of his proposed letter. He denied that anything he said in private in New Delhi about laicized priests was different from his public statements. Garrone's final letter was sent to all presidents on January 10, 1976.[46]

The months between Murphy's and Garrone's letters (October, November, and December) were filled with meetings and communications
with Cardinal Garrone. Various bishops, representatives of NCEA,
and presidents of colleges visited Rome in a manner that could well
be turned into a novel of intrigue. Some of the visitors were opposed to
NCEA leadership and felt strongly that another viewpoint should be
heard.[47]

By now, suspicion was growing that indeed, Rome intended to bring
the non-ecclesiastical universities under more direct surveillance. As a
collective response to such a possibility, Msgr. Murphy and the NCEA
College and University Department's board of directors developed a
document, "Relations of American Catholic Universities and Colleges
with the Church,"[48] explaining the context of American higher education within which the Catholic colleges and universities functioned.
Praising the freedom that they had to establish and govern their own
institutions because of the Constitution of the United States and its
Bill of Rights, the document at the same time insisted that the universities must also be free from a juridical relationship with the church.
The document was regarded as a response to Cardinal Garrone's invitation to comment on the formulation of a new academic law of the
church. Drafts were submitted to the presidents in February and one
was sent to Rome.

Msgr. Murphy, encouraged by the apostolic delegate, Archbishop
Bernardin, and the Bishops and Presidents' Committee, arranged for a
delegation to meet with Cardinal Garrone in March 1976 and to present
a copy of "Relations" to him. After three lengthy discussions, the visit
concluded satisfactorily, and it was understood by the delegates that
there would be no further action.[49]

But Garrone was also hearing from the group in the United States
that did not agree with the NCEA position. The Institute for Catholic
Higher Education sent innumerable representations to Rome concerning the "political" actions of NCEA and insisting that it did not speak
for all of Catholic higher education. Dr. S. Thomas Greenburg of the
Institute for Catholic Higher Education and others believed that the
Catholic colleges were indeed on the way to the loss of their Catholic
identity and had absorbed the secularist philosophy surrounding them
in American higher education. Rev. Joseph Cahill, C.M., president of
St. John's University, criticized the NCEA "Relations" on the grounds
that it did not really respond to Garrone's questions but rather had become a comprehensive statement on American Catholic higher edu-

cation. If so, he pointed out, the bleak side has not been presented. Nothing has been said about the students' loss of commitment to the faith and to its ideals.[50]

The opposition continued throughout the next year to urge strong measures by the Vatican. According to George Kelly, Cardinal Garrone in 1977 suggested to Father Cahill that he bring his point of view to the NCCB. Cardinal Cooke then set up a meeting for him with Archbishop Bernardin, but, according to Cahill, there was no response to his representation. Kelly quotes Garrone as saying to him: "Is there no other voice within American Catholic education than that of the NCEA and Father Hesburgh?"[51]

According to Msgr. Kelly, the founding of the Fellowship of Catholic Scholars in 1977 was a direct response to this query of Cardinal Garrone. It attempted to present an alternate position to the bishops. In 1979 Rev. Ronald Lawlor, O.F.M. Cap., the first president of the Fellowship, had a talk with Bishop Thomas Kelly, General Secretary of NCCB. In the same year, Dr. James Hitchcock led a delegation which met with Archbishop John Quinn. Both meetings were unsatisfactory. Unfortunately, unfriendly relations continued between NCEA and the Fellowship, so that very often Rome received contradictory messages from these two groups. Although the Fellowship represented only a handful of institutions, its leadership was influential with certain persons in Rome. When the document *Sapientia Christiana* was published in April 1979, it stated explicitly that it pertained only to ecclesiastical faculties. Nevertheless, Greenburg and his colleagues continued to press for Vatican supervision of other Catholic universities because of what they regarded as "the liberal establishment" that ruled there.[52]

The death of Paul VI in August 1978 removed a very valuable ally of the Catholic universities, one who had been willing to temper the actions of the Congregation and whose apostolic delegate in Washington, Archbishop Jean Jadot (1973–1980), kept him well informed about American higher education. Paul VI had been supportive of the role of Hesburgh in the IFCU and always kept the door of his office open to him. The new pontiff, John Paul II, visited the United States in October 1979. His remarks on the occasion of a meeting of the Catholic college presidents will be discussed below, but they served as an introduction to the basic concerns that he would focus on: (1) the relationship that should exist between the university and church authority, and (2) the role of the Catholic theologian vis-à-vis the magisterium. These issues were clearly the centerpiece of the work of the Commission for the

Revision of Canon Law in its consideration of universities and in the many discussions and drafts which culminated in *Ex Corde Ecclesiae.*

Canon Law Revision

The matters we have been considering were an important context for the work going on in the Commission for the Revision of Canon Law. The question about alienation of property from the religious community to an independent board of trustees has already been discussed in chapter 3. Now that the universities no longer acted through the authority structures of the founding religious communities, it was necessary, from the point of view of the Congregation, to establish "norms" in canon law to spell out their relationship with the church. Garrone had expressed concern about the transfer of property from religious communities to predominantly lay boards of trustees without indults of alienation, an action which led him to question the Catholicity of the universities. His requests for information about the way that the institutions were following up on the document of 1972 and his simultaneous preparation of the norms for ecclesiastical faculties in what would become *Sapientia Christiana* made the university presidents very nervous about Rome's intentions in their regard.

Despite the efforts of the leadership on both sides to develop a spirit of collaboration, the clouds over the relationship with the Vatican had become ever darker as the seventies wore on. Basic positions were simply restated without any new insights being heard. While the many meetings were being held under the auspices of the IFCU and NCEA College and University Department with the Congregation for Catholic Higher Education between 1965 and 1975, another group in Rome was working to revise the Code of Canon Law, the body of laws that govern the Latin Church in matters of discipline.[53] In the earlier Code of 1917 there had been no reference to Catholic higher education, although there was mention of "teachers of religion" (1381). Why did it now seem appropriate to insert some laws to govern relations of the church with higher education?

One of the reasons was that religious orders were no longer actually governing the universities. While this was something new in the United States, it had been the case in Europe since the nineteenth-century secularization of the universities. The Holy See had developed a way of safeguarding the orthodoxy of theology faculties attached to these universities. It did so by requiring those who accepted appointment on the theological faculties to have a "canonical mission" from the appropriate ecclesiastical authority. In Latin America, Asia, and Africa, Catholic universities had generally been chartered by Rome or by local Ordinaries, and the degrees given were in virtue of the link to the Vatican. Protection against interference by anti-clerical governments was guaranteed by the requirement of the "canonical mission" for theologians, who were chosen by the local bishop rather than by state ministries of education as was customary for other faculties.

In the first unofficial draft of the proposed Revision of the Code (1976), this requirement of a canonical mission was extended to all Catholic university theology faculties.[54] This innovation took no note of the unique American system, where the total institution was under the direction of an independent board of trustees and not the state, and where the selection of theology faculty was done by the administrators of the university and not by a ministry of education. Hence, the proposed canon was received in the United States with disbelief and opposition. In addition, the whole new section of the Code dealing with higher education suggested a new and more authoritative role for the bishop in the life of the university.[55] This was due, in part, to the renewed emphasis on the authority of local bishops within their dioceses as promulgated by Vatican Council II.

Nationally respected canonists, working with the Association of Catholic Colleges and Universities (formerly NCEA College and University Department), developed a critique of the 1978 draft, the first official draft, which was submitted to the Commission for the Revision of Canon Law and to the Congregation for Catholic Education.[56] College and university presidents, having just labored through the years of articulating the nature of a Catholic university, had assumed that the 1972 document was the last word on the subject. They found it almost inconceivable that Rome could now propose something so contrary to the spirit of that document. The Association was working with the Bishops and Presidents' Committee to study the ways in which the institutions were carrying out the recommendations of Vatican Council II and of "The Catholic University in the Modern World," as requested by Cardinal Garrone. They had just had lengthy meetings with the cardinal in Rome discussing their document, "Relations," in which the unique situation in the United States precluding external interference in internal policies was clearly put forth.[57] How were the proposed canons to be reconciled with the respect for academic freedom and institutional autonomy so recently articulated in the 1972 document and seemingly accepted by Cardinal Garrone? What of the conversations with him at New Delhi and in Rome in 1975? The inconsistency was explained once again by authorities in Rome by the fact that two different Roman offices were involved: the Commission for the Revision of Canon Law and the Congregation for Catholic Education. Such inconsistency did not seem to bother them. Additional negative comments on other parts of the 1978 Revision received from countries around the world did, however, lead to the pope's appointment of additional members to the Commission in 1981. From the United States it was a welcome choice: Cardinal Joseph Bernardin, chair of the Committee on Canonical Affairs of NCCB. In his previous role as president of the National Conference of Catholic Bishops, the cardinal had been a friend of Catholic higher education, and he now attempted to bring its concerns to the Commission. He was unable to get time on the agenda for a discussion of the issue of canonical mission, but he did succeed in bringing about a change of language to "mandate"; canon 767 (1980 draft) would now read, "All those who teach theological disciplines in Catholic universities or institutes of higher learning must receive a *mandate* (not a *canonical mission)* from the appropriate ecclesiastical authority."[58]

While it did seem a slight concession, this change in language allowed the Catholic universities in the United States to distinguish themselves from ecclesiastical faculties (those erected by Roman authority) and thus to conclude that they were not covered by the document-in-progress that would become *Sapientia Christiana.*[59] They were reassured on this point at the 1980 IFCU Assembly in Louvain-la-Neuve by the delegate from the Congregation.[60]

The continued work on the revision of the Code was accompanied by two other events related to the discussion of identity. The first was the 1979–80 National Congress of Church-Related Colleges and Universities and the second was the visit of Pope John Paul II in October of 1979. The ecumenical Congress will be discussed in chapter 7, but here we note its significance in promoting interdenominational relations of the American Catholic community.

Visit of Pope John Paul II

The meeting of Pope John Paul II with the presidents of Catholic colleges and universities took place at The Catholic University of America on October 7, 1979.[61] In the context of the recent apostolic constitution, *Sapientia Christiana*, the Holy Father's reference to "all Catholic universities, colleges, and academies of postsecondary learning in your land, those with formal and sometimes juridical links with the Holy See, *as well as all those which are 'Catholic'*" gave hope that the distinction sought by the college presidents had been accepted by Rome. They took this statement to mean that not all Catholic universities needed to have a juridical connection to the church, and the pope made it clear that the ecclesiastical faculties which gave special Vatican degrees were in a class by themselves.

The core of his message was one that inspired general agreement as to the mission of the Catholic universities and colleges in the United States:

> A Catholic university or college must make a specific contribution to the Church and to society through high quality scientific research, in-depth study of problems and a just sense of history, together with the concern to show the full meaning of the human person regenerated in Christ, thus favoring the complete development of the person. Furthermore, the Catholic university or college must train young men and women of outstanding knowledge who, having made a personal synthesis between faith and culture, will be both capable and willing to assume tasks in the service of the community and of society in general, and to bear witness to their faith before the world. And, finally, to be what it ought to be, a Catholic college or university must set up, among its faculty and students, a real community which bears witness to a living and operative Christianity, a community where sincere commitment to scientific research and study goes together with a deep commitment to authentic Christian living. This is your identity.[62]

Agreement with John Paul II's vision as expressed here was consonant with many of the universities' own description of their mission. But the call to count on "a deep commitment to authentic Christian living" on the part of students and faculty was seen as unrealistic, and, in fact, would continue to be the source of tension between the universities and the Holy See. How would "Christian living" be assessed?

The pope said further: "If then your universities and colleges are institutionally committed to the Christian message, and if they are part of the Catholic community of evangelization, it follows that they have an essential relationship to the hierarchy of the Church." It was not clear how this "essential relationship" was to be understood or how institutional commitment to the Christian message might be expressed or judged. Confusion was increased by the fact that the pope immediately followed this statement by consideration of the role of theologians and the importance of their fidelity to the magisterium. To some in the audience, it appeared that it was the theologian and his or her adherence to the official teaching of the church that would constitute the "essential relationship" of the institution to the church. On the other hand, many of the presidents saw their "Catholic identity" in the university's broad mission of research, teaching, and service rather than in the orthodoxy of their theology departments.

The pastoral letter of the American bishops, issued the following year, was more in harmony with the latter perception. The Bishops and Presidents' Committee, founded in 1974, had proved to be an excellent channel for communication between the universities and the hierarchy in the United States. Cordial relations had predominated in the annual meetings of the group, and by 1979 they saw the desirability of issuing a pastoral letter on Catholic higher education. Under the leadership of Bishop Daniel Pilarczyk of Cincinnati, the committee provided a draft, and the supportive and challenging pastoral was issued by NCCB in 1980, a step which the ACCU saw as lessening the need for the canonical approach being taken in the revision of the Code. By reference, the bishops' letter acknowledged the 1972 "The Catholic University in the Modern World" as well as the American response, "Relations of American Catholic Colleges and Universities with the Church" (1976). It strongly affirmed the importance of Catholic higher education, "both for its own sake and for the life of the church."[63]

Any hope that this effort would alter the Roman action was dashed when the next draft of the Code (1980) showed no improvement over the earlier one. The demand for the canonical mission was retained. It was at this point that the ACCU board determined to ask Archbishop Bernardin to intervene with the Commission when he attended its session in October 1981. Meanwhile, the level of anxiety among the college and university presidents grew, particularly since their institutions were now highly dependent on federal and state assistance to students to keep their enrollments high and their facilities adequate for new programs. During the summer of 1981 several documents circulated among the bishops reminding them of the need to press for Roman acknowledgment of the unique American situation. President Timothy Healy, S.J., in a letter to Bernardin on August 28, 1981, wrote:

> Just at the time that Catholic colleges have come fully to accept this custom [rules for hiring, firing, and tenure in American higher education] both

because they must in order to preserve the integrity of their secular being, and because they wish to follow the Church herself in honoring secular structures and realities, this same autonomy is challenged on narrow canonical lines, hostile to both the letter and the spirit of the Second Vatican Council.

Healy pointed out that some have suggested moving the theology faculty into a separate institute in order to avoid ecclesial intrusion into the university itself. But he resisted the idea: "it would accomplish at one stroke and by Roman authority what in Georgetown's case almost two hundred years of protestant and secular pressure have not been able to do; that is, drive formal teaching about God and His Church out of the University curriculum."[64]

A month earlier Hesburgh had written a circular letter to all of the bishops, recounting in detail the story of American Catholic higher education and its interaction with church authorities and urging them to defend the way in which the universities had benefited from the American system of government, being able to pursue their mission of higher education in freedom for two hundred years. As a participant in the many meetings of IFCU and in the joint sessions with the Congregation for Catholic Higher Education, Hesburgh argued that the provisions of the new Code would do irreparable harm and would force the universities out of a relationship with the church.[65]

Even the change in the language to "mandate" which was achieved by Bernardin's intervention in 1981 did not diminish the concern that such a requirement would constitute "external control" of the university. Bernardin reported to ACCU that Archbishop Lara of the Code Commission had made it clear to him that the intent of canon 767 (canon 812 in the final Revision) was "to establish a relationship between the teaching of theological disciplines in institutions of higher learning and the magisterium." The "mandatum" would be the minimal way of accomplishing this.[66]

At the end of December 1981, Charles Wilson, legal counsel at Georgetown, prepared a memorandum for Father Healy, which was shared with ACCU, on the potential dangers in the proposed Code. The canonists who had done the critique of the 1978 draft for ACCU prepared another one of the 1980 draft. They were not sanguine about the outcome.[67]

Preparations were now made for a delegation from the United States to meet with Pope John Paul II and to lay the case before him prior to the promulgation of the revised Code. The delegation was instructed by the ACCU board to seek to have canon 812 removed from the Code or, at least, to secure a dispensation for the American institutions. With the support of the General Secretary of the NCCB, Bishop Thomas Kelly, arrangements were made through Archbishop Pio Laghi, the Apostolic Nuncio in Washington, for a group of five to seek an audience with the pope for mid-March, 1982. The delegation was led by the Executive Director of ACCU, Alice Gallin, O.S.U., and included four other persons: the vice chair of NCCB, Most Rev. Bishop James Malone; the chair of the ACCU Board, Msgr. Frederick R. McManus; and two presidents, Rev. Theodore M. Hesburgh, C.S.C., of the University of Notre Dame and Rev. William Byron, S.J., of the University of Scranton. Unfortunately, the date for the audience was not firm until the day before the appointment, and Father Hesburgh had to leave Rome for El Salvador, where he was to monitor the national elections. The other four delegates visited with the pope on March 18, 1982, and in the fifteen minutes allotted to them explained the American situation which made the concept of a mandate unacceptable. The Holy Father listened attentively and asked for a follow-up memorandum stating their position. This suggested to the delegates that he had never seen the correspondence previously sent to Rome regarding the problems. He told the delegates that Cardinal Felici, the head of the Code Commission (with whom the delegates had had a very unpleasant interview) wanted to have "canonical mission" reinstated.[68] The pope said that he had the text for his review at the moment and would consider the delegates' position with regard to the mandate.

When the delegates returned to Washington, Archbishop Laghi suggested that some alternative wording to canon 812 be submitted. This was done, and Father McManus and Sister Alice Gallin presented them to the archbishop and also sent them, through the diplomatic pouch, to Cardinal Baum, Secretary of the Congregation for Catholic Education, and to Pope John Paul II under date of April 5, 1982. They were not accepted.

In this whole matter, the support of the American bishops for the universities' arguments was unwavering. In both 1981 and 1982 the NCCB Administrative Board reaffirmed the position taken by ACCU with regard to the proposed canons. The collaboration experienced on the Bishops and Presidents' Committee was strengthened and broadened and would become increasingly important when the new Code was promulgated on January 25, 1983, to take effect on November 27. Both

Bishop William Hughes as chair of the Bishops and Presidents' Committee and Archbishop John Quinn as chair of NCCB spoke to the bishops about the dangers of hasty implementation and suggested regional meetings with university presidents to explore the implications of the Code. The canons regarding institutions of higher education were now numbered 807–814, with the one on the mandate being canon 812.[69] This canon would be the subject of many journal articles, speeches at the Canon Law Society of America, the Catholic Theology Society of America, the College Theology Society, and debates at public and private meetings. What did the canon mean for the United States? Was it retroactive? If theology teachers did not request a mandate, what would happen? What would be the civil law consequences if there was perception of external control of the universities? Under the leadership of the ACCU and the Bishops and Presidents' Committee, commentaries on the final Code were requested from both canon and civil lawyers. A "confidential" paper written by Charles Wilson reminded the presidents that, despite the decisions in *Tilton* and *Roemer*, there were five essential characteristics needed for colleges to be eligible for public aid:

1. They must not discriminate in student admissions or faculty hiring on religious grounds;
2. They must not compel participation in religious exercises;
3. Theology must be taught as an academic discipline;
4. There must be no proselytizing;
5. There must be an atmosphere of academic freedom.

Wilson made a presentation at an executive session of the presidents attending the ACCU annual meeting in February 1984, discussing with them the implications of the canons vis-à-vis civil law. The meeting was not open to others for fear that recognition of difficulties with the new canons would encourage the opponents of Catholic higher education to challenge the public support received by the colleges and universities under various programs.

Ex Corde Ecclesiae

The issue of the relationship of these institutions with the hierarchy in Rome became even more troubling when Cardinal Baum forwarded the first draft of a document which would be a "correlative Pontifical regulation" to complete the new Code with reference to universities. It would be analagous to *Sapientia Christiana*, issued earlier for seminaries and ecclesiastical faculties.[70] This first draft was to be held "in strictest confidence" by qualified "experts" (*periti*) to whom it was sent, to be shared only with "closest colleagues." In May 1983 it was therefore shared with the ACCU board of directors and it was discussed as well at the IFCU Assembly which met in Toronto that summer. Delegates from other countries were not nearly as disturbed as those from the United States, but as the discussion continued they too began to recognize the problems that might occur if the draft were implemented.

After several preliminary drafts for the purpose of consultation of "experts," the Congregation issued a "Schema" to be studied by "all interested parties" who, in "full freedom and frankness," would submit their opinions by November 30, 1985, after which an International Congress would be convened in the course of 1986. The Schema had two parts: the "Proemium" and the "Norms." The former dealt with the philosophical, theological, and pastoral reasons for the church's interest in universities and other institutes of higher studies and presented an inspiring task of inculturation[71] "through scientific research, university teaching, and the higher education of her members." Again, it referred to the fact that "the ecclesial conditions of Catholic universities differ from place to place. Some in fact have been canonically erected and approved, and others, though being really Catholic, do not have such a juridical status." Nevertheless, the second part of the Schema, the Norms, contained forty-nine specific regulations for all Catholic universities regardless of their canonical standing.

Under date of February 11, 1986, the ACCU submitted a synthesis of the responses to this draft received from its members, and on February 14 its board of directors submitted a strongly critical paper. Basic to both documents was a commitment to academic freedom and institutional autonomy as lived in the American higher education community and therefore part of the culture within which Catholic colleges and universities sought to live out their mission. Both also expressed criticism of the inconsistent ecclesiology given expression in the Schema; was the "ecclesial community" the same as "the Church" or, in the latter instance, did it really mean the hierarchy? In June 1986 a concise critique was forwarded to Rome by Father Hesburgh after a meeting he had hosted in September 1985 for the leaders of the major Catholic universities of North America.[72] The next step in the consultation was the publication by Rome of the responses to the 1985 Schema received from around the world and an analysis of them, which was distributed to all universities and colleges for further response.

Pope John Paul II visited the United States in September 1987 and was hosted by the Association of Catholic Colleges and Universities at Xavier University of New Orleans on September 12. The impressive size of the audience of college presidents underscored their concern about the Schema, and reflected their desire to express their service of both the church and society even while resisting canonical regulations. The pope recognized the fact that it was the bicentennial of the United States Constitution and praised the work done by the American colleges. He spoke to them as a colleague committed to university education and well aware of the interaction of the institutions of higher learning and the particular cultures of the countries in which they existed. Nevertheless, his message once again emphasized the need for the university to be explicit in its profession of Catholicity. Yet, given the warmth of the pope's personal expression of confidence in them, the presidents believed that the next version of the Schema might be less juridical.

The revised draft was circulated under date of November 8, 1988. It was indicated that this draft would serve as the working paper for an international Congress of delegates to be held in Rome in April 1989. This time the United States was awarded eighteen places in the Congress for university delegates, and since the Congregation left the method of election up to each country, the board of directors of ACCU, by common consent, selected them. An attempt was made to choose presidents from various types of colleges and universities (previously they had all come from universities) and to include persons who had not been involved in earlier Congresses, so that some new points of view might emerge and a new generation of leaders might experience an international Congress of this type. The NCCB was also asked to select four bishops to participate.[73] The Executive Director of the ACCU was one of the eighteen presidential delegates and two resource persons, Msgr. Frederick R. McManus and Rev. Avery Dulles, S.J., were invited to accompany the delegation.

The eight days in Rome from April 18 to April 25, 1989, were full ones. The agenda as it had been submitted to the delegates was not acceptable because it only provided for discussion of the draft document in small groups and a written report with observations at the end of the several days. The IFCU gave leadership to a movement to change the agenda, a strategy reminiscent of the actions at the beginning of

Vatican Council II. The proposal for a new process of discussion, debate, and voting was accepted by the representative of the Congregation.[74] Working groups were organized by language and therefore by cultures, and within each group consensus soon emerged on many points. Interactions with the total group at general assemblies and in social settings soon created a unanimity, collected in ten recommendations for changes to the document.[75] These were then included in a revised draft sent out in July 1989. A final opportunity for input was provided by the committee of fifteen, elected at the Congress, who returned in September 1989 to assist in the final wording of *Ex Corde Ecclesiae* before it went to the Plenarium for acceptance.[76]

What can be said of all this dialogue? On the one hand, in the final drafts of the document there was growing appreciation of the important role that universities play in evangelizing and handing on cultural traditions. For this reason, the language is sensitive to cultural values and diversity among cultures within the world community and also within the church community. The final text of *Ex Corde Ecclesiae* is inspirational and encouraging for those engaged in the difficult task of education in contemporary society. Much of the document reflects Pope John Paul II's own professorial background and his appreciation of the intellectual task to be accomplished. Yet, in each of the drafts and in *Ex Corde Ecclesiae* the section of Norms belies the positive bias of the main text. The number of these Norms in the earlier versions, reaching as many as forty-nine separate injunctions in the 1985 draft, indicated the overriding concern of the Roman hierarchy for particular ways that bishops could control the life of the university.

By the time of the final text, the Norms were greatly reduced. A major difference was that in accord with the wishes of the delegates to the 1989 Congress, the Norms were to be implemented by the bishops' conferences in the various parts of the world.[77] Seen as a significant admission of the inherent relationship of universities to cultures, this mode of implementation was welcomed. It has, however, proved more difficult than envisioned, and what was expected to be accomplished early in 1991 had not yet been achieved in 1999. In the United States the task was entrusted to a committee of bishops, headed by Bishop John Leibrecht of Springfield–Cape Girardeau, Missouri. Members of this "implementation" committee were appointed by Archbishop Pilarczyk, chair of NCCB, and included Cardinal Hickey, Cardinal Maida, Archbishop Schulte, Archbishop Lipscomb, Bishop Malone, and Bishop Griffin. In addition, seven presidents of Catholic colleges were asked to serve as consultants to the committee: Rev. J. Donald Monan, S.J., Rev. Edward Malloy, C.S.C., Dr. Dorothy Brown, Dr. Matthew Quinn, Rev. William J. Byron, S.J., Dr. Karen Kennelly, C.S.J., Brother Ray Fitz, S.M., and Dr. Norman Francis. Additional resource persons named were Rev. Frederick R. McManus, Dr. Alice Gallin, O.S.U., and Dr. Sharon Euart, R.S.M. After the first "ordinances" for implementation were rejected by the presidents in 1993, a full-time staff person was appointed to assist the committee in setting up further consultation. Rev. Terrence Toland, S.J., accepted this assignment. Another set of norms was prepared and accepted by a vote of the NCCB of 224 to 6 in November 1996. This decision was, however, not acceptable to Rome, and so the dialogue continues.

The quest for an acceptable definition of Catholic identity has not been solved by *Ex Corde Ecclesiae,* although the ideals it expresses regarding the nature and mission of Catholic universities have become a resource of great value in the ongoing dialogue on college campuses. Since 1991, and as a specific part of the implementation process in the United States, local conversations involving ecclesiastical authorities have been convened. Together with university leaders, bishops are seeking creative ways to share in the intellectual and religious life of the campus community without endangering institutional autonomy and academic freedom.

Thus, the eighties and nineties seem to have brought new possibilities of answering the question about the Catholic identity of the colleges and universities. It does seem that the presidents want to answer Cardinal Garrone's question "Are they still Catholic?" in the affirmative, but there is still no agreement as to the appropriate ways that an American Catholic college or university shows forth its Catholicity. There is still a gulf between the universities and the canon lawyers as to the understanding of "norms" and how they can be interpreted in the American context, the task entrusted by *Ex Corde Ecclesiae* to national conferences of bishops.

SEVEN

Confrontation or Convergence?

Sorting out the tasks of a college or university and evaluating them within the framework of an ecclesial mission have continued to preoccupy the leaders of Catholic higher education through the late seventies into the nineties. As they accepted the standards of American higher education and the regulations of federal and state government, they also continued to carry on a dialogue with the church about their "Catholic" identity. Could and would the values of these different constituencies converge or would they exist in a mode of confrontation with one another?

Catholic colleges and universities were not alone in their struggle to articulate their mission in confusing times. In its report to the Carnegie Foundation for the Advancement of Teaching in 1973, the Commission on Higher Education stated that "There has been a basic erosion of affection for and interest in education, including higher education."[1] To deal with the severe crises that existed, political, financial, and demographic, the Commission suggested certain priorities which would, if adopted by the universities, clarify the purposes of higher education. According to the Commission, this clarification of mission was essential if higher education were to regain favor with the public. Some of these priorities for all American colleges and universities were to preserve and enhance quality and diversity, to advance social justice, to enhance constructive change, to achieve more effective governance, and to assure more resources and effective use of them.[2]

Whether or not they read the Commission report, the Catholic college and university presidents focused on these very goals. They were aided in their task by the call of the church to many of these same objectives—social justice, diversity in students and faculty, fidelity to the intellectual heritage of the Catholic tradition, and constructive change.

This latter priority, illustrated by the shift in governing authority which had occurred in the late sixties, was apparently acceptable to the religious communities and the American bishops.[3] For the moment it seemed as if the adaptation to the demands of the academic world would not necessarily contradict the goals of a truly Catholic university. The values espoused by Edmund Pellegrino in his 1979 inaugural address as president of The Catholic University of America suggested that they were complementary:

> To be truly universities, Catholic universities must recognize more clearly the conditions which define a valid intellectual mission infused by faith. Reason and faith have been, and will often appear to be, in conflict. Each has offended the other in the past. If this is to be avoided, and if Catholic universities wish to be regarded seriously as constructive critics of culture, some distinctions must be made and respected. They must learn to speak with authority and without authoritarianism, of morality without moralizing, of the spirit of the law without idolizing the letter, of licit limits to dissent without repressing new explorations of all truths—scientific, sociopolitical or theological.[4]

The bishops' pastoral letter issued in 1980, *Catholic Higher Education and the Pastoral Mission of the Church,*[5] also witnessed to a possible convergence of values by stressing the importance of attending to issues of peace and justice, meeting the needs of new groups of students, and responding to the powerful call for change issued by Vatican Council II. At the same time, the bishops emphasized the need for the universities to be clear about their Catholic identity. In the discussions within the Bishops and Presidents' Committee, which drafted the pastoral letter, a common understanding of the role of the Catholic university in American society was being forged, one which emphasized the relationship of the hierarchy to the universities as pastoral rather than juridical. The bishops saw themselves as assisting the colleges and universities in their attempts to meet the needs of the times rather than as controlling the trustees and administrators in the development of policies. Yet, the area of theology faculties remained problematic. What was the responsibility of theologians teaching in Catholic colleges and universities to the magisterium or official teaching authority of the church? Correlatively, what was the oversight required of the bishop for all "Catholic" institutions in his diocese? This would continue to be an area of tension.

The 1980 pastoral letter built upon the pope's October 1979 address discussed in chapter 6, but added to it the concern of American bishops about the challenges facing the universities in the areas of financing and government regulation. The bishops recognized the fact that the institutions' Catholic identity must be expressed in terms that were far more ecumenical than previously and should not focus primarily on the role of theology or religion. Quoting Vatican Council II, they reminded the Catholic community of the reason for the church's commitment to higher education: "people who devote themselves to the various disciplines of philosophy, history, science and the arts can help elevate the human family to a better understanding of truth, goodness, and beauty, and to the formation of judgments which embody universal values."[6] The language quoted here with approval reflected the bishops' determination to be inclusive in expressing "Catholic" identity, and to avoid giving justification to the opponents of church-related education in their claims that such universities and colleges were "pervasively sectarian." Reliance on the words of the Fathers of Vatican Council II was a way of expressing commitment to the church's mission without alienating either non-Catholic Christians or members of other religious traditions involved in the mission of Catholic higher education in the United States. Nevertheless, the bishops stated clearly: "The Catholic identity of these institutions should be evident to faculty, students, and the general public. Policies, practices, programs and general spirit should communicate to everyone that the institution is a community of scholars dedicated to the ideals and values of Catholic higher education." They did recognize, however, that there were legal restrictions in some states that made such overt Catholic character impossible at the time, and they expressed the hope that such policies might be modified.[7]

The combination of American values such as independence and individual freedom with church values such as fidelity to revealed truth and the transmission of the Catholic heritage, according to the pastoral letter, is the ideal. The bishops wrote: "Academic freedom and institutional independence in pursuit of the mission of the institution are essential components of educational quality and integrity; commitment to the Gospel and the teachings and heritage of the Catholic Church provide the inspiration and enrichment that make a college fully Catholic."

The bishops recognized the task of achieving academic excellence as defined by the wider academic community. They strongly endorsed the colleges' traditional emphasis on the liberal arts and praised recent efforts to upgrade the teaching of theology. They also noted an important new aspect of an institution's "Catholicity": its commitment to educate its students in issues of peace and justice and to continually review its own practices and policies from this perspective. This may well be one of the most significant challenges in the bishops' document, and it was one that many of the colleges took seriously as they sought to express their Catholic identity.

Another concern of the bishops, the education of minorities, caught the attention of some college presidents. The same institutions which had educated the immigrants of the nineteenth and early twentieth centuries were now called on by the bishops to offer access and support to new groups, particularly to Hispanic-Americans because of their numbers and their Catholic background.[8] The decade ahead witnessed serious efforts in this direction, notably among the colleges founded by women religious, where the percentage of minorities in twenty of them rose to 20 percent or above by 1990.[9] This effort, indeed, was seen as a logical continuation of the Catholic women's colleges' mission to offer education to underserved populations.

The compatibility of the bishops' goals for Catholic higher education with the objectives of the colleges and universities augured well for future relationships. The fears of losing federal aid because of a specific "Catholic" mission seemed to abate somewhat as the ecclesial understanding of "Catholic" was broadened within the church. The presidents' determination to retain their Catholic identity was strengthened by the in-depth conversations with their colleagues in other church-related institutions, also suffering from identity challenges voiced by their respective church bodies. The opportunity for this exchange of ideas came in the National Congress of Church-Related Colleges and Universities held in 1979 and 1980. Prepared for by two years of study, planning meetings, and position papers on various topics of mutual concern, the Congress took place at the University of Notre Dame in the summer of 1979 and in a follow-up session in February 1980. At the summer gathering there were approximately six hundred institutions representing twenty-three different denominations. Sessions explored legal issues, changes in curriculum, definition of mission, ecclesial expectations and financial concerns. An "inventory" was developed to assist institutions in their efforts at self-identification as church-related.[10] The environment of the Congress on the clearly-Catholic campus of Notre Dame was appreciated by the delegates, and the fact that each day had provision for ecumenical church services created a context of prayer for the lengthy general discussions. The second session of the Congress was held in Washington, D.C., at the time of the ACCU and NAICU meetings, and although it lacked the leisure and time of the first session,

it served to concretize some of the recommendations made in the previous summer and to encourage the executives of the church-related
colleges to meet at least annually in order to share common concerns.[11]

For the decade of the eighties, these concerns focused on the economic and cultural changes in American society and how best to educate students for a global and multi-cultural future. The "new" students
described earlier brought with them attitudes toward traditional values which were often contrary to the teaching of Christian communities, and the issues of public policy and individual life-styles called for
collaborative approaches by those who identified themselves as church-
related institutions. Programs in international education as well as community service and peace and justice education were often on the agenda
and the sharing of ideas on these topics increased the bonds among the
executives. Philosophically, the questions often came to a focus on the
dilemma posed by the recruitment of a more diverse campus population and the ongoing attempts to preserve and enhance the Christian
mission of the institution. Underneath many of these discussions was a
growing fear that in their desire to be one with their peers in other institutions of higher learning they were becoming "secularized." Many
of the position papers at the Congress had dealt with this question, and
the annual meetings of the church-executives continued to probe the
meaning of this term.

Colleges founded by different Protestant denominations had usually
distanced themselves from their founding churches as they became universities.[12] Catholic universities, on the other hand, remained overtly
Catholic until the 1960s. Relying on the teaching of *Gaudium et Spes,*
they tended to adapt to American higher education as embodying the
"modern world" without separating themselves radically from the ecclesial community which gave them their distinctive character. However, some observers deplored the direction in which they were moving.
David Riesman, as we have seen, viewed them as already "secularized."[13]
James T. Burtchaell, C.S.C., worried that they would indeed follow the
same path as their Protestant colleagues.[14] The discussion hinged on
the relationship of faith to the modern world and the degree of adaptation to secular reality that could be regarded as a positive value from a
religious point of view.[15]

In an attempt to handle this question, Harry Smith had defined *secularization* in a way that contrasted it to *secularism:*

> Secularization is herein defined as that historical process within Western
> thought in which man has undergone a radical transformation in his under-
> standing of the nature of the world, truth, history, and religious authority.

As long as the Christian roots of these insights, man's responsibility for the world, and the possibility of ultimate wholeness and meaning are recognized, secularization remains a creative process in which man discovers what it means to be truly human.[16]

However, Smith cautioned that "when the derivedness or relativity of human existence is denied or man seeks to dissolve the tension by all-inclusive or religious world-views, then secularism results and man forfeits his freedom and puts himself in bondage to a 'spurious' worldliness or inhuman religiousity."

Between 1965 and 1980 the secularization of the college was a key question at many meetings and in many journals. Very often, the word "secularization" was used pejoratively, and when the epithet was hurled at church-related higher education by those who favored a clear religious identity, the debate resulted in confrontations and defensive postures. Catholic universities, called to mediate the faith to cultures (the world), struggled to keep their focus on the best way to promote their distinctive mission in dialogue with the various publics they served without sacrificing the special worldview which arose from their Catholic tradition. For this, they relied heavily on the documents of Vatican Council II and the subsequent allocutions of Pope Paul VI and John Paul II on inculturation. The university presidents regarded the changes they had made and were making as adaptation to American academic culture, not an acceptance of godless "secular" values. This distinction was a hard one to maintain.

In a memorandum drawn up for the board of trustees of Fordham on July 31, 1968, Rev. Edmund Ryan, S.J., described the misuse of the word "secularization" by those who were concerned about developments at Fordham. He insisted that what was happening was "declericalization," not "secularization," and that the changes being made were in accord with the decrees of Vatican Council II and the Jesuits' Thirty-First General Congregation. He urged a positive understanding of Christian secularity which was basic to an Incarnational view of human existence. The Christian "looks at and lives in the secular with God, with Christ."[17]

This positive understanding of the secular world was not universally accepted by the leaders of the Catholic colleges, but to many of them it made sense. The world in which they lived was the only one in which they had a role to play, and they interpreted the task of the university as one of inculturation rather than one of domination and imposition of cultural norms. On the other hand, some university leaders wished to reverse the trend toward accommodation to the culture because they believed it diminished their Catholic character. A few of these joined hands with the Institute for Catholic Higher Education formed at St. John's University and linked to the Fellowship of Catholic Scholars. An issue of the Fellowship's newsletter in February 1980 called Catholic universities and colleges to "once more express their commitment to the Catholic faith." The leaders of the Fellowship maintained that unless the institutions remained "authentically Catholic," they ought not to survive. Msgr. George A. Kelly was Executive Secretary of the Fellowship, and its board of directors at the time included persons affiliated with Loyola Medical School, University of Santa Clara, Molloy College, the Josephinum School of Theology, The Catholic University of America, Rosary College, Loyola University, Holy Cross Fathers, Southern Province, Saint Louis University, University of Scranton, Darlington Seminary, and St. John's University. None of them were university presidents or official representatives of their institutions. But their statement is significant as a sign of the internal tensions hovering over any discussion of the Catholic character within the colleges as well as with the Congregation in Rome. The group represented by the Fellowship made it clear that their concern was the secularization of Catholic colleges and universities. As they pointed out, "it is an undeniable fact that Catholic universities recently have understressed the importance of witnessing the Catholic faith, choosing instead to adopt a university model designed mostly by unbelievers."[18]

In order to place the debate over secularization in context, it is helpful to review a few of the areas of concern and the ways in which they color decisions up to the present: demographics, public policy, cultural shifts, and ecclesial expectations. What should be the response in these areas by colleges committed to a distinctive mission as Christian, and more precisely, as Catholic?

Demographics

The tremendous growth in enrollment in Catholic institutions after 1960 has already been noted. In 1988 a report based on the 229 colleges on the ACCU membership list claimed a total student enrollment in the Catholic sector of 609,350, of whom about 400,000 were full-time students. These 229 institutions included 11 research/doctoral universities, 100 comprehensive colleges, 91 liberal arts colleges, and 24 two-year colleges.[19] It should be noted that the Catholic cohort included a larger percentage of comprehensive institutions than the total independent college sector, indicating the area in which enrollments in Catholic institutions had grown the most, probably because of the increase in adult part-time students. Since most of the Catholic colleges had always focused on undergraduate programs, these figures presented a challenge. From 1982 to 1988 the growth in enrollment in Catholic colleges and universities was almost entirely among part-time students. Having had a strong cadre of women's colleges, the Catholic sector continued to uphold that tradition, still maintaining forty-three of them. These forty-three colleges, however, were only about one-third of the colleges originally founded for women by women religious; the others had closed, merged, or become coeducational.[20] Only one single-sex college for men remained at the end of the eighties, St. John's University in Collegeville, Minnesota. By 1988, 59 percent of all students in Catholic colleges and universities were women. The geographic distribution of Catholic campuses remained steady: 80 percent were located in the Northeast and Midwest, and many of the large universities were in urban areas. We should also note that in the eighties the distinction between full-time and part-time became increasingly blurred. As colleges began to use these terms to describe the number of credit hours being taken in a semester rather than actual residence on campus or a "full" program of study, the division into two classes of students became less meaningful.

Efforts to increase the diversity of students by focused recruitment of black, Hispanic, Asian, and Native American men and women were not very successful. Although the statistics indicate that Catholic colleges in 1988 had a 7.7 percent Hispanic population, 49 percent of that group were from the three Catholic universities in Puerto Rico. In 1988 only 6 percent of the student population at Catholic colleges was black. Those institutions with larger adult part-time programs tended to have higher percentages of black and Hispanic students, but the necessary figures are not available, except for the Neylan group of colleges, several of which had outstanding success.[21]

Why has the desired increase in minorities not been realized? One important reason is the dearth of sufficient scholarship funds to make attractive offers to the students of color who have the ability to do college work but not the money to pay the tuition. As the nation awakened to the need to educate all of its citizens, the better endowed universities and colleges worked at locating and recruiting students who needed special financial help. Secondly, for many black students the Catholic culture was an alien one; added to a white middle-class environment, it was not an attractive option. One route that did work was that of sports; both football and basketball lured players with scholarships and, for the most part, managed to give them enough academic assistance to maintain high graduate percentages within NCAA criteria. Although Hispanic students often came from Catholic cultural backgrounds, the white liberal Catholicism on many Catholic campuses after the sixties was not a hospitable environment, either. The lack of openness to their piety and values made them feel like outsiders. Finally, the desired diversity required proper preparation of faculty with regard to learning styles and cultural biases, and the tension between academic standards and adaptability was often unresolved.

Unfortunately no data have been systematically collected regarding the number of Catholic and non-Catholic students in the colleges and universities. Obviously, the ratio has been changing in most of the institutions, and as the number of adult-learners has increased, the religious identity of the students has been harder to ascertain. Their choice of a Catholic college or university generally has little to do with its religious identity.[22] With over 50 percent of the students falling into the category of "adult learners" (although some universities report 85 or 90 percent Catholic "traditional" undergraduate students), most of the colleges no longer see themselves as "educating Catholic young people." Indeed, many of them are now serving large numbers of adult students who are not Catholic; this seems to be especially true of urban universities. Hence, the identity question arises once again. Can one have a Catholic university without a large percentage of Catholic students? Certainly, there are places that seem to have done so. We can turn to colleges such as Christian Brothers College in Memphis, Tennessee, where the surrounding population is only 2 percent Catholic and where many of the students come from the local area. The usual number of Catholic students is between 25 and 30 percent of enrollment, and yet CBC is recognized as "Catholic."[23] What then is the relationship of the faith of the students who come to the Catholic colleges and the identity of the college itself?

Public Policy

We have already described the educational assistance provided by the federal government, which was essential for the viability of the colleges and universities. Beginning in 1944 with the Servicemen's Readjustment Act (G.I. Bill), aid was extended to all students in 1965 and

1972. By 1981, even with the lessening of enthusiasm for higher education, the federal government was giving over 6 billion dollars in student aid and another 3.4 billion for research, much of which was channeled through universities.

However, the public's dismay over the radical response on some campuses among those opposed to federal policies, and especially to the Vietnam War, meant that each year's allocation for higher education had to be fought for. Lobbyists from the business community regarded college faculty as always dissatisfied, demanding higher salaries and benefits while teaching fewer and fewer hours of class and encouraging students' negative behavior.[24] The Republican administrations preferred to reduce taxes rather than to increase support for higher education.

Increased efforts on the part of the higher education community to lobby Congress involved many compromises among the various national associations located at Dupont Circle in Washington, D.C. Differences between the public and private sectors, always a factor in collaborative efforts, sometimes became acrimonious, but most of the time these sectors were able to present a united front to the public. From the perspective of the Catholic colleges and universities, NAICU, the National Association of Independent Colleges and Universities, carried the main responsibility for representing independent higher education. NAICU and ACCU were among the thirty different organizations that worked together in the Secretariat of the American Council on Education to try and develop win-win situations for the public and private sectors.[25] On the whole, their efforts were successful. The Middle Income Assistance Act, enacted in 1978, was welcomed by colleges, both public and private, which served many middle-class students. However, the emphasis gradually became more focused on loans than on grants, resulting in the unfortunate burden of debt carried by most young alumnae/i as they left their alma mater. On another level, the Catholic colleges came into conflict with the other sectors of Catholic education in the late seventies when the lobbying effort for tuition tax credits heated up. As a department of the National Catholic Educational Association, Catholic colleges and universities were expected to support their colleagues engaged in elementary and secondary education. However, the higher education lobbyists, fearing that any program of tuition tax credits or vouchers would siphon funds from student aid programs already in place, opposed the bill. The ACCU was clearly caught in the middle and worked with both sides in order to achieve a compromise. While not supporting the NCEA position, ACCU managed to avoid public opposition on the part of the higher education community.[26]

In the eighties, the states faced the rising costs of public universities as well as the demands for continued subsidies in the form of scholarships, special programs for minorities, and outright grants for independent institutions. Since the number of students continued to increase year after year, the costs continued to do the same. State associations of independent college and university presidents became very active, playing a significant role in pressuring the legislatures every year at budget time. Students also organized to lobby for financial aid and other benefits. Universities which raised tuition beyond the cost-of-living increase felt the wrath of the media as well as of the parents.

As a result of enrollment concerns, the public policy issues often dealt with the question of aid to students. In the mid-eighties there was open disagreement between public and private sectors as to the extent that residential costs should be covered and what the ratio of loans to grants should be. In various ways, support for graduate education was reduced and grants for faculty became an endangered species. Higher education found itself continually interacting with government agencies regarding EEOC regulations, OSHA mandates, accessibility for the disabled, and drug and alcohol policies. All of these laws were costly to implement. There was some concern that the university's autonomy was being undermined by government regulations. Years earlier, in the 1957 *Sweezy v New Hampshire* case, the Supreme Court had reaffirmed the university's freedom from state interference, stating that "the four freedoms of a university are: to determine for itself on academic grounds who may teach, what may be taught, how it shall be taught, and who may be admitted to study."[27] In the 1980s it seemed that the freedom of the university to determine these matters, especially admissions policies, was hemmed in by governmental regulations and public polls.[28] The public perception of the ivory tower, as reflected in public policy, was ambiguous at best and decidedly negative at worst. Recourse to litigation based on noncompliance with governmental regulations became common and this, in turn, led to increased costs for the institutions.

Cultural Shifts

The delegates to the National Congress of Church-Related Colleges and Universities, assembled together in 1979, expected great cultural shifts but they could hardly have imagined the extent of these shifts. When one contemplates the changes in the demography of students in American colleges, recalled above, it is clear that the culture of the campuses was bound to change dramatically. During the seventies, students had become increasingly job-oriented in their educational goals and more socially liberal in their attitudes toward premarital sex and the use of drugs and alcohol. By the end of the decade, of the 11.7 million students entering as freshmen, more than half held jobs and over 40 percent attended some night classes; only 28 percent lived with their families or relatives. They chose to major in business, engineering, and scientific and technical fields, rather than in the humanities and social sciences. Writers deplored the individualism and self-centeredness of this generation of students and their lack of political involvement.[29] In 1979, 63 percent of entering freshmen gave as an "essential or very important objective" the desire to be prosperous, in contrast to only 45 percent a decade before. According to one author, this was not surprising; they mirrored the opinions of the broader society, which was suffering from inflation and rising unemployment. She writes: "College students did not create the 'Me-ism' of the decade; it merely came with them to campus."[30] In reaction to the sixties, the students of the seventies had become more conservative (except in sexual mores) and more concerned about doing well in the world of business than about changing the structures of society. In 1979 two out of three students intended to follow a professional career, with law and medicine at the top of the list. With such aspirations came increasing emphasis on grades, expressed by one writer thus: "In some minds the mere fraction of a grade became the nail-in-the-horseshoe that could wreck life's best-laid battle plan: for want of a high enough fraction, a student's semester grade point average could suffer, which in turn could impair his year-end GPA, ruining his chance to be accepted by a top law school and, later, by a prestigious firm that would make him a partner within ten years, assuring him a minimum salary of $100,000 a year and lifetime security."[31]

In this kind of atmosphere a spirit of community was hard to engender. Honor systems were frequently violated; cheating on examinations and term papers increased. Some students manifested hostility to the enrollment of disadvantaged minorities, and the women now admitted to previously all-male institutions had to fight for respect. A few Catholic institutions, such as the University of Dayton and LeMoyne College, were already coeducational, but the vast majority of men's colleges became coed only in the seventies. The experience of women on their campuses is an important indicator of the cultural climate. Some male faculty and students at schools like Notre Dame and Holy Cross did not take kindly to the advent of women and in some instances were overtly hostile, despite the administration's commitment to coeducation.[32] At larger urban universities, such as Marquette, Loyola, and Fordham, which had already enrolled women in graduate programs and in schools of education, the inclusion of undergraduates was relatively peaceful. Some colleges agreed to have women as day-students but postponed the acceptance of residents.

One of the arguments in favor of coeducation, often used by presidents of Catholic colleges, was that women were more committed to liberal arts and would thus help to stem the tide of professionalism. But it was the declining enrollments and the consequent financial pressures in the men's colleges between 1970 and 1972 that was decisive in the vote of the trustees in favor of coeducation.[33]

What effect the climate of the campus might have on the women who came was a question ignored by both those who favored and those who resisted coeducation. The conversation focused on what they might bring to the campus. What went without attention was the overall change this might make in the mission and identity of the college. Earlier articulations had emphasized the manly virtues to be acquired by the students and their preparation for leadership in male-dominated professions. Cocurricular life at the all-male college had been sports-oriented, and social events were quite different from the typical Catholic women's college. The physical changes needed to accommodate women on the campus were hardly touched upon in preliminary conversations, and the cultural shift that would result was simply ignored. Although church teaching had long opposed coeducation, that consideration did not enter into the recorded discussions. There was also no discussion by the Catholic all-male colleges with the Catholic women's colleges, their neighboring "sister-colleges" for many years, about the decision to go coed and the effect it might have on the women's colleges' enrollment. Anger at this lack of concern still simmers below the surface when the leaders of Catholic women's colleges meet.

As we have pointed out, overall enrollments in the 1970s at Catholic colleges and universities increased from 450,000 to 535,000, and by 1988 reached 609,350. By that time, women had become 59 percent of the student population, but of the approximately 360,000 women, only 27,295 were enrolled at Catholic women's colleges.[34] This redistribution of gender had serious consequences for Catholic higher education, especially in the area of student life. Simultaneously, restrictions arising from a philosophy of *in loco parentis* were removed, and teachers of moral theology shifted their focus from the traditional elements in the formation of conscience, including sin, to an emphasis on Christian service of others as the essence of Christian faith. Without the structured socio-religious environment which had predominated on campuses, student affairs officers now had a more difficult task than their predecessors. Nevertheless, the professionally trained young men and women who now appeared in student personnel offices and in residence halls had skills and positive attitudes toward developmental tasks which made their presence on campus a real gift. They approached the issues of sexuality and discrimination against minorities within a framework of values that highlighted the importance of each individual person and the need for each person to grow in self-confidence based on respect for his or her own integrity. There was less emphasis on moral teaching as traditionally understood, and spiritual formation was less overt and less specifically Catholic than it was under the priests and religious who previously had been in charge of student life.

A task force formed in 1980 by ACCU to study campus life at Catholic colleges submitted a report on two groups of colleges, eight in Minnesota and eight in Illinois and Indiana.[35] The report suggested several ways that student personnel officers dealt with such ever-present problems as alcohol and drug abuse, date rape, pregnancy, and lack of respect for other students. The need for clear policies, with room for flexibility, was seen as of utmost importance, and the inclusion of students in the development of such policies was strongly recommended. Consistency was often lacking when policies were carried out by persons from a variety of backgrounds rather than from a single religious community tradition, as had existed among the priest-rectors, monks, brothers, and sisters once in charge of resident halls and student activities. Workshops focusing on team collaboration among the lay professionals became a priority for presidents and deans. Experiments with parietal visitation rules, coed dormitories, and honor houses (those with no supervision) provided opportunities to educate students in moral decision making, but required staff who could handle difficult situations and who were themselves committed to a life based on faith and principle.

By the end of the eighties, college administrators began to reconsider some of the policies adopted in response to student demands in the previous decade and to search for better ways of promoting community building based on Christian moral principles. A program begun in 1995 for student affairs officers, the Institute for Student Affairs at Catholic Colleges (ISACC),[36] has been evaluated very positively by the teams from eighty institutions that have participated. Basically, it seeks to reunite the decisions about personal and community behavior with the principles of Christian morality. It has four explicit goals: (1) to learn about the Catholic intellectual tradition; (2) to network with colleagues at Catholic colleges and universities across the nation and internationally; (3) to discuss how to ground student affairs practice in the Catholic identity of the institutions; and (4) to apply this understanding to practical concerns on campus. This Institute has already resulted in presentations at the National Association of Student Personnel Administrators and the Institute for College Student Values. It has also spawned a new organization, the Association for Student Affairs at Catholic Colleges and Universities. Under the leadership of Rev. Robert M. Friday, Vice President for Student Affairs at The Catholic University of America, this new group hopes to carry on the work begun at ISACC.

ISACC is one example of a response to the cultural context that had shifted so dramatically that it presented little or no support to traditional values on the Catholic college campus. In general, a collaborative effort among the leaders of Catholic higher education is essential to reinvigorate the commitment to a "value-added" educational experience based on the Judaeo-Christian tradition, an experience that would assist students in their struggle to live by principle in a world where that has become the exception rather than the rule.

Ecclesial Expectations

Christian churches which had founded colleges expected them to produce good citizens and moral persons. From the beginning of American higher education the training in character had been a high priority. The presidents of the early church-related colleges often taught the capstone course in Moral Philosophy. In Catholic institutions, with the high number of priests and religious on the faculty and supervising residence life, the opportunities for moral guidance abounded and were well utilized. In addition, the formation of a community was easier when there was a central liturgical life as well as an academic and social one. But with the new lifestyle on college campuses and the lack of cohesiveness among the students, it was more difficult to find ways and means of inculcating the Gospel values previously taken for granted. Now distinct programs needed to be developed to accomplish the same ends.

Colleges were in the forefront of liturgical experimentation in the post–Vatican Council II days. It was hoped that active participation in the worship experience would attract the students to attend services voluntarily. In most cases, the immediate response of excitement at new forms of celebration gave way in subsequent years to a diminution in attendance at the Eucharist. Campus ministers have struggled to find ways of communicating to students the importance of the Christian assembly at worship. This reflects, of course, the larger problem in the parishes, where the emphasis on the obligation of going to Mass is no longer sufficient to bring people to church on Sunday, and the new liturgical rituals have not been sufficiently developed to encourage attendance.

Another channel for value-added education was found in the university's commitment to developing the virtues of concern for the common good and unselfish service of others as an expression of Christian faith. On many campuses this translated into peace and justice education.

To focus on this aspect of campus life was to carry out a mandate from the church in its effort to spread the Gospel in the twentieth century. In 1971 at a synod meeting of Catholic bishops, the concern for the poor was voiced loud and clear. The resulting document boldly proclaimed that "the concern for justice was constitutive of the church." In other words, it was not an option. How would this message be spread in the American church? One of the recommendations of the Call to Action Conference, described in chaper 4, was that Catholic colleges and universities should develop programs of education in the issues of peace and justice. This proposal was further expanded by Archbishop William Borders in an address to the presidents at the ACCU meeting in early 1977,[37] and it was then examined and studied by the staff at ACCU. In 1978 a process was initiated by which colleges could volunteer to be "pilots"; the associate director of ACCU visited each pilot campus to help start its peace and justice program. Using the same basic process that had worked well at the Detroit Call to Action Conference, she insisted that "local" injustices be addressed as well as global ones. This meant, for example, that if "world hunger" were to be the target of their efforts, some attention should be given to the waste of food in the college cafeteria. Each college developed its program according to the interests of faculty and students, and support, both moral and financial, from the president was a *sine qua non*. The seven colleges with pilot projects reported each semester for three years to an Advisory Council set up by ACCU and were given assistance in refining goals or gaining greater support from the campus community.[38]

Prior to this effort, several academic programs in peace and justice education had already been introduced, the most notable at Manhattan College, where an Institute for Peace Studies had been established in 1971. The "Urban Plunge" was an annual activity promoted by the Center for Social Concerns at Notre Dame, which brought students for a live-in experience in an inner-city parish. Villanova had already begun to organize campus ministry activities around the issue of world hunger. The pilot programs attempted to bring these and new endeavors together, with each project including curriculum innovations, experiential learning, and Gospel reflection. The spread of these programs during the eighties is attested to by reports from about thirty different colleges which were periodically gathered and published by ACCU. While there is, as yet, no analytical study of them, the impact is clear but minimal. In 1998 Bishop Joseph Sullivan, addressing the annual meeting of ACCU, insisted on the imperative of handing on the commitment to social action that is inherent in the Catholic tradition. Such a commitment, he pointed out, is part of the "identity" that the Catholic colleges are seeking to retain.

The bishops repeatedly call for persons who will be leaders in the quest for justice; certainly the Catholic colleges are providing some of them. Lay Associate programs have multiplied, and the number of volunteers for community service reaches into the thousands. The colleges and universities have been assisted in their efforts by some remarkably dedicated persons. Over the years, workshops and annual meetings consistently featured Rev. J. Bryan Hehir, Rev. Peter Henriot, S.J., Dr. David O'Brien, Dr. Joseph Fahey, Rev. Ray Jackson, A.A., Dr. Kathleen Weigert, Rev. Don McNeill, C.S.C., William J. Byron, S.J., Loretta Carey, S.D.C., and Marjorie Keenan, R.S.H.M. A coordination of efforts was brought about by the presence of several of these leaders on the ACCU Advisory Council on Peace and Justice.

However, at almost all of the national or regional meetings on this topic, there have been voices expressing fear that the attention to social action will undermine the intellectual work of the faculty and students. This attitude has delayed introduction of courses on the church's social teaching into the curriculum, and it is clear that the church's teaching on war and peace, economic injustices, human rights, and the evangelization of cultures has not been widely studied by Catholics, even those teaching in Catholic schools and colleges; hence, there is need for continuing faculty development if the richness of the tradition is to be kept alive and shared with others in American society.

What are other ecclesial expectations? It is evident from the discussion in chapter 6 that the Roman authorities continue to expect a juridical relationship with Catholic universities around the world. On the other hand, the work of the Bishops and Presidents' Committee and the collaboration of the American hierarchy in gatherings such as the National Congress and annual meetings of the ACCU suggest another approach to the definition of Catholicity as it pertains to the institutions. Development on campus of faith communities, solid but contemporary courses in theology, freedom coupled with assistance toward mature responsibility in decision making, education around faith and justice issues—all of these aspects of the university are seen by the American bishops as important pieces of a Catholic identity. It is important to recall, however, that the bishops do not think or act as a single person. Within their ranks are those who would be happier with the Roman rather than the American approach, with a clear and binding juridical relationship rather than reliance on mutual trust and dialogue. Annual meetings of the NCCB testify to differences of opinion on many topics, including the mission and ecclesial standing of Catholic universities.

Unlike other Christian colleges and universities which participated in the National Congress, Catholic institutions have a sense of church authority which is universal as well as local. Hence, ecclesial expectations which may vary from diocese to diocese and from Catholic community to Catholic community are ultimately subject to a challenge by Roman authority. Events of the eighties, including the revision of the Code of Canon Law with its new section on universities and the many meetings of delegates leading up to *Ex Corde Ecclesiae,* underscored the accountability of the institutions and the concept that the term "Catholic," when used with "university," had to have a meaning agreed to by both church and university. Without repeating all that has been written in earlier chapters about this question, it can be said that this remains a central point of conflict as the American bishops attempt to implement the norms set forth in *Ex Corde Ecclesiae.* Although the bishops approved by an overwhelming vote the pastoral approach to their relationship with the universities and colleges, the Congregation for Catholic Education, in its review, insisted on greater attention to a juridical statement.[39] The end has not yet come.

Ecclesial expectations can also be extended to include the local Catholic community, the parents, alumnae/i, trustees, and donors, who are essential to the continued prosperity of the colleges. It is difficult to find data on their expectations, but there is enough anecdotal information to suggest that they can never be ignored when the "Catholic identity" question is raised. What president has not had a phone call from these various parties demanding to know what has happened to the university's Catholic character? Pressure groups within the church as well as outside of it express outrage over invited speakers, honorary degree recipients, student behavior, and so forth. Whatever the juridical link to the church, the living and vital relationships which the college has with its many constituencies determine how "Catholic" it is in the public's eye and, on a fundamental level, how Catholic it really is or wants to be.

EIGHT

Tolerance, Pluralism, and Beyond

At the end of his book *The Soul of the American University,* George Marsden raises the question: "Is there room for Institutional Pluralism?"[1] In the final decade of the twentieth century, Catholic colleges and universities seem to be saying that there must be such room, that they have a distinctive tradition at the root of their institutions which claims to be recognized, and that strengthening such a tradition will constitute a major contribution to American higher education. In this they are joined by many of their Christian church-related college colleagues.[2] They share Marsden's concern about the uniformity that has been imposed on American colleges and universities in the name of academic excellence. They express their awareness that in adapting to the standards of AAUP and the various government and accrediting agencies they may have lost some of their distinctiveness, their very reason for being.[3] They often ask the questions: "In seeking diversity of faculty and students in every institution of higher learning, have we overlooked the need for a diversity among institutions? If homogeneity takes over, then how can a community hand on its distinctive educational tradition?" Without a core of faculty and administrators committed to the institution's particular mission, the tradition will most assuredly be lost.

At the same time it is clear that among the Catholic colleges and universities today there is no uniformity. This is true internationally as well as nationally, and the existence of some nine hundred institutions of Catholic higher education around the world provides a laboratory for exploring the ways in which the faith tradition is mediated to a new generation within the context of different cultures.[4] For this is the heart of the matter. How does the process of inculturation affect the way in which we understand Christian faith and develop a mode of evangelization appropriate to higher education? Hence, what is the role of American culture in the life of American Catholic higher education? And what is the role of American Catholic higher education in American culture?

Inculturation is a major theme in the writings of John Paul II and is treated by him in relation to universities in *Ex Corde Ecclesiae*. Brian Hehir, in his address at the St. Thomas meeting in 1995, suggested that this document needs to be read through the lens of *Gaudium et Spes*. Father Hehir points out that the understanding of the church as found in the documents of Vatican II moves Catholics from a confrontational theology to a theology-in-dialogue, so that in conversation with other cultures and traditions we seek to learn as well as to teach. This shift in the perceived relationship of the church to the world causes a loss in solidity and surety about one's arguments, but provides a catalyst for rediscovering the Catholic intellectual tradition. Hehir stresses the importance of this ecclesiological perspective as basic to an understanding of the identity of a Catholic university:

> *Gaudium et Spes* takes you into a discussion of the world as a theological object of reflection, not simply a political and social arena where certain tasks must be achieved. *Gaudium et Spes* is about how we read history as Christian Catholics. *Gaudium et Spes* is about issues of vocation, intellectual and civil, as well as ecclesial. *Gaudium et Spes* is about how we understand the logic of the disciplines, secular and sacral, and their relationship.[5]

If we move into a discussion of the world as a theological object of reflection, as Hehir urges us to do, what do we find? What is the state of things in "the world"? In recent years society in the United States has suffered severe divisions among its members, divisions which necessarily are reflected in the life of the colleges and universities. Reports issued by government and private research institutes repeatedly point to the growing gap between the rich and the poor, the educated and the ignorant, the new immigrants and the old ones. These divisions surface whenever issues of global concern, whether of health, education, or commerce, are raised. The economic policies of the Reagan and Bush administrations did not aim directly at closing that gap but rather at promoting prosperity by reducing taxes at the top and presuming that the benefits would "trickle down" to those below. By the end of the eighties it was clear that that vision had not been realized. Instead, an increase in the national deficit and various international crises reduced funds available for education, health, and welfare. Even though the Soviet Empire had collapsed, the arms race had not ceased and was promoted now more for profit than for national security. The economic prosperity of the nineties, linked closely to international markets, has not yet dealt with the needs of the underdeveloped countries or with the health and education of the marginalized within the United States. Nor have we as a country decided what role is appropriate for a nation that is the most powerful in the world. These are questions that the graduates of Catholic universities should be particularly concerned about; they also should be confident about their ability to contribute to the answers.

The second half of the twentieth century witnessed Catholics moving from a position of being merely tolerated to one of being active players in the economic and political life of the nation. The post-World War II expansion of state universities and community colleges testified to the need for a variety of institutions in the academic arena to meet the needs of a diverse population now seeking higher education. While the Ivy League still set the pace, others, including Catholic universities, were seen as adding to the availability of educational opportunity and doing so in such a way that they contributed to the diversity and strength of the enterprise. What had been "tolerance" of such schools gave way to a necessary acceptance of "pluralism" among institutions. Catholic colleges benefited from this shift in perception and gradually moved into the mainstream. On their part, the Catholic cohort after Vatican Council II was able to demonstrate a growing recognition of academic freedom and institutional autonomy. They showed themselves willing to meet the standards of accrediting agencies and to abide by the AAUP guidelines for faculty and student rights. Of necessity, they conformed to the government regulations regarding equal opportunity, affirmative action, and nondiscrimination.

Unfortunately, the greater the homogenization engendered by such standards and regulations, the less the respect for true pluralism. Marsden argues for a less slavish accommodation to such standards, as if they were normative for all time:

> There is no necessity that so vital a part of society as its higher intellectual life should be pressured to fit one monolithic mold into which all sub-traditions are poured. Rather it seems there ought to be encouragement of institutional variety, including variety based on substantive religious concerns. Instead of following the pattern of having nonsectarian national standards set by a dominant establishment and then classing dissenting religious perspectives as at best second-rate, it should be recognized that re-

ligiously defined points of view can be intellectually as responsible as non-religious ones.[6]

This struggle against a mentality of homogenization was an issue within the Catholic community. An image or ideal of a Catholic college based on the overt Catholicity of the campuses in pre–Vatican II days was deeply implanted in alumnae/i, and it was difficult to explain to them as well as to parents, donors, and other friends of the colleges why changes in curriculum and student life were being made. On the other hand, as the new generation of the seventies saw it, the only unchanging feature of life was change itself. This seemed to be true not only in the university but also in the life of the church itself. As the reforms of the Council were implemented, contrasts between those who welcomed change and those who hated it deepened. One result was the the gradual development of sharper categories among Catholics; the terms "liberal" or "conservative" were used by the media and often by persons who wished to identify opinions of those with whom they disagreed. It became increasingly difficult to articulate what Cardinal Bernardin would later call "common ground," and so discussions about the Catholic identity of colleges and universities and attempts to formulate statements about it usually came to a dead end or, at best, the publication of an ambiguous text. A good example of this was the ACCU Committee on Purpose and Identity, discussed earlier.

In 1985 Pope John Paul II convened an Extraordinary Synod to study and evaluate the effects of the Council. Twenty years had passed since John XXIII and Paul VI had blessed its work; the implementation of its decrees worldwide had been varied and, in some cases, contradictory. The ambiguity about Catholic discipline that arose in the wake of changes made by the Council was being challenged, and the Synod was asked to sort through the evidence presented by the local churches and to clarify doctrinal and disciplinary teachings that may have been misunderstood.[7]

The papers prepared for the Synod by the bishops participating in it shed light on the tensions involved in trying to work out the meaning of the church being *in* the world as contrasted to an earlier vision of its being *in relationship to* the world. This was the shift evident in the very title of *Gaudium et Spes*, "The Church in the Modern World," and explained the importance of the 1972 document, "The Catholic University in the Modern World." In the *Final Report* of the Synod of 1985, six principles were enunciated for the interpretation of the documents of Vatican Council II :

1. Each passage and document of the Council must be interpreted in the context of all the others, so that the integral meaning of the Council may be rightly grasped;

2. The four major constitutions of the Council are the hermeneutical key for the other decrees and declarations;

3. The pastoral import of the documents may not be separated from, or set in opposition to, their doctrinal content;

4. No opposition may be made between the spirit and the letter of Vatican II;

5. The Council must be interpreted in continuity with the great tradition of the Church, including earlier councils;

6. Vatican II must be accepted as illuminating the problems of our own day.[8]

In his analysis of the Synod, Avery Dulles suggests that its language was deliberately irenic so as to avoid increasing the divisive tendencies in the church of the mid-eighties. Yet he points out that its conclusions clearly moderate the enthusiasm of the sixties, interpreting the signs of the times in a more negative way. A few of the bishops now regarded some of the statements of the Council as naive and as relevant to a time when "secular society all over the world seemed to be converging toward greater freedom, prosperity, and universal harmony," as compared with 1985, when they saw a world of "misery, division, and violence" under the power of the Evil One.[9]

Much of the Synod's evaluation of the effects of the Council show signs of such a more pessimistic worldview. This neo-Augustinian group of bishops (as characterized by Dulles) undoubtedly had an impact on the future development of structures that were intended to promote the participation of the "people of God" in the life of the local church. One senses a withdrawal from the Council's determination to seek full involvement of the church, the people of God, in the secular sphere, unless supervision by the hierarchy would protect orthodoxy of faith and traditional discipline. A somewhat limited interpretation of *Gaudium et Spes* has colored subsequent papal documents on evangelization, on social questions, and on universities. It has even led to serious questioning of the role of Episcopal Conferences as instruments for the development of church teaching.[10]

By 1985 the responsibility for governing American Catholic colleges and universities in harmony with their distinctive mission as Catholic had passed from the religious communities that founded them to independent boards of trustees. After 1970 most of these boards were self-perpetuating and were composed of lay and religious members. During the eighties it became obvious that lay trustees, now having full fiduciary and legal responsibility for the institution, would need more orientation to the history of the institution, its Catholic character, and the responsibilities of trusteeship in seeing that decisions were in line with that tradition. The Association of Catholic Colleges and Universities offered workshops for trustees which emphasized the responsibility of testing decisions within that context, but only a small number of trustees had the opportunity of attending. It has not been an easy task to educate trustees who come from the corporate world, even when they sincerely believe in the importance of the Catholicity of the institutions in which they serve. Men and women who sit on the boards of Catholic universities, while expressing appreciation for the religious heritage of the institution, often have more concern for its fiscal stability and want to leave the educational and religious aspects to the founding community as long as some of them are around. What will happen when they are not? Clearly, this is a greater problem for the Neylan colleges, since there are very few religious women choosing higher education as a ministry, but among some congregations of brothers and priests one senses the same unhappy phenomenon. It suggests that the "window of opportunity" for the religious who founded the colleges and universities to pass on the torch to their lay successors may not be open for very much longer.

As we have seen, the new trends in American Catholic higher education were not easily understood or accepted by Roman authorities. The movement of the colleges into mainstream American higher education, with its professionalization, its emphasis on autonomy and academic freedom, and its a-religious environment, led Cardinal Garrone and others to reiterate their insistence that "being Catholic" must be more than a semantic cover for a secular reality. This instruction was met with a defensiveness by the leaders of Catholic higher education, who saw what they were doing as simply a different mode of "being Catholic" as independent institutions within the church. From the first draft of the Schema for an apostolic letter to the final issuing of *Ex Corde Ecclesiae,* some of the participants in the dialogue talked right past each other.

Since 1990 the focus has been on the implementation of the apostolic constitution. The difficulties in reaching agreement on this with Roman authorities have already been discussed. However, the positive side effect has been the numerous regional meetings between bishops and representatives from the campuses. Here they have often been able to identify common interests and to provide for communication on a regular basis. Position papers by theologians have been helpful in developing a common vocabulary when the connection between the church and the Catholic university is the central issue. On-campus committees of faculty are studying the Catholic intellectual tradition and are beginning to explore the ways in which their teaching and research might extend it to another generation of students. One example of this is the extensive commitment of resources to seminars for faculty at the University of Dayton, a good model for other universities interested in promoting research that addresses ethical dimensions of many different professions. At the same time, the faculty is working to strengthen the core of humanities and sciences required of all students. At Georgetown University, a seminar of faculty and administrators from across the schools of the university met during the 1995–96 academic year and produced a document for discussion called "Centered Pluralism." It focused on the Jesuit and Catholic identity of Georgetown and struggled to reconcile the effort to cultivate that identity with the actual pluralism of the university. Rather than simply dealing with an abstraction called "identity," the Georgetown document is self-critical and honest about the university's shortcomings, and it suggests many courses of action that would reinvigorate its Catholic mission.

Another way of attacking the problem has been found in the creation of various institutes for the study of contemporary issues from the perspective of the Catholic tradition. Several of these can be found at the University of Notre Dame—for example, the Cushwa Center for the Study of American Catholicism, the Center for Civil and Human Rights, and the Erasmus Institute. St. Thomas University in Miami, University of San Diego, Marquette, DePaul, Holy Cross, and Loyola in Baltimore, among others, give witness to the increased support for programs of Catholic Studies on campuses both large and small. Saint Louis University has produced and shown to faculty and staff videos on the mission of the Jesuits, and the showing is accompanied by small group discussions, relating the story to the university today. New publications such as those coming from the Interdisciplinary Program in Catholic Studies at the University of St. Thomas at St. Paul are spreading the word about the Catholic intellectual tradition.

These new efforts testify to the fact that the danger to the identifiable Catholic character of most of the colleges was and is not imaginary. Although the presidents have reacted strongly against any proposal for a clear juridical relationship with the hierarchy, they have not been able to articulate with precision the characteristics of their institutions which they regard as giving it its Catholic identity. Vatican Council II, in strengthening the role of the local bishop and recommending national conferences of bishops, had not attended to the consequences of such a strengthened position vis-à-vis the institutions already established in their dioceses and recognized as Catholic by both the civil and local church communities. The work of clarifying the mission of the Catholic university *in* the church and at the same time *in* the world remains to be done. The 1972 "Catholic University in the Modern World" came close to doing so, but the four characteristics given therein are not clear enough for Roman authorities, nor have they been sufficiently visible in many Catholic colleges and universities.

The Synod of 1985 on the implementation of Vatican Council II did not address the issue of higher education, and the recently promulgated Code of Canon Law (1983) contains contradictory signals. On the one hand, the Catholic university is recognized as having autonomy necessary for its work, but on the other hand, the degree to which it is recognized as Catholic is circumscribed by canonical requirements. The new canons (especially 810 and 812) suggest an authoritative role for the local Ordinary which could override the decisions of trustees, both lay and religious. Was this seen as necessary because religious communities no longer controlled the universities? The 1990 Apostolic Constitution, *Ex Corde Ecclesiae,* incorporates the canons by reference but sheds no light on how the contradictions might be resolved. Of particular difficulty is the question of a mandate for those who teach theology in Catholic institutions of higher learning and how that could be implemented in the American context.

But *Ex Corde Ecclesiae* did make a major contribution to the ongoing conversations about Catholic identity. Its focus on the university's task of mediating faith to cultures inspired a number of creative innovations on Catholic campuses and a renewed determination to hold on to their Catholic heritage in the face of multiple pressures. Linking this way of understanding their mission to the already existing programs of peace and justice education on many campuses has led to more intensive consideration of the church's social teaching and an appreciation of the contribution it can make to contemporary issues. The growth of these programs was attested to by a national symposium held at Iona College in June 1998, where over 180 participants from sixty Catholic colleges gathered to share ideas and experiences in the promotion of such initiatives.[11]

It is recognized that more must be done to instill the community service programs that now flourish on many campuses with the Catholic social teaching tradition developed in the last hundred years. Many of the colleges have expanded their earlier mission of offering education to Catholic families, often from immediate immigrant background, to include the marginalized in today's American society. Large numbers of students and faculty engage in volunteer service to the segments of society in need of special help. This is seen as Catholic social doctrine in action. There remains the need to strengthen the mechanisms for a serious reflection by faculty as well as by administrators and students on the Gospel basis for social justice and for their own active participation in programs of community service. By encouraging one another, the colleges are moving forward in developing this mark of their Catholic identity.

Many problems remain, stemming from the increased pluralism on faculties and within student bodies. Ecumenical outreach in the seventies added to the richness of faculty competencies and insights, but it also diminished the number of now-tenured faculty with a deep commitment to the Catholic faith at the root of the tradition of the institution. While individual non-Catholic faculty have been highly supportive of the mission of the college, the "culture" of Catholicism has undoubtedly been weakened or, in some cases, lost. This may simply be a phase in the inculturation process, but it calls for conscious attention on the part of trustees and administrators. A culture that could be called "Catholic" no longer exists in most families or social institutions; yet, at the same time, there has been an enormous increase in the active participation of many of these same families in parish life, Catholic schools, religious education programs, and diocesan offices and councils. What we witness may be a shedding of a religious culture rather than of a loss of faith. In its place has come to our campuses contemporary academic culture, a reality which Marsden sees not only as a-religious but often anti-religious. While it is true that the shift in consciousness, underscored at Vatican Council II and in the writings of John XXIII, Paul VI, and John Paul II on inculturation, has led to a new understanding of the richness of other cultures and their religious traditions which we need to study carefully rather than simply confront, it also remains true that there must be a significant number of serious and theologically educated Catholics on the faculty and in administrative posts if there are to be the necessary conversations about the mission of the Catholic college or university in American culture in the twenty-first century.

The pluralism or diversity among student bodies certainly continues to be a challenge. Embracing the call to educate all those who are willing to be educated, regardless of race or socioeconomic status, has led to a proliferation of ethnic groups, religious faiths, and wide-ranging educational backgrounds on Catholic college campuses. What can be the common core of the educational experience? How will the richness of Christian literature, art, and music be transmitted to persons of such divergent cultural experiences?[12]

Further, Catholic colleges are concerned about the role of religion in higher education and the ecclesial dimensions of theological education. How "Catholic" can they be without violating certain governmental regulations on nondiscrimination? How can they avoid being considered as controlled by the church and hence ineligible for academic and professional recognition? What can they do to promote the moral and faith development of students who come from such different backgrounds? How can contemporary problems on campus such as alcohol abuse, date rape, cheating, and plagiarism be dealt with among students with little or no prior moral education? How can the college focus on the "common good" in the building of community?

To deal with many of these questions, a variety of special programs have been developed: Black Studies, Women's Studies, Native American Studies, and lately, Catholic Studies. But in this effort to welcome the cultural diversity of the students, the faculties then have the problem of a lack of coherence in the curriculum. They frequently revise the "core" of the degree programs; they establish honors programs which stress the liberal arts; and, to a limited degree, they create interdisciplinary courses. With flexibility and creativity as the watchwords, the colleges have sacrificed required courses that once communicated a common fund of knowledge to all students. As a result, the elements of the Christian tradition that were found in European history, English literature, the study of a language, and heavy doses of philosophy and theology are no longer a "given." Can Catholic colleges be satisfied with an education that lacks acquaintance with the known world and the cultures at the time of Christ, with the work of Milton and Shakespeare, with the icons and cathedrals of medieval Europe, with the reform of Martin Luther, the case of Galileo, the colonization movement and its positive and negative effects on the non-European world? One interesting attempt to meet this lacuna is that of the faculty at St. Bonaventure University, who redesigned the freshman year of studies according to the *Journey of the Mind to God* of St. Bonaventure. This opens a door to the Christian classics and suggests a framework to approaching the Catholic intellectual tradition.

The change in faculty brought about by new hiring guidelines under EEOC and the debate over tenure (in view of the end of mandatory retirement at age 65) has had a significant effect on students as individuals as well as on the institutions themselves. The need for specialists in professional fields and the unwillingness of administrators to commit resources to liberal arts courses when students are free to avoid them (and thus when registration declines) has led to significant expansion of part-time or adjunct faculty. While this allows colleges to offer some highly qualified professionals to students, it reduces the number of full-time and tenured faculty who constitute the core community of the university. There is also a question of justice involved here: adjuncts are paid by the course (as little as $2,000 for a semester, or even less) and are rarely able to find full-time employment. In some institutions they teach two or three courses, yet remain part-timers receiving a small stipend and no benefits. A reduction in the number of full-time faculty surely makes it more difficult to carry on the tradition of interpersonal relations which has been one of the advertised strengths of Catholic colleges, which have been relatively small and intentional communities. And how does this situation of low-paid adjuncts square with the social doctrine of the church?

Finally, the role of religion and/or theological studies in the institutions poses a continued challenge. While leading secular universities such as Chicago, Michigan, Boston, and Vanderbilt offer programs in religion, they are not regarded as central to the educational experience of undergraduates. Some scholars, such as George Marsden, have moved from secular universities to Catholic universities precisely to seek a community of scholars who are not ashamed to discuss significant questions of meaning and the diverse religious traditions that have something to say about them. The earlier curricula in theology and religious studies have been critically examined and radically altered during these thirty years. This has had bad as well as good effects. A conference convened at Marquette University in 1995 described and evaluated the changes made in theological education since 1960 and the papers presented there explain a great deal about the present state of theology at Catholic colleges.[13] As Catholic universities and colleges attempted to make the study of Catholic teaching relevant to the current students in their programs, they sometimes hired new faculty who lacked rootedness in the tradition and consequently presented new ideas without the necessary nuances. Some faculty in Catholic universities have also been challenged by ecclesial authorities concerning the orthodoxy of what they teach. This tension has already been described in previous chapters, but it is important to reflect on it within the broader context of the changes in the church consequent on Vatican Council II. What consonance is there between theology classes and sermons in the parishes? How does seminary training impact on the possibility of priest-scholars? What light is shed by the Catholic press? How are the divergent theologies of leading theologians communicated and analyzed?

A national symposium dealing with some of these issues was held in the summer of 1995 at the University of Saint Thomas in St. Paul, with 450 participants from about sixty institutions, including presidents, vice presidents, academic deans, student life and campus ministry personnel, faculty, and staff. Under the general title "Catholic Higher Education: Practice and Promise," several of the papers from the conference were published by ACCU and became resources for many campus discussions. Peter Steinfels, in his address at the meeting, said that the Saint Thomas conference was "potentially as important as Land O'Lakes—a gathering that, if you so choose, has every likelihood of entering the history books as signaling a new moment in Catholic higher education, in American Catholicism and, just maybe, in our society's effort to achieve an authentic pluralism." And Margaret Steinfels challenged the audience in strong words: "I believe we have a decade—ten years—in which this question of identity must be honestly addressed and definitively taken on as a commitment and core project of institutions that hope to remain Catholic."[14] Note that she said this in 1995; the target is 2005, not very far away.

Ms. Steinfels described the characteristics of the Catholic intellectual tradition, a list I would suggest could well be taken as the "non-negotiables" for Catholic colleges and universities in their continuing attempt to recover the intellectual heritage that is theirs. Whatever the cultural context and the needs of the times, the institutions must embody the elements of the tradition as she describes them:

1. In this tradition reason and faith are not seen as antagonistic or unconnected;
2. The tradition takes philosophy and philosophical thinking seriously;
3. It challenges the belief that facts come in pristine form—no baggage, no assumptions, no preconditions, no ends, no language that fills it with meaning.

4. It resists reductionism; it does not collapse categories; we do not deny reason in order to profess faith nor deny faith because we trust reason. Both are part of the picture.

American Catholic colleges and universities, in the continuing process of inculturation in which they are necessarily engaged, cannot sacrifice these fundamental elements, nor can they deny the centrality of Jesus Christ to that tradition without giving up their Catholic intellectual heritage; this is the profound truth beneath the years of negotiations that we have studied. True pluralism in American higher education will benefit from the distinctive contributions that will flow from the clarification of this educational goal on the part of Catholic colleges and universities and their recommitment to achieving it.

Appendix 1

QUESTIONNAIRE ON ELIGIBILITY FOR NEW YORK STATE AID TO HIGHER EDUCATION, 1968

THE UNIVERSITY OF THE STATE OF NEW YORK
THE STATE EDUCATION DEPARTMENT
OFFICE OF THE PRESIDENT OF THE UNIVERSITY
AND COMMISSIONER OF EDUCATION
ALBANY, NEW YORK 12224

August 12, 1968

Memorandum to : Chief Executive Officers of Institutions of Higher Education

From: James E. Allen, Jr., Commissioner of Education

Subject: *Constitutional Eligibility of Certain Non-Public Institutions of Higher Education for State Aid Pursuant to Chapter 677 of the Laws of 1968*

As you know, Chapter 677 of the Laws of 1968, which implements recommendations of the Select Committee of the Future of Private and Independent Higher Education in New York State, provides that in order to qualify for state aid apportionments, an institution must be eligible for state aid under the Federal and State constitutions.

Responsibility for determining eligibility rests with the Commissioner of Education. To assist me in making this determination, I am asking each institution which intends to apply for aid pursuant to Chapter 677 to provide the information requested in the attached memorandum.

Submission of that information, within the time specified, will be deemed to constitute an indication of the intention of your institution to apply for aid under Chapter 677, and I will advise you as promptly as possible of my determination with respect to the constitutional eligibility of your institution.

If you have any questions or comments about the material in this memo-randum, please do not hesitate to communicate with me or with my Counsel, Mr. Robert D. Stone.

Sincerely,
James E. Allen, Jr.

Attachment

THE UNIVERSITY OF THE STATE OF NEW YORK
THE STATE EDUCATION DEPARTMENT
STATE EDUCATION BUILDING
ALBANY, NEW YORK 12224

CONSTITUTIONAL ELIGIBILITY OF CERTAIN NON-PUBLIC INSTITUTIONS
OF HIGHER EDUCATION FOR STATE AID
PURSUANT TO CHAPTER 677 OF THE LAWS OF 1968.

Chapter 677 of the Laws of 1968, which implements recommendations of the Select Committee on the Future of Private and Independent Higher Education in New York State, provides that in order to qualify for state aid apportionments pursuant to the chapter, an institution ". . . must be eligible for state aid under the provisions of the constitution of the United States and the constitution of the state of New York."

The relevant provision of the United States Constitution is contained in the First Amendment, and is set forth in the following language:

"Congress shall make no law respecting an establishment of religion, or pro-hibiting the free exercise thereof; . . ."

The relevant provision of the New York State Constitution is contained in Article 11, §3, and is set forth in the following language:

"Neither the state nor any subdivision thereof shall use its property or credit or any public money, or authorize or permit either to be used, directly or indi-rectly, in aid or maintenance, other than for examination or inspection, of any school or institution of learning wholly or in part under the control or direction of any religious denomination, or in which any denominational tenet or doctrine is taught, but the legislature may provide for the transportation of children to and from any school or institution of learning."

In order to determine the eligibility of a given institution for apportionments of State aid under the quoted constitutional provisions, the Commissioner of Educa-tion will require information concerning the purposes, policies and governance of the institution, and concerning its faculty, student body, curricula and programs.

While each applying institution is free to submit whatever information it con-siders relevant to the question of its constitutional eligibility for the receipt of State aid under Chapter 677, it is requested that specific answers be provided to the questions set forth below.

An institution seeking an apportionment of aid for the period commencing July 1, 1969 should submit its statement with respect to eligibility, in duplicate, together with any supporting documents, likewise in duplicate, no later than November 1, 1968 to:

> Robert D. Stone
> Counsel and
> Deputy Commissioner for Legal Affairs
> State Education Building
> Albany, New York 12224

Each statement with respect to eligibility should provide full information with respect to the following:

1. What are the stated purposes of the institution, as set forth in its charter or legislative authority (please quote verbatim), and in other relevant documents?
2. Is the institution wholly or in part under the control or direction of any religious denomination? If the answer is in the affirmative, indicate the nature and extent of such control or direction in all areas of the life of the institution.
3. Does the institution receive financial assistance from any religious body? If the answer is in the affirmative, please indicate fully the nature, extent and frequency of such assistance and indicate the proportional relationship which such assistance bears to other sources from which the institution derives funds.
4. Do the policies of the institution with respect to the selection of members of its governing board, its administrative officers or its faculty provide that the faith or creed of a candidate shall be relevant in any way to his selection? If the answer is in the affirmative, please set forth in full the text of any such policy which is in writing, and indicate fully the nature and extent of any such policy which is not in writing.
5. Do the policies of the institution with respect to the admission of students provide that the faith or creed of an applicant shall be relevant in any way to his admissibility to the institution? If the answer is in the affirmative, please set forth in full the text of any such policy which is in writing, and indicate fully the nature and extent of any such policy which is not in writing.
6. Do the policies of the institution with respect to the awarding of scholarship, fellowship or other financial assistance to its students provide that the faith or creed of an applicant shall be relevant in any way to the awarding of such assistance? If the answer is in the affirmative, please set forth in full the text of any such policy which is in writing, and indicate fully the nature and extent of any such policy which is not in writing.
7. Is any denominational tenet or doctrine taught in the institution? If the answer is in the affirmative, please provide full information concerning the nature and

extent of such instruction and indicate whether it is mandatory or optional. If mandatory for some students, but not for all, please indicate the circumstances under which it is mandatory.

8. Does the institution award any degree or degrees in the field of religion? If the answer is in the affirmative, please indicate the name of such degree or degrees and provide full information with respect to the requirements for the conferring of such degree or degrees.

9. Does the institution include within its structure, or is it affiliated with any seminary or school of theology? If the answer is in the affirmative, please provide a full description of the seminary or school of theology, and indicate the nature and extent of the relationship or affiliation.

10. What is the place of religion in the programs of the institution? (Please indicate the character and extent of required religious observance, if any.)

11. Do the policies of the institution with respect to the use of any institutional facility or program by others than the staff, faculty and student body provide that the faith or creed of an individual applicant, or the denominational affiliation of an organizational applicant is relevant in any way to the granting of such use? If the answer is in the affirmative, please set forth in full the text of any such policy which is in writing, and indicate fully the nature and extent of any such policy which is not in writing.

12. Has the institution filed with the State Education Department a Certificate of Religious or Denominational Institution pursuant to Education Law section 313? If so, please indicate the date of filing, and indicate whether such certificate was subsequently withdrawn.

13. Is there any other information which the institution deems pertinent to a determination of its eligibility for state aid under the constitutional provisions referred to above?

August 5, 1968.

Appendix 2

NEW YORK STATE COMMISSIONER
OF EDUCATION TO PRESIDENT OF THE
COLLEGE OF NEW ROCHELLE, 1969

THE UNIVERSITY OF THE STATE OF NEW YORK

THE STATE EDUCATION DEPARTMENT

OFFICE OF THE PRESIDENT OF THE UNIVERSITY

AND COMMISSIONER OF EDUCATION

ALBANY, NEW YORK 12224

Wednesday

December 31

1969

Sister Mary Robert Falls, O.S.U.
President
The College of New Rochelle
New Rochelle, New York 10802

Dear Sister Mary Robert:

In my letter of July 22, 1969, I advised you that on the basis of all the information then at my disposal, I was compelled to reach the tentative conclusion that The College of New Rochelle is not eligible for State aid pursuant to Education Law Article 129 under the provisions of Article XI, Section 3 of the New York State Constitution.

I am grateful to you for availing yourself of the invitation which I extended in that letter to meet with key members of the Education Department staff to assist us in insuring that our information about the institution is current, complete and accurate. The information which you provided during and subsequent to that meeting, as well as all information previously provided, has been thoroughly reviewed.

On the basis of all information now at my disposal, I find that I must still conclude that The College of New Rochelle is not eligible for State aid under the relevant provisions of the New York State Constitution. While my conclusion is based not on any single factor, but rather upon my understanding of the institution as a whole, I have noted that the institution characterizes itself as a "Catholic college"; that the catalog and other publications of the institution evidence a strong religious commitment; that members of the sponsoring religious order comprise a substantial minority of the board of trustees, occupy the presidency and many of the key staff offices, and comprise approximately one-third of the faculty; the College states, in its submission to us, that responsibility for administering the College is shared by the community of Ursuline Nuns, the sponsoring religious order; that all students are required to complete at least three credit hours in courses in religious studies; and that College-sponsored religious activities appear to be exclusively Christian and specifically Roman Catholic in style.

If, as a result of any future development at the institution, you believe that further consideration should be given to its eligibility for State aid, a new application may of course be submitted.

Despite our inability to apportion State aid to The College of New Rochelle at this time, we shall of course continue to work with you in every way possible in pursuit of our common goals.

Faithfully,
Ewald B. Nyquist
Commissioner of Education

Abbreviations for Archives

AAAUP   Archives, American Association of University Professors

ABC   Archives, Boston College

ACHC   Archives, College of the Holy Cross

ACNR   Archives, College of New Rochelle

ACUA   Archives, The Catholic University of America

ACUA/NCEA   Archives, The Catholic University of America/ National Catholic Educational Association collection. This includes the records of the Association of Catholic Colleges and Universities, referred to between 1904 and 1978 as the College and University Department of NCEA.

AFU   Archives, Fordham University

ALUC   Archives, Loyola University at Chicago

AMC   Archives, Mundelein College

AMHC   Archives, Manhattanville College

ANCCB   Archives, National Conference of Catholic Bishops

ASBU   Archives, St. Bonaventure University

ASLU   Archives, Saint Louis University

AUND   Archives, University of Notre Dame

Notes

One: The Winds of Change

1. Philip Gleason, *Contending with Modernity* (New York: Oxford University Press, 1995). The very title of this work suggests Gleason's thesis. On the other hand, the historical record he presents also demonstrates a constant move toward adapting to the modern world.

2. Andrew M. Greeley, *From Backwater to Mainstream: A Profile of Catholic Higher Education* (New York: McGraw-Hill, 1969).

3. Basic documents of AAUP used by the author can be found in the 1990 edition of *Policy Documents and Reports* (Washington, D.C.: AAUP).

4. J. Bryan Hehir, "The Church in the World," in James L. Heft, S.M., *Faith and the Intellectual Life* (Notre Dame, Ind.: University of Notre Dame Press, 1996), 106.

5. Ibid., 112. Note the positive use of the word "secular."

6. Neo-scholasticism is examined in detail with reference to its impact on the Catholic worldview in the inter-war period by Gleason, *Contending with Modernity*, 115ff. It was a philosophical system based on the realism of Aristotle harmonized with Christian revelation by Thomas Aquinas. In that understanding of reality there could be no conflict between faith and reason (116).

7. The long and painful experiences suffered by theologians who sought to use such new methods of research is described by Henri de Lubac, *At the Service of the Church,* trans. by Anne Elizabeth Englund (San Francisco: Ignatius Press, 1993). The original French edition was *Mémoire sur l'occasion de mes écrits* (Namur: Culture et Vérité, 1989). The life of de Lubac witnesses to an inspiring degree of integrity under very difficult circumstances.

8. Gustave Weigel, S.J., "American Catholic Intellectualism—A Theologian's Reflections," *Review of Politics,* vol. 19, no. 3 (July 1957). The Catholic Commission on Intellectual and Cultural Affairs (CCICA) had been formed in 1946 for faculty on both secular and Catholic campuses, but most of its members were at secular universities. Although lay members predominated, the first Executive Director was Rev. Edward Stanford, O.S.A. (1946–53), and he was succeeded by Rev. William Rooney. At the annual meeting of CCICA in 1954, John Tracy Ellis delivered his paper on Catholic intellectual life that became a catalyst for self-criticism among

Catholic colleges and universities. See "American Catholics and the Intellectual Life," *Thought* (Autumn 1955): 351–388.

9. Ernan McMullin, "Philosophy in the United States Catholic College," in *New Themes in Christian Philosophy*, ed. Ralph M. McInerny (Notre Dame, Ind.: University of Notre Dame Press, 1968), 372–373, as quoted in Gleason, *Contending with Modernity*, 409 n. 76.

10. It is impressive to scan the NCEA *College Newsletter* of this period and note announcements of the lectures given on Catholic campuses, both large and small. It explains, at least in part, the preparation of those in higher education for the reception of the work of Vatican II.

11. Patrick Allitt, *Catholic Intellectuals and Conservative Politics in America, 1950–1985* (Ithaca, N.Y.: Cornell University Press, 1993), 7. See also his *Catholic Converts* (Ithaca, N.Y.: Cornell University Press, 1997). British and American converts had predominated in Catholic intellectual circles for most of the nineteenth and twentieth centuries.

12. See William Buckley, *God and Man at Yale* (Chicago: Regnery, 1951), and various contributors to Buckley's new publication, *National Review* (1955–).

13. This is well documented in Ellen Schrieker, *No Ivory Tower: McCarthyism and the Universities* (New York: Oxford University Press, 1986). Regrettably, neither the AAUP nor the AAU was vocal in defense of the faculty so defamed, a reminder of the fragility of academic freedom. Another useful example from recent history is the failure of the academic community to safeguard its independence in the pre-Hitler period in Germany, thus paving the way for the Nazi program of *Glichshaltung*. See Alice Gallin, *Midwives to Nazism: German Professors in the Weimar Republic, 1925–1933* (Macon, Ga.: Mercer University Press, 1986).

14. Philip Gleason, "Academic Freedom: Survey, Retrospect and Prospects," address to NCEA College and University Department, March 28, 1967. Typescript in ACUA/NCEA.

15. A photocopy is in the AAAUP, Committee A file.

16. Cited in a Memo to the file of November 21, 1958, from Louis Joughin, AAAUP.

17. AAUP, "Statement of Principles on Academic Freedom and Tenure," *Policy Documents and Reports*, 1990 edition, p. 3.

18. Sidney Hook, *Heresy, Yes—Conspiracy, No!* (New York: J. Day, 1953), 161–172.

19. John Cogley, "The Future of an Illusion," *Commonweal*, June 2, 1967.

20. Jacqueline Grennan, "Convocation Address," November 21, 1966, in Grennan, *Where I Am Going* (New York: McGraw-Hill, 1968).

21. Journet Kahn, in *Proceedings of the American Catholic Philosophical Association*, 1957.

22. Copy of this invitation, dated May 9, 1955, ACNR.

23. This remark of Bannan is cited in his defense papers, described later. The explanation for Bannan's statement is given in the written document. It may not have been said at the time, but rather included in his written defense. Dr. Fontinell

seemed to recall that it had been he, not Bannan, who made this remark; in any case they clearly agreed with one another. When I began my research in the college archives I found no records of this unpleasant affair. However, I was able, through personal contact with the faculty members involved, to recapture the documentation that will be referred to here and to provide copies for the college archives. I also interviewed the former chaplain, the only cleric involved who was still living in 1996. I am deeply grateful to all of them for their cooperation. Recently (1998) the archivist discovered a file on this subject affirming the materials used by the author. All are now in the archives of the College of New Rochelle.

24. Gleason, "Academic Freedom: Survey."

25. An important confrontation took place on February 27, 1956, when faculty members, particularly Joseph Cunneen and Francis Sullivan, disagreed vehemently with a guest lecturer, Godfrey Schmidt, whose topic was "Subversives in Higher Education." Schmidt was a rabid McCarthyite and had a manner of speaking that was inflammatory. The audience was made up of a number of older women in Westchester who sponsored this series of lectures, the college allowing them the use of facilities. In a report of the event it was pointed out that "The women that make up the supporting group are not open-minded on many current issues and cherish deep national and racial prejudices as well as a strong political bias." Even the college president, when reprimanding the faculty members for their discourtesy, could only recommend greater self-restraint in the future, noting that Mr. Cunneen "was not intemperate in language until provoked to it by the insulting remarks of the speaker." ACNR, Cunneen file. Unfortunately, there is no indication of who wrote the report on this event or to whom it was addressed. It is possible that it was simply a memo to the file in the dean's office. It is dated February 27, 1956, the day of the lecture.

26. The Index of Forbidden Books listed books detrimental to faith, and permission from the bishop was needed to read them. Faculty would submit a list of books to be used in their courses and the dean would get the needed permission. The Index was abolished in 1966.

27. The details of the accusations are taken from the papers submitted to Cardinal Spellman for review and from interviews with the lay faculty members and the chaplain in 1995–96.

28. The view from the dean's office is found in three letters sent by the acting dean, Mother Mary Alice Gallin, to Mother Mary Peter Carthy, the dean, who was studying at The Catholic University of America during this year. October 6, 11, and 16, 1956, ACNR.

29. When interviewing the principals in the case (1995), I sought information about the person who brought the matter to the cardinal's attention, but without success. Their assumption was that the president sought help from the cardinal, possibly through Msgr. John Voight, Secretary of Education for the archdiocese.

30. See the file on Augustin Léonard, O.P., in ACNR, especially his letters to Mother Mary Peter Carthy. He would have found similar intellectual excitement

speakers, was considered outrageous by many, including bishops on the board of Catholic University. Joseph Nuesse, *The Catholic University of America: A Centennial History* (Washington, D.C.: The Catholic University of America Press, 1990). John Tracy Ellis was particularly distressed by such high-handed decision making, which ignored faculty and student points of view.

59. Gleason, "Academic Freedom: Survey." For an excellent overview of developments in the 1950s and 1960s, see Gleason, *Contending with Modernity*, part 3.

60. Pastoral letter of Archbishop Joseph E. Ritter of St. Louis, June 17, 1960, ACUA/NCEA.

61. The English version of these two works is *The Mystery of the Church*, trans. A. V. Littledale (Baltimore: Helicon Press, 1960).

62. *Pacem in Terris*, April 11, 1963 (NCWC, Washington, D.C.), no. 157. Pope John had already expressed these sentiments in *Mater et Magistra* in 1961.

63. This is the translation given in one edition of *Pacem in Terris* (New York: Ridge Press, 1964). It seems to go further than the same text in the NCWC edition, no. 158, where we read: "For Catholics, if for the sake of promoting the temporal welfare they cooperate with men who either do not believe in Christ or whose belief is faulty because they are involved in error, can provide them either the occasion or the inducement to turn to truth."

64. In the case of sisters, the number receiving their doctorates at Catholic universities went from 77 percent in 1951–60 to 63 percent in 1961–70, and to 30 percent in 1971–80 and 1981–90. Marie M. Cooke, R.S.M., and Mary Chinery, "Doctoral Degrees Earned by United States Women Religious 1907–1992," in *Women Religious and the Intellectual Life: The North American Achievement*, ed. Bridget Puzon, O.S.U. (San Francisco: Catholic Scholars Press, 1995), 33–34.

65. Hans Küng was a popular speaker among those working toward church unity in other churches as well as on college campuses. He made an extended tour of the United States in 1963 and was welcomed everywhere except at The Catholic University of America. The examples of ecumenical discussions are found in *College Newsletter*. They do not pretend to cover events on all campuses during these exciting years leading up to the decree on ecumenism adopted at Vatican Council II. As indicated above, Küng was the keynote speaker at the NCEA convention in St. Louis in 1963, where he received an honorary degree from Saint Louis University.

66. This decree, *Unitatis redintegratio*, was adopted on November 21, 1964. Flannery, *Vatican Council II: Conciliar and Post Conciliar Documents*, 452–471.

67. Ibid., 516.

68. Eugene Grollmes, S.J., report of November 12, 1969. ASLU, Reinert papers.

69. The built-in contradictions of the late sixties are well described in Charles Kaiser, *1968 in America* (New York: Weidenfeld and Nicolson, 1968).

70. ABC, JEA collection.

71. Gleason, *Contending with Modernity*, 296.

72. Morris Pollard, "Thirty-two Years at Notre Dame," and Timothy O'Meara, "A Personal Reflection," are two of the essays published in Theodore M. Hesburgh,

C.S.C., *The Challenge and Promise of a Catholic University* (Notre Dame, Ind.: University of Notre Dame Press, 1994).

73. Introduction by Theodore M. Hesburgh, in *The Challenge and Promise.*

Two: The Americanization of Catholic Colleges and Universities

1. Attempts have been made to analyze the so-called "Catholic vote" in the 1960 election, but no interpretation is definitive. For an immediate analysis, see *U.S. News and World Report,* November 21, 1960. For an indication of the continuing disagreement about interpretation, see a letter to the *New York Times* by Rev. Andrew Greeley, October 16, 1996. During the thousand days of Kennedy's presidency little or nothing of his "dark side" was glimpsed by most Americans. He was admired by many young students for his exciting projects, such as the Peace Corps.

2. Report of the Presidential Commission on National Goals, 1960. Quoted in Logan Wilson, *Shaping American Higher Education* (Washington, D.C.: American Council on Education, 1972), 16.

3. Ibid.

4. Ibid., introduction.

5. Clark Kerr, *The Great Transformation in Higher Education, 1960–1980* (New York: SUNY Press, 1991), prologue.

6. The question of what drives the selection of topics for research in Catholic universities has been raised recently by John C. Haughey, S.J., "Catholic Higher Education: A Strategy for Its Identity," *Current Issues in Catholic Higher Education* 16, no. 2 (Winter 1996): 25–32. A follow-up project is reported on by Raymond Benton Jr. and Marc D. Hayford in *Current Issues* 18, no. 1 (Fall, 1997): 67–80.

7. The court challenges to this act will be treated below.

8. The role of the private foundations in the financing of higher education is dealt with later in this chapter. The work of the Carnegie Foundation for the Advancement of Education was particularly significant.

9. This debate would continue into the seventies. See, for example, the variety of opinions in Sidney Hook, Paul Kurtz, and Miro Todorocich, eds., *The University and the State: What Role for Government in Higher Education?* (Buffalo, N.Y.: Prometheus Books, 1978).

10. Theodore Distler, "Report of the President," AAC *Bulletin,* vol. 47 (1961): 135–142.

11. *College Newsletter,* vol. 25, November 1961.

12. *College Newsletter,* vol. 25, January 1962.

13. *College Newsletter,* vol. 27, November–December 1963.

14. *College Newsletter,* vol. 27, December 1964.

15. For this and subsequent interpretations, see Wilson, "Catholic Colleges and Civil Law." Mr. Wilson had been with the firm of Williams and Connolly in Washington, D.C., and was a participant in several of the cases regarding aid to church-related colleges and their students.

16. *Horace Mann League v Board of Public Works of Maryland*, (1966). The suit was directed against the state of Maryland, since only a governmental unit can violate the establishment clause, but the four colleges chose to be defendants so that their side of the argument could be presented. See Wilson, "Catholic Colleges and Civil Law," note 12. The other two institutions were Western Maryland (Methodist) and Hood College (Church of Christ). Hood was among the four whose grants were challenged, but it was exempted from the final court ruling.

17. Gallin, *Independence,* chapter 3.

18. Samuel J. Thomas, "After Vatican Council II: The American Catholic Bishops and the *Syllabus* from Rome, 1966–1968," *Catholic Historical Review* 83, no. 2, (April 1997): 233–257. The text of the letter, which is appended to Thomas's article, was clearly intended to exert some control by the bishops over theologians, thus indirectly suggesting some intervention in the universities where they taught. It was this kind of control that might have affected the status of the Catholic institutions in the various cases that would question their "pervasive sectarianism."

19. Wilson, "Catholic Colleges and Civil Law," note 77. The quote is from White's opinion in the cases *Lemon v Kurtzman*, 403 US 602 (1971), and *Tilton v Richardson,* 403 US 672 (1971).

20. *Tilton v Richardson,* cited above. See Charles H. Wilson, *Tilton v. Richardson: The Search for Sectarianism in Education,* a brochure printed by the Association of American Colleges, Washington, D.C., 1971.

21. In addition to the study by Wilson in "Catholic Colleges and Civil Law," there is an excellent overview of the changes that occurred in the relationship of higher education to federal law in William A. Kaplin, "Law on the Campus 1960–1985: Years of Growth and Challenge," *Journal of College and University Law,* vol. 12, no. 3 (Winter 1985): 269–301. This entire issue deals with the law and American higher education and has several useful articles.

22. Ellen Condliffe Lagemann, *Private Power for the Public Good* (Middletown, Conn.: Wesleyan University Press, 1983). The new direction, i.e., focusing on student aid, was favored by the Carnegie Foundation for the Advancement of Teaching but was opposed by the lobbyists in the Higher Education Secretariat in Washington, where the conflict between the research-oriented universities and liberal arts colleges was very clear.

23. See Wilson, "Catholic Colleges and Civil Law," on the underlying conflict over the meaning of the establishment clause which entered into all these decisions.

24. Ibid., 20.

25. Even in the way they secured a tax exemption, Catholic colleges aligned themselves with private colleges rather than with the church, which had its own religious exemption. The Executive Secretary of the College and University Department of NCEA advised members to secure a separate educational tax exempt status rather than be included in the group ruling of USCC (United States Catholic Conference) for all institutions of the church listed in the *Official Catholic Directory.* Some colleges, particularly those in New York, withdrew from the *OCD* listing, but

most wanted to remain identified as Catholic colleges. The dilemma was solved in the 1980s when ACCU (Association of Catholic Colleges and Universities) secured an agreement from the USCC to list them but not include them under the umbrella of the USCC tax exemption. Colleges wishing to retain their individual tax exemption and not be included under USCC are advised to place an asterik next to the name of the college in the listing. They are then not included in the exemption of the church and its institutions. ACUA/NCEA.

26. Report of the Executive Secretary of the College and University Department (NCEA), April 15, 1971. A trust fund was also established to collect money to defray the expenses, and Dr. Willis Tate, president of Southern Methodist University, served as honorary chair. AAC and AGB paid for the amicus brief supported by the several associations. Dr. Friedman reported that he was especially gratified by the participation of the National Association of State Universities and Land Grant Colleges, which thus brought in public education. A discussion of various higher education associations is found in chapter 4.

27. *Roemer v Board of Public Works*, 426 US 736 (1976).

28. Wilson, "Catholic Colleges and Civil Law," 37.

29. See Gallin, *Independence*. The strengthening of the role of the laity in the governance of Catholic higher education was perhaps the most important factor in changing the public image of these institutions.

30. See Wilson, "Catholic Colleges and Civil Law," 10–53. These regulations impinged on hiring faculty and staff, recognition of student organizations, and unionization of faculties.

31. Some early examples of Catholic college fund-raising efforts are given in Gleason, *Contending with Modernity*, 99–199.

32. James R. Day to Henry S. Pritchett, February 28, 1910, cited in Lagemann, *Private Power*, 185.

33. Lagemann, *Private Power*. The Carnegie classification of institutions is still significant in ranking them and affects the current rankings by news magazines and college guides. TIAA did not discriminate against church-related schools.

34. Rev. James Burns, C.S.C., to Sister Irene Gill, April 17, 1921, Correspondence of Mother Irene Gill, ACNR. See also Minutes of the CNR Board of Trustees, January 16, 1924, ACNR.

35. ACNR, Empire State file.

36. The attitude of the Catholic Church toward endowments is an interesting aspect of this question. Since the collection of funds for good causes was generally focused on the neediest members of the community, it was a principle that nothing collected should be saved or invested but rather, all should be used immediately to meet the need. See Mary Oates, *The Catholic Philanthropic Tradition in America* (Indianapolis: Indiana University Press, 1995), 133–139. Although endowing colleges, academies, and universities was acceptable, it did not fulfill one's obligation for charitable giving. Since higher education was considered the preserve of the socially and economically well-off, a general church collection for endowment pur-

poses was never favored by the hierarchy. It was even difficult for them to agree to national collections for The Catholic University of America and for the American College in Rome. By the 1940s a number of outstanding lay Catholics took up the challenge of endowing the universities of their choice. Catholic foundations today are an important part of that support and are coordinated in their philanthropic efforts by an association established in 1976, Foundations and Donors Interested in Catholic Activities (FADICA).

37. Manning M. Pattillo and Donald M. Mackenzie, *Church-Sponsored Higher Education in the United States: Report of the Danforth Commission* (Washington, D.C.: American Council on Education, 1966), 207.

38. Reinert's role is described in detail in chapter 3. See his own account in Paul Reinert, S.J., *To Turn the Tide* (Englewood Cliffs, N.J.: Prentice-Hall, 1972).

39. See Carnegie Commission on Higher Education, *A Digest and Index* (December 1968–June 1972), Berkeley, 1972. Clark Kerr was the Chair of the Commission from 1967 to 1980. In writing his own recollections of the period, *The Great Transformation in Higher Education, 1960–1980*, he makes little reference to Catholic or other church-related colleges. A record of the work of the commission can be located in AUND, CPHS 79/13 and 80/08.

40. See chapter 3.

41. *Priorities for Action: Final Report of the Commission on Higher Education* (New York: McGraw-Hill, 1973).

42. Charles Ford and Edgar Roy, *The Renewal of Catholic Higher Education* (Washington, D.C.: NCEA, 1968), 7–14.

43. Gallin, *Independence*, 1.

44. See chapter 5. For a detailed analysis of this movement and seven case studies (College of New Rochelle, Saint Louis University, University of Notre Dame, University of Portland, Mundelein College, Fordham University, and Saint Michael's College), see Gallin, *Independence*.

45. In a study done by Earl McGrath and Gerald Dupont, S.S.E., in 1967, it is reported that 125 of the 159 respondents (administrators of Catholic colleges and universities) claimed that the *Horace Mann* case had no influence whatsoever on the composition of their governing boards (*The Future Governance of Catholic Higher Education in the United States* [n.p., 1967], 23). In retrospect this judgment seems to have been a hasty one; records of trustee minutes and articles in the Catholic press suggest that *Horace Mann* was decidedly a factor. There is little doubt that the refusal of the New York State legislature to delete the Blaine Amendment to the constitution, by which any aid to "sectarian" institutions was forbidden, had a significant impact on the colleges in New York State in their move to independent boards. See the discussion of this question in Gallin, *Independence*, 91 ff.

46. Martin J. Stamm, "Emerging Models of Governance in Contemporary American Catholic Higher Education," *Current Issues in Catholic Higher Education* 2, no. 1 (Summer 1981). This article is based on Stamm's doctoral dissertation on

the laicization of boards, University of Pennsylvania, 1979. Copy in the ACCU office, Washington, D.C.

47. Middle States report on replies to a questionnaire by presidents of sixty-six Roman Catholic institutions for lay students, 1969. ACUA/NCEA.

48. Ford and Roy, *Renewal,* 9.

49. A description of eight different "models" used by Catholic institutions is given in Stamm, "Emerging Models."

50. Rev. Leo McLaughlin, S.J., president of Fordham, was unable to bring about a peaceful change of governance. See Gallin, *Independence,* 85–100. Walsh became president of Fordham in 1969.

51. It is interesting to note that even without the New York Blaine Amendment, as it was incorporated into the criteria for so-called Bundy money, lawyers were very cautious about any unnecessary statements about institutional Catholicity.

52. Gallin, *Independence.* This can be verified in each of the seven institutions studied.

53. John McGrath, *Catholic Institutions: Canonical and Civil Law Status* (Washington, D.C.: The Catholic University of America Press, 1968).

54. A recent study of enrollments in Catholic higher education has been done by Thomas M. Landy, "Demographic Snapshot: Catholic Higher Education, 1960–1990," a paper delivered at Saint Louis University, May 9, 1997.

55. Ernest Bartell, C.S.C., *Project 80: Enrollment, Finances, and Student Aid at Catholic Colleges and Universities* (Washington, D.C.: ACCU and NIICW, 1980).

56. Pettit, *Enrollment and Finances.*

57. These data are from the U.S. Department of Education, National Center for Education Statistics, Digest of Education Statistics, as reported in the *Washington Post,* March 5, 1996. See chapter 6 for implications of these data for Catholic institutions.

58. See the splendid address of the president, Mother Grace Dammann, R.S.C.J., to the alumnae who were questioning this decision. It was, she said, simply a matter of justice to provide a Catholic education for all Catholics, black or white. Text of her address in Mary Oates, ed., *Higher Education for Catholic Women* (New York: Garland, 1987). Mother Dammann had been preparing the way for the inclusion of blacks as essential to the movement of Catholic Action. See Gleason, *Contending with Modernity,* 153–154.

59. The decision at Saint Louis to adopt a nondiscrimination policy was not reached easily, and there is still debate about the role that Rev. Claude H. Heithaus, S.J., and Archbishop Glennon played. See Paul Shore, "The Message and the Messenger: The Untold Story of Father Claude Heithaus and the Integration of Saint Louis University," in William Shea and Daniel Van Slyke, eds., *Trying Times: Essays on Catholic Higher Education* (Atlanta: Scholars Press, forthcoming).

60. Bartell, *Project 80.*

61. The hesitation of Catholic colleges and universities to admit full-time residential black students reflected the general attitude of the Catholic commu-

nity at the time. In an article on July 5, 1969, in *America*, Benjamin Masse, S.J., wrote that Catholics were "paying less attention than they did 20 years ago" to the social teaching of the church. There was even some concern expressed about priests and religious who took part in civil rights demonstrations, and several guidelines were drawn up for major superiors of men's congregations in September 1969. The previous year about 170 sisters from eighty communities had founded the National Black Sisters' Conference to develop a sense of solidarity. There were three black religious communities at the time, and the black sisters in the established "white" communities were aware of their minority status. *America*, August 2, 1969.

62. The use of the term "minority" has its own difficulties, but since the studies use the term, it is used here. See Yolanda T. DeMola, S.C., "Let's Get Rid of 'Minority,'" *America*, October 31, 1987.

63. Ernest Bartell, C.S.C., "Catholic Higher Education: Trends in Enrollment and Finance 1978–82," in *Current Issues in Catholic Higher Education* 4, no. 1, (Summer 1983): 9. A special study was undertaken by the Neylan colleges and published by ACCU in 1991, entitled *Recruitment and Retention of Minorities*, which gives detailed information about ten of the colleges.

64. Such actions were one obvious effect of the impact of students coming from other campuses and from national student organizations to the Catholic campuses.

65. The numbers of enrolled minorities have remained low, despite efforts in the 1970s and 1980s to increase them. The average in Catholic colleges and universities in 1988 was only about 17 percent, and that includes black, Hispanic, and Asian students. See Pettit, *Enrollment and Finances.*

66. AAUP, *Policy Documents*, 153.

67. The Association of Governing Boards did not favor a concept of "representative" boards of trustees which would give faculty and students membership; instead it urged adding them to committees of the board and suggested that a few new graduates might be given a single term on the board in order to bring the ideas of students to the discussion.

68. Helen Lefkowitz Horowitz, *Campus Life* (New York: Alfred A. Knopf, 1987), 250–251; the quotation paraphrases Arthur Levine, *When Dreams and Heroes Died* (San Francisco: Jossey-Bass, 1980), 103.

69. Pettit, *Enrollment and Finances*, 6.

70. David Riesman viewed the changes with dismay. He bemoaned the grade inflation, pass/fail options, and credit given for non-college level work. Riesman, *On Higher Education: The Academic Enterprise in an Era of Rising Student Consumerism* (San Francisco: Jossey-Bass, 1980), 82. For a development of the responses, see chapter 3.

71. The need for radical changes was often highlighted by recommendations from the accrediting agencies. In a 1960 report to Villanova University, Middle States laid out a vast blueprint for self-improvement covering most of the topics

mentioned. North Central pointed out many areas in need of improvement to Loyola University, Mundelein, and Saint Louis, among others.

72. Elizabeth Campling, *The 1970's* (London: B. T. Batsford, 1989), introduction.

73. Report of the Executive Secretary, April 15, 1971, ACUA/NCEA.

74. Friedman to Mother Elizabeth McCormack, R.S.C.J., president of Manhattanville College of the Sacred Heart, July 22, 1966, ACCU, Member files.

75. Friedman, Memo to the members, October 24, 1968. The article by Gallagher was "The Maryland College Aid Case," in the July 9, 1966 issue of *Ave Maria.* ACUA/NCEA.

76. These included St. Catherine (1938); The Catholic University of America (1940); University of Notre Dame and Saint Louis University (1968); Boston College, Manhattan College, Marquette University, and Trinity College (1971); Holy Cross (1974); Santa Clara and Georgetown (1977). For the history of PBK and the charges of prejudice, see Richard Nelson Current, *Phi Beta Kappa in American Life* (New York: Oxford University Press, 1990).

77. Information on the Select Commission is from AUND, CPHS 127.

78. See Appendix 1 for the questionnaire, contained in the memo of James E. Allen, Jr., August 12, 1968. ACNR.

79. Letter from Robert D. Stone, Deputy Commissioner for Legal Affairs, New York State Department of Education, to the committee working on the criteria for the Bundy money, June 13, 1968. Stone clearly references the *Horace Mann* case as the basis for the twelve considerations he lists as material for the questionnaire. Since the criteria were not stated but were rather to be inferred from the questions, there was always a certain amount of ambiguity as to what constituted eligibility. Stone's letter is found in ACNR, Special Issues 1968–78.

80. The complications that arose from the attempts to prove eligibility for Bundy money are discussed in detail in Gallin, *Independence.* There have been some attempts to measure the far-reaching consequences of the colleges' attempts to become eligible and of the changes made in their internal policies that were influenced by the quest for Bundy money. See, for example, Stephen J. Sweeny, "State Financial Assistance and Selected Elements Influencing Religious Character in Catholic Colleges Sponsored by Women Religious," Ph.D. diss., New York University, 1991. Of the three original grantees, only Manhattanville considered it necessary to declare that it was no longer a Catholic college but rather a "secular" college. It withdrew, and did not resume, its membership in the College and University Department of NCEA. Trustee minutes of Manhattanville indicate that not all trustees understood what was implied in this change to a "secular" college. On the other hand, Paul Reiss, vice president at Fordham, recalls a trip to Albany to argue that "non-sectarian" was not the same as "secular." Interview with author at Saint Michael's College, June 14, 1995.

81. See the long debate over whether or not to apply for Bundy money among the trustees at St. Bonaventure University. A decision to do so was reached in October 1975. ASBU, Minutes of Trustees.

82. The author participated in a conversation in Albany with Commissioner Ewald J. Nyquist in which this point was made explicitly.

83. *College Newsletter,* April 1971. Manhattanville and St. John Fisher had dropped their membership. *College Newsletter,* December 1970.

84. See the questionnaire in Appendix 1.

85. Stephen J. Sweeny compared such changes in Catholic women's colleges located in New York and other states with programs of state aid to changes in similar institutions in states without any state aid program. He found no difference in the "liberalizing" of the rules, suggesting that such changes had less to do with meeting funding requirements than with the general lessening of discipline in the society at large. Sweeny, "State Financial Assistance." Several other dissertations also deal with the impact of Bundy aid on the decisions of the Catholic colleges.

86. The concept of *in loco parentis* was struck down in *Goldberg v Regents of the University of California,* 1967.

87. Gleason, *Contending with Modernity,* 265.

88. See the discussion in chapter 1 of Ellis and others who were critical of the status quo in the 1950s.

89. Appendix 1 (the questionnaire for Bundy money). In the preparation for the *Tilton* case, the documents requested from the defendants raised similar fears. Among such things as the charter, its amendments, bylaws, handbooks, etc., the prosecution also asked for a copy of the rules and regulations of the sponsoring body; copies of letters used for fund-raising within the past three years; syllabi, application forms, forms used by interviewers of applicants for faculty positions, policies regarding chapel attendance, and a numerical breakdown of students and of faculty by religious affiliation. A copy of this list of documents was sent to all NCEA College and University Department members by the Executive Director, under date of February 6, 1969. ACUA/NCEA. It is also enlightening to note the way that the New York Commissioner of Education explained denial of Bundy money in his letter to the president of New Rochelle; see Appendix 2.

90. This difference between American Catholic universities and other Catholic universities around the world became very clear to the author in her years of attending IFCU Council meetings as an official observer representing ACCU (1978–92).

91. The IFCU assembly in Tokyo in 1965 has been dealt with in chapter 1. From 1965 until 1990 there would be many attempts to finalize a statement on "The Catholic University in the Modern World." See chapter 6. The various versions can be found in Alice Gallin, *American Catholic Higher Education: Essential Documents 1967–90* (Notre Dame, Ind.: University of Notre Dame Press, 1992).

92. Ibid., 7–12. Father Hesburgh gives credit to Father Robert Henle, S.J., for the text.

93. Compare, for example, the references in *America* and *Commonweal* with the *Newsletter* of the Fellowship of Catholic Scholars during the thirty years after Land O'Lakes. For a particularly negative view, see George Kelly, *The Battle for the American Church,* chapter 7.

94. This will be studied in detail in chapter 6.

95. Rev. Robert Henle, S.J., described this new sense of freedom in a position paper for the IFCU meeting in Kinshasa in 1968. ASLU, Reinert papers (Henle, IFCU). For those who lived with students and worked with them both inside and outside the classroom, this new freedom was a major factor in the changes in rules and regulations of the seventies. Some remain affirmative about the new freedom; others remember those days with dismay and some anger toward the leadership that permitted such changes.

96. Swords to Flanagan, July 16, 1962, ACHC. Evidently attendance at daily mass was still required.

97. An official definition offered by the College Theology Society in 1967 endorsed the statement of the Commission on Religion in Higher Education of AAC entitled "Religion as an Academic Discipline." See Patrick W. Carey, "Changing Conceptions of Catholic College Theology/ Religious Studies, 1965–1995," in Shea and Van Slyke, *Trying Times*. See also Rosemary T. Rodgers, *A History of the College Theology Society* (Villanova,Penn.: College Theology Society, 1983).

98. Carey, "Changing Conceptions," 7.

99. For this and other documents, see AAUP, *Policy Documents & Reports*, 1990 edition.

100. At the time of the strike at St. John's University in 1965, AAUP tried very hard to persuade the Middle States Association to adopt as part of the accreditation process a statement to the effect that failure to abide by the AAUP Principles on Academic Freedom and Tenure would be cause for loss of accreditation. Middle States refused to bind itself to this kind of statement but in practice has often seemed to accept the AAUP view.

101. Gleason, "Academic Freedom: Survey."

102. Gerald F. Kreyche, "American Catholic Higher Learning and Academic Freedom," NCEA Convention, 1965, NCEA *Bulletin* 62 (1965).

103. Edward Manier and John W. Houck, eds., *Academic Freedom and the Catholic University* (Notre Dame, Ind.: Fides, 1967).

104. Letters concerning the Garaudy affair are in ASLU. Father Reinert reported on the action taken to the board of trustees on November 21, 1966. Board of Trustees Minutes, 1959–66, ASLU.

105. Gerald McKevitt, S.J., *The University of Santa Clara: A History, 1851–1977* (Stanford,Calif.: Stanford University Press, 1979).

106. C. Joseph Nuesse, *The Catholic University of America* (Washington, D.C.: The Catholic University of America, 1990), 394–395. In a letter to his friend, Bishop Robert E. Tracy, Father John Tracy Ellis called the affair "an unmitigated tragedy." ACNR, Carthy file.

107. For a brief history of these cases, see Charles Curran, *Catholic Higher Education, Theology, and Academic Freedom* (Notre Dame, Ind.: University of Notre Dame Press, 1990), chapter 3. Cases involved Mercy College in Detroit (1962), Gonzaga University (1960), St. Mary's College in Winona (1968), Dayton (1966), and The Catholic University of America (1967).

108. The documents involved are to be found in AAAUP.

109. David Fellman, a former president of AAUP, made the point in his comments at the 1966 Notre Dame symposium that many of the same problems experienced by St. John's could be found on other, non-Catholic campuses. On the Notre Dame meeting, see Manier and Houck, *Academic Freedom and the Catholic University*.

110. Extensive records of the St. John's case are in the AAUP archives in Washington, D.C. The documents include not only the official reports of Committee A but correspondence between AAUP and the Middle States Association. The case is summarized in the AAUP *Bulletin* (Spring 1966 and Winter 1967).

111. Bertram Davis to Dr. Edward J. Monahan, associate Executive Secretary, Canadian Association of University Teachers, March 4, 1966, AAAUP.

112. "A Report from Committee D," in AAUP *Bulletin* (Autumn 1966). It presents the letter of April 29, 1966, from the Commission on Institutions of Higher Education to Committee D of AAUP. Committee D protested the position taken by Middle States as "a totally inadequate response." AAAUP. Evidently the AAUP tried to get Father Cahill to accept the mediation of Fathers Reinert and Hesburgh, but in Reinert's opinion, the administration was not open to assistance. Dr. William Fidler, AAUP to Reinert and to Hesburgh, February 16, 1966, and Reinert's response, February 16, 1966. AUND, UPHS file.

113. Commission on Institutions of Higher Education, Middle States Association of Colleges and Secondary Schools, in the Matter of St. John's University, November 18, 1966, AAAUP.

114. "College and University Government: St. John's University (NY)," in AAUP *Bulletin* (Autumn 1968): 325–361.

115. Ibid., 357–361. It is interesting to note that this change in the wording of St. John's objectives had no relationship to the Bundy money. The concern for state funds is often cited as the reason for the change in the self-description of Catholic colleges, but since St. John's never applied for Bundy money and the 1968 statement resulted from AAUP and Middle States pressure, it is clear that other factors were at least as important as government funding.

116. Statement submitted by Professor Robinson of St. John's at the annual AAUP meeting in April 1965. AAAUP; Subcommittee on Academic Freedom at Church-Related Colleges. A retrospective study dealing with this matter of the limitations clause was published in *Academe* (September/October 1988). There was still some ambiguity about the meaning of the clause in the 1940 document as well as in the attempt to interpret it in 1970.

117. For details see Curran, *Catholic Higher Education*, 194–202, and Nuesse, *Catholic University*, 399–401.

118. There was a strong opinion that the 1940 limitations clause was not intended to allow institutions to contravene academic freedom merely by announcing it ahead of time, but rather, it sought to allow institutions to require doctrinal fidelity if they chose to do so. However, if they did, they were denied "the moral right to proclaim themselves as authentic seats of higher learning." *Academe* (September/October 1988): 54–55.

119. Response from C. Clarence Friedman to draft from the Committee on Church-Related Institutions, December 21, 1967, AAAUP. There is a concurring opinion from Rev. Gerard J. Campbell, S.J., president of Georgetown University, April 23, 1967. AAAUP, CRI file.

120. "Report of Committee A, 1969–70," AAUP *Bulletin* (Summer 1970).

121. *Academe* (September/October 1988). This suggests that the clarity which had been sought regarding the limitations clause was never really achieved. Comments by Leon Pacala, Executive Secretary of the Association of Theological Schools in the United States and Canada, and Professor William W. Van Alstyne of Duke offer further questions about the committee's presentation.

122. See Ernest Boyer, ed., *Control of the Campus* (Princeton, N.J.: Princeton University Press, 1982). This is a report to the Carnegie Foundation for the Advancement of Teaching from a commission set up to study governance structures in higher education.

123. See chapter 6.

124. For the Dayton case, see Mary J. Brown, "The Heresy Affair at the University of Dayton," April 29, 1997, dissertation in progress at the University of Dayton.

125. The statement (undated, but referring to the September 21st decree and asking for a response of support by October 4th) is in the Archives of Mundelein College of Loyola University. The members of the committee are from DePaul, Mundelein, Barat, Loyola, and St. Xavier. The representative from Loyola was John Bannan, one of the philosophers at New Rochelle in 1956 who were attacked by clerical members of the faculty. See the full account in chapter 1.

126. Report of the first annual meeting of the Loyola University chapter of AAUP, Tuesday, October 11, 1966, AMC.

127. Paper prepared for Mundelein faculty giving a report on the steering committee's meeting of November 9, 1966, AMC.

128. The questions posed in the survey (AMC) are of particular interest, both because they address issues that have never been definitively settled, and because they were asked at a time when most Catholic colleges and universities were still governed by trustees who were exclusively members of the sponsoring religious body:

1. Are church-related colleges public institutions?
2. Are they "ecclesiastical" entities?
3. Who owns your college?
4. What problems are posed by a religious or clerical administration?
5. What problems are posed by episcopal authority a) with regard to doctrinal matters, and b) with regard to a local ordinary's concern to coordinate all on (*sic*) the various apostolic work within his diocese?
6. What role does the faculty play in your institution, particularly in policy-making?

7. What are the particular problems of religious and/or clerical faculty in their functioning as faculty members?

129. Catherine A. L. Jarrott for the committee to Philip Denenfeld, February 25, 1967, AMC. In his response of March 3, 1967, Denenfeld asked if the interfaculty committee could assist the special AAUP committee that had been set up to deal with academic freedom in church-related colleges. He suggested that their discussion might cover preferential hiring on a religious basis; distinction, if any, between religious and lay faculty; faculty participation in the development of policies; ex post facto application of religious limitations. Denenfeld to Jarrott, March 3, 1967, AMC.

130. AMC, no date given.

131. Curran, *Catholic Higher Education*, 74.

132. The work of this committee is described by Nuesse, *Catholic University*, 402–410.

133. In a much later case against Professor Charles Curran (1989), the university pointed out that the trustees had never formally adopted the AAUP guidelines. *Charles E. Curran and Julia Fleming et al. v The Catholic University of America*, Civil Action No. 1562–87, Superior Court of the District of Columbia, 1989.

134. John Courtney Murray, S.J., convocation address, printed in *The University in the American Experience* (New York: Fordham University Press, 1966), 9.

135. *College Newsletter*, December 1966. This was a talk given by President Walsh to the faculty at Boston College.

136. *College Newsletter*, December 1967.

Three: Uncertainty and Ambiguity

1. Kerr, *The Great Transformation*, 55. See also Earl Cheit, *The New Depression in Higher Education* (1971), which stated that over 60 percent of colleges and universities are "in a financially precarious position," quoted in Richard Freeland, *Academia's Golden Age: Universities in Massachusetts 1945–70* (New York: Oxford University Press, 1992), 97.

2. Robert J. Henle, "A Report on the American Catholic University," April 1968. ASLU, Henle papers. In Henle's opinion, some would survive the financial crisis and develop a new and distinctive role with new opportunities to contribute to the church, nation, and mankind. Henle was vice president for academic affairs at Saint Louis University and would soon be president of Georgetown University. When he arrived at Georgetown in 1969, he found a precarious financial situation.

3. See, for example, the variety of opinions in Hook et al., *University and State: What Role?*

4. Theodore M. Hesburgh, "Resurrection for Higher Education," an address to the American Council on Education Annual Meeting, October 6–8, 1971, in

Arthur Levine and John Weingart, *Reform of Undergraduate Education* (San Francisco: Jossey-Bass, 1974), 333.

5. AAUP, *Policy Documents and Reports*, 1990 ed.

6. For an interesting analysis, see Thomas Bender, "Politics, Intellect, and the American University, 1945–95," *Daedalus* (Winter 1997): 1–38.

7. Richard W. Waring, "A Study of the Fiscal and Personnel Resources of Catholic Colleges Founded by Women Religious," Ph.D. diss., University of Toledo, 1985. Waring points to a great decline in cash gifts from the religious communities of sisters between 1973 and 1983, due in large part to the decreased number of sisters working as teachers and administrators in the colleges. In the colleges studied by Waring there were 1360 sisters in 1973–74; in 1983–84 there were 991; for 1989–90 he projected 843. The overall statistics regarding sisters engaged in higher education are equally dismal. They reflect the changes in apostolic commitment on the part of religious communities as their numbers declined and the calls to meet other needs in society increased. Waring cites some tentative studies which indicated a movement away from employment in institutions founded and sponsored by a religious community to positions in other institutions of higher education. For data on trends in religious communities, see Neal, *Catholic Sisters in Transition*.

8. Ford and Roy, *Renewal*, 124.

9. See chapter 2.

10. Bender, "Politics, Intellect, and University."

11. Minutes of the Board of Trustees, Saint Louis University, January 20, 1970, ASLU.

12. Minutes of the Board of Trustees, Saint Louis University, July 25–26, 1970, ASLU.

13. It is interesting that in his book of recollections, *Seasons of Change* (St. Louis: Saint Louis University Press, 1996), Reinert does not refer to this external effort which had such favorable results for all of private higher education.

14. Interview with Hennesey, November 30, 1995.

15. Alexander W. Astin and Calvin B. T. Lee, *The Invisible Colleges* (New York: McGraw-Hill, 1972).

16. The boycott of classes by students occurred on February 27, 1970, and was related to the nonrenewal of a contract for a popular sociology teacher. The decision had been made by the faculty Rank, Salary, and Tenure Committee and, after an appeal, was reaffirmed by the committee. At the request of the president, student leaders of the boycott met with faculty representatives; this ad hoc faculty-student committee decided to have a full faculty meeting the following week. Eventually, an open meeting of faculty with 800 students (out of 900) passed certain resolutions leading to a more participative form of governance for the college. Students joined all faculty committees except RTS and Faculty Affairs, and faculty joined all student committees except residence life. This collaborative arrangement proved to be of great benefit in May 1970, when the college confronted the question of canceling classes, exams, and commencement in the aftermath of Kent State.

ACNR. It should be noted that at this time New Rochelle was appealing the negative decision regarding the Bundy money.

17. Letter to students, February 16, 1969, AUND. Hesburgh, after wide internal consultation, stated that he believed he had a clear mandate to require that (1) lines of communication are kept as open as possible, with all legitimate means of communicating dissent assured, expanded, and protected; (2) civility and rationality are maintained; and (3) violation of others' rights or obstruction of the life of the university is outlawed as illegitimate means of dissent. He therefore announced that if any individual or group substituted force for rational persuasion, they would be given fifteen minutes of meditation to cease and desist. Suspension would follow failure to comply.

Other university presidents expressed admiration for Hesburgh's clarity and moral courage. Reinert was able to negotiate most of the demands made by students, but was then criticized by alumni for giving in to them. See the correspondence in the Reinert papers, ASLU.

At several Catholic colleges, following the Kent State shootings of protesting students, the device of the "teach-in" was used to educate students, faculty, administrators, parents, and alumni/ae about the war in Vietnam. The advantage of the teach-in over simple demonstrations was that it allowed for education on the issues and often brought faculty and students together for discussion and debate.

18. Reinert, *To Turn the Tide.*

19. The story of this failed effort is in AUND, UPHS 88. The stumbling blocks seemed to be doubt that Saint Mary's College would keep its identity, and resentment over the attitude that some at Notre Dame expressed toward Saint Mary's, as bringing little or nothing to the merger. Alumnae of Saint Mary's became stalwart defenders, not only in word but in financial support, of its independent existence.

20. McKevitt, *University of Santa Clara.* See especially chapter 18 on the years 1958–1977.

21. This is made clear in the discussions reported in the trustees' minutes in 1969–70 when the option was under consideration. ACHC. The results of the move to coeducation at Holy Cross are told in a personal story of the women who were the first coeds. Ann J. Cahill, *Women on the Hill* (Worcester, Mass.: Center for Interdisciplinary and Special Studies, College of the Holy Cross, 1993).

22. As late as 1957 a decree was issued by the Vatican requiring an indult for a Catholic school to engage in coeducation. However, in response to a later query in 1970, the Congregation for Catholic Education remanded the question to the local Ordinary or the Bishops' Conference. S.C.C.E. Instructio a Sacra Congregatione, 1 February 1971. Cited in Flannery, *Vatican Council II: Conciliar and Post-Conciliar Documents,* 678. It would be interesting to know how many conversations with the local bishop concerning the switch to coeducation actually occurred.

23. A good analysis of this mood is found in a study for the Carnegie Foundation for the Advancement of Teaching, Arthur Levine's *When Dreams and Heroes*

Died. Levine notes the loss of confidence in leaders in higher education and in organized religion on the part of society at large and of college students in particular (p. 10). The two words most used to describe the students' earlier experience of life were Watergate and Vietnam.

24. Kerr, *The Great Transformation,* 55.

25. David R. Contosta, *Villanova University 1842–1992* (University Park: Pennsylvania University Press, 1995), 217. Protests at Villanova in the seventies seemed to focus on grievances about the university rather than on the national and political issues. Yet, see Contosta's chapter entitled "Counterculture," 197–225, for context.

26. Kerr, *The Great Transformation,* 130. Kerr's view was, of course, colored by his term as chancellor at UCLA during some of the worst days of rebellion.

27. Riesman, *On Higher Education,* preface.

28. Ibid., 82.

29. Ibid., 176.

30. The task force was to address purposes and goals of colleges. It had two subcommittees, one on theological instruction and the other on social concerns. Minutes of the Executive Committee Meeting, January 13, 1970, ACUA/NCEA.

31. In a letter of October 28, 1970, to the president of the AAC, Dr. Frederic W. Ness, Dr. Richard A. Matre of Loyola University Chicago informed him that the Executive Committee, acting on the recommendation of the task force which he chaired, had decided against such a merger since there was a need for a forum to discuss specifically Catholic issues. At this time, the Protestant Council of Colleges did merge with AAC. There is also a report of a task force meeting held earlier with Dr. Ness on September 11. Father William Crandell, S.J., head of the Association of Jesuit Colleges and Universities, was also a party to the meeting with Ness. Pressure for such a merger was coming from foundations, which were being asked for support by the various associations in the Washington Secretariat, and Dr. Ness said that AAC would welcome a merger with the College and University Department of NCEA.

32. Philip Gleason in his Marianist Award Lecture at the University of Dayton in 1994, "What Made Catholic Identity a Problem?" maintains that as long as Catholic colleges remained self-consciously a subculture in American higher education, their identity was not questioned.

33. For the text, see Gallin, *Essential Documents,* 5–16. For the genesis of the document and the reaction to it, see chapter 2 in this book. This document was the target of many critics during the next three decades. See, for example, George A. Kelly, *The Battle for the American Church* (Garden City, N.Y.: Doubleday, 1979), chapter 4, "The Battle for the Catholic Campus." See also his *The Battle for the American Church Revisited* (San Francisco: Ignatius Press, 1995), chapter 6, "John Paul II vs. the Catholic College System." Kelly likens Land O'Lakes to the loss of the Philippines in World War II, but he believes that the Catholic campus, unlike the Philippines, is still "in the hands of insurgents."

34. Whatever the theory about the canonical status of the property used by the colleges, the operational understanding was that it belonged to the religious community. An explicit reference to this fact is found in a paper delivered by Rev. James Hennesey, S.J., of Fordham University, to the Annual Conference of Finance Administrators of Jesuit Institutions, October 13, 1967, ACHC. Under a cover letter to this paper sent to "Bob" [at Holy Cross] on October 10, 1967, Hennesey comments that previously, "The restraining and moderating influence on an active President and Administration has come not from the Legal Trustees, but from Society [meaning S.J.] and Canon Law." See also the comments of Sister Hildegarde Marie Mahoney, S.C., in a memorandum prepared for the Fiscal Concerns Committee of the Leadership Conference of Women Religious on February 2, 1974. She described the difficulties met by presidents in trying to get all the necessary permissions from Rome or even to know what was required. Committee on Law and Public Policy, file on McGrath/Maida, ANCCB. Trustee minutes of the institutions in the pre-1967 days often refer to "permissions" for spending large sums of money being requested from Provincials, Generals, or Roman Congregations; this clearly suggests recognition of the obligations under canon law.

35. McGrath, *Catholic Institutions: Canonical and Civil Law Status.* McGrath had been a popular consultant on the question since 1965 and clearly influenced the thinking of many presidents. His opinion was a focus at the meeting that Reinert held at Saint Louis University for Jesuit presidents and their attorneys in May 1967. For a study of this question, see Gallin, *Independence,* chapter 3.

36. Auturo Cardinal Tabera and Gabriel Cardinal Garrone to John Cardinal Krol, Chair of NCCB, October 7, 1974. ANCCB, Committee on Law and Public Policy file, PROT.N.SCRIS 300/74; SCI 427/70/23.

37. Adam Maida, *Ownership, Control, and Sponsorship of Catholic Institutions: A Practical Guide* (Harrisburg: Pennsylvania Catholic Conference, 1975). This was the first work that took a clear position opposite that of McGrath. It was not endorsed by the Bishops' Conference but was simply distributed as an opinion that might be useful. However, if the goal of distributing the book was to stimulate discussion of the issues with the colleges, why was a copy not sent to the Executive Director of the NCEA College and University Department for dissemination to the colleges? Msgr. Murphy first saw the book when Rev. Fabian Bruskewitz at the Sacred Congregation for Education handed him a copy as he was leaving Rome after a visit in April 1975. Letter of John F. Murphy to President Norbert J. Hruby, at that time chair of the board of the NCEA College and University Department. ACUA/NCEA.

38. Archbishop Joseph Bernardin to Auturo Cardinal Tabera and Gabriel Cardinal Garrone, March 6, 1975; ANCCB PROT.N. SCI 427/70/23; SCRIS 300/74. Archbishop Bernardin at that time was president of NCCB. Garrone's response of April 16, 1975, indicated that the scope for the Bishops and Presidents' Committee was far wider than the Commission on Ownership of Property. However, the request to set up a commission of bishops and representatives of the conferences of

men and women religious to discuss the property issues had excluded any representation of the colleges themselves. The Executive Director of NCEA College and University Department protested this exclusion to both Borders and Bernardin. See Murphy to Borders, April 29, 1975, and Murphy to Bernardin, April 30, 1975, ACUA/NCEA. Since the commission met only once, the issue died a natural death. Ultimately the task of studying the property and control issues led to the formation of a committee by NCEA (COPCU) and publication of several works by the Center for Constitutional Studies, set up at the University of Notre Dame in 1977.

39. David Burrell and Francesca Kane, *Evangelization in the American Context* (Notre Dame, Ind.: University of Notre Dame Press, 1976).

40. Call to Action Conference papers, ACUA/NCEA. The spirit of the Call to Action Conference was picked up and invigorated by a group in Chicago named simply the "Call to Action." They sponsored a celebration in 1996 to mark the twentieth anniversary of the Detroit meeting.

41. Minutes of the Purpose and Identity Committee, December 6, 1974, ACUA/NCEA.

42. Maguire papers, ALUC. Maguire cited the St. John's University case, the Maryland case (*Horace Mann*), and the possibility that such an attempt on the part of the church to control decisions of the university would lend credence to Jacqueline Grennan's claim that ecclesiastical control precludes the mission of a true university.

43. This opinion is quoted in the Minutes of the Purpose and Identity Subcommittee, ACUA/NCEA. Mr. Charles Horgan had been very active in promoting the idea of independent boards of trustees in Catholic colleges. See Gallin, *Independence.* He had been successful in the suit against New York State to secure Bundy money for the College of New Rochelle and was strongly influenced in his legal opinions by the attitude of New York to "sectarian" colleges. He was president of the National Association of College and University Attorneys in 1974–76 and was highly esteemed by his colleagues. He was also a strongly committed Catholic and served religious orders and the archdiocese in many ways.

44. See publications of the Center for Constitutional Studies.

45. Although the author of the subcommittee's paper, Rev. James T. Burtchaell, C.S.C., did not wish it to be published as his private opinion (a suggestion made to him by the committee), he did agree to publication ten years later in *Current Issues in Catholic Higher Education* (Summer 1988): 19–21. In the intervening years many articles on the topic had been presented in *Current Issues,* which served as a useful forum for divergent opinions.

46. David J. O'Brien in *Conversations* 6 (Fall 1994), The National Seminar on Jesuit Education.

47. American Provincials, "The Jesuit Mission in Higher Education," Jesuit Conference, Washington, D.C., 1978.

Four: New Horizons

1. The Association of Catholic Colleges was the original name of the group of college presidents who came together under the leadership of The Catholic University of America in 1899. In 1904 it joined forces with the Association of Seminaries and the Association of Parish Schools to form the Catholic Educational Association. In 1927 the word "National" was added to the title. Within NCEA there were different departments for various levels of education; the College and University Department was one of them. In 1978 the department reverted to its original name, Association of Catholic Colleges and Universities, indicating a greater autonomy in external affairs. However, it retained its internal relationship to NCEA in matters specifically Catholic.

2. One can follow this development in the publications of the various organizations as well as in the NCEA *College Newsletter*.

3. For Stanford's role at Villanova, see Contosta, *Villanova University*.

4. Edward V. Stanford, *A Guide to Catholic College Administration* (Westminster, Md.: Newman Press, 1965). The foreword is written by Theodore A. Distler, President Emeritus, AAC. Stanford was involved in the discussions that were carried on by Catholic college leaders in the mid-sixties concerning a shift in governance to independent boards and was mentioned as a consultant in the records of several colleges. He died suddenly in 1967. See Gallin, *Independence*.

5. See chapter 2, 64–65, for a discussion of the effort to interpret the limitations clause.

6. *College Newsletter* 28, no. 3 (February 1966) notes that Shannon was the first bishop so to serve, although four priest-presidents had already held the office. Shannon was president of the College of St. Thomas in St. Paul, Minnesota.

7. Richard A. Matre to Dr. Frederic W. Ness, October 28, 1970, ACUA/NCEA. In the judgment of the NCEA Executive Committee, it was necessary to have an organization which would address specifically Catholic issues. A full discussion of the issues had preceded the meeting of the Executive Committee. Representatives (Msgr. John F. Murphy, Richard Matre, and Father Friedman) had met with Dr. Ness on September 11. Father William Crandell, S.J., chairman of AJCU, had also attended. The reason for the AAC overture was the concern expressed by foundations about the proliferation of organizations with similar purposes. Some colleges also found the multiple dues a problem. The task force did not recommend the merger. Report on the meeting of September 11, ACUA/NCEA. Although the year is not given, it would appear that it was 1970.

8. At its meeting of February 3–5, 1979, the ACCU board affirmed its decision to act "normally" through NAICU unless there was some special "Catholic" angle to an issue. ACUA/NCEA.

9. ABC, Research file.

10. Interview with Mr. Joseph Kane, April 29, 1996. In her position as Executive Director of the Association of Catholic Colleges and Universities, the author was a member of the Secretariat and served two terms as chair and thus *ex officio* on the board of directors. She can therefore testify to the strength of Mr. Kane and his colleagues in defending the interests of their constituencies from 1976 through her retirement in 1992.

11. For a full-length study of the AJCU and events leading up to its formation, see Paul A. Fitzgerald, S.J., *The Governance of Jesuit Colleges in the United States 1920–1970* (Notre Dame, Ind.: University of Notre Dame Press, 1984).

12. Father General Arrupe, while committed in principle to the idea of separate boards, wanted each institution to apply for permission to make the change. Between 1967 and 1977 they all created independent boards, some of which left control over property and mission in the hands of a board of "members," all Jesuits, but all of which placed the normal governance of the university in the hands of a board of trustees which included laypersons.

13. The files of the AJCU are located in the archives at Boston College. The association, no doubt, has had the strengths and weaknesses of most voluntary associations, but it does serve well for communication and mutual support among the Jesuit presidents. The agenda for AJCU often overlaps with that of ACCU, NAICU, and several other higher education organizations; consequently, it has tended to emphasize issues of particular relevance to Jesuit concerns and to promote "Conferences" of various administrative personnel, e.g., student affairs officers, deans, and admissions directors.

14. See, for example, the representation of Jesuits on the board of NAICU, in Minutes of NAICU Secretariat and Board. In the eighties the president of AJCU was also on the board of ACCU, a factor that led to increased collaboration.

15. In a Memo to Member Presidents of October 24, 1968, Executive Associate Secretary Friedman of NCEA reminded them that he had urged establishment and/or strengthening of state associations of private colleges now being organized under AAC auspices.

16. *College Newsletter* was issued quarterly from 1937 to 1964. After 1964 there was a publication in the form of a communication from the Executive Director or the Executive Committee. In 1975 a regular newsletter entitled *Update* began, with vol. 1 dated January 24. This has been continued at different time intervals; by the 1980s it was published regularly six times a year. A journal called *Occasional Papers* was issued from 1975 to 1979, when it was succeeded by *Current Issues in Catholic Higher Education,* published twice a year. In the nineties *Occasional Papers* has again come to life, carrying papers on specific themes. Information about ACCU activities can also be found in the general NCEA publications, especially the CEA/NCEA *Bulletin* from 1904 to 1969 and the current journal *Momentum.*

17. In Gallin, *Essential Documents,* 135–151.

18. This was often a very sensitive issue; one example was when the higher education community opposed the idea of tuition tax credits because it was as-

sumed that money that went to non-public schools as tuition tax credits would be subtracted from the other programs of higher education, such as Basic Education Opportunity Grants. The United States Catholic Conference was strongly in favor of tuition tax credits, as was NCEA. ACCU worked to persuade the higher education group not to oppose the effort in public. However, by not supporting tuition tax credits, ACCU was at odds with the bishops and the NCEA position. See Memorandum of Understanding, January 29, 1981, ACUA/NCEA.

19. An interesting account of the "identity" crisis among women religious which spilled over into their attitudes toward their colleges is V. V. Harrison, *Changing Habits* (New York: Doubleday, 1988). This deals with Religious of the Sacred Heart. Another more negative view of what happened is found in Kelly, *Battle for the American Church*, chapter 9. He presents the "cases" of the Sisters of the Immaculate Heart of Mary in California, the School Sisters of St. Francis in Milwaukee, and the Sisters of Charity of New York. Data relevant to this development can be found in Marie Augusta Neal, S.N.D.deN., *Sisters' Survey*, done for the Conference of Major Superiors of Women in 1966. Some later and more reflective essays can be found in Bridget Puzon, O.S.U., ed., *Women Religious and the Intellectual Life* (Bethesda, Md.: International Scholars Publications, 1995).

20. The sisters who attended this meeting were Irenaeus Chekouras, R.S.M. (St. Xavier College), Marie Immaculee Dana, R.S.M. (Carlow College), Kathleen Feeley, S.S.N.D. (College of Notre Dame of Maryland), Rose Ann Fleming, S.N.D. (Trinity College), Alberta Huber, S.S.J., and Mary Thompson, S.S.J. (College of St. Catherine), Dorothy Ann Kelly, O.S.U. (College of New Rochelle), Jeanne Knoerle, S.P., and Ruth Eileen Dwyer, S.P. (Saint Mary-of-the-Woods), Mary Elizabeth Loomis, S.H.C.J. (Rosemont College), Colette Mahoney, R.S.H.M. (Marymount–Manhattan College), Joel Read, O.S.F., and Austin Daugherty, O.S.F. (Alverno College), Doris Smith, S.C. (College of Mt. St. Vincent), and Alice Gallin, O.S.U., Associate Executive Director, ACCU. List taken from the minutes of the first Neylan meeting, June 30–July 2, 1978, ACUA/NCEA.

21. The two sisters who funded the organization were Genevieve and Edith Neylan. Their gift was made at a time in the fifties when women religious were attempting to prepare numerous young members for teaching. Very little is known of the Neylan sisters, but their benefaction has been very productive. In the group's study on minorities (*Recruitment and Retention of Minorities*, 1991), it was found that there were twenty "Neylan" colleges with a 20 percent minority enrollment (at a time when the national average was 17 percent), and that five had a 50 percent minority enrollment. The three conferences were held at Marymount College in 1983, Alverno in 1986, and Notre Dame of Maryland in 1989. Annual meetings have been held at the time of the ACCU meeting for the past several years. ACUA/NCEA.

22. Everett Walters, "The Rise of Graduate Education," in Walters, ed., *Graduate Education Today* (Washington, D.C.: American Council on Education, 1965).

23. Ibid., 9.

24. Ibid., 18. The question about master's programs and their development in non-research universities was often a topic of conversation at the NCEA College and University Department during the seventies.

25. Hugh Davis Graham and Nancy Diamond, *The Rise of American Research Universities: Elites and Challengers in the Postwar Era* (Baltimore: Johns Hopkins University Press, 1997). As used by these authors, the word "rise" has two meanings, first, the rise in the position of American universities in international circles and second, the rise of the challengers, the post–World War II universities. This work provides a helpful context for studying the efforts and successes of the Catholic research universities in the post-war period.

26. For the history of graduate education in Catholic institutions, see Gleason, *Contending with Modernity*, chapter 8, and pp. 197–206, 220–226. There were several efforts to coordinate degree programs and research activites, but to no avail. Even the Jesuit universities, despite directives from the Father General, were never able to agree on a plan for coordination. However, both the JEA and the NCEA had committees on graduate studies, so that the questions were kept alive in the years prior to World War II. The influx of refugee scholars to the United States due to conditions under the Hitler regime aided in the drive to upgrade the academic reputation of the universities, but there was no serious effort to become research universities until after World War II.

27. Gleason, *Contending with Modernity*, 204. Opposition to the centrality of research in graduate education was expressed by George Bull, S.J., of Fordham University in a 1938 article in *Thought*. He considered research as "diametrically opposed to the whole Catholic tradition of learning." "The Function of the Catholic Graduate School," *Thought* 13 (September 1938).

28. In a report done at the University of Notre Dame in 1967 entitled "Sponsored Research and Other Sponsored Programs," which covered grants from foundations as well as from government, there is clear evidence of such growth. From 1958, with a total of $1,143,600 in grants ($924,100 from the government), to 1966, with a total of $5,680,102 ($5,103,778 from the government), one can easily see the increasing importance of outside funding. AUND, UPHS 78. During the same period, foundation and government support at the University of Dayton grew from $1,212,203 to $4,580,622 (James Heft, S.M., letter to author enclosing a report on research grants).

29. John Tracy Ellis, *American Catholics and the Intellectual Life* (Chicago: Heritage Foundation, 1957). Ellis pointed to the lack of appreciation among Catholics for the intellectual life and noted the absence of Catholic scholars from the national dictionaries of science and letters. His remarks were reinforced by the much-quoted phrase of Rev. John J. Cavanaugh, C.S.C., former president of Notre Dame: "Where are the Catholic Salks, Oppenheimers, Einsteins?" Commented on by Philip Gleason, *Contending with Modernity*, 294. Cavanaugh's quote was from a talk given to the Carroll Club in Washington, D.C., December 15, 1957, in Gleason, *Contending with Modernity*, chapter 13 n. 49.

30. Nuesse, *Catholic University*, 376.

31. William Trombley, "Changing Catholic Colleges," syndicated column in *Journal-Bulletin, Washington Post,* and *Los Angeles Times,* March 6, 1966. Although Trombley suggests a list of "first-rate Catholic schools," including Fordham, Georgetown, Notre Dame, and Saint Louis, "with Boston College, Duquesne and Marquette moving up," he does not mention any scholars from the universities other than Saint Louis and Notre Dame. It is also not possible to know from the article what criteria were used for his judgment.

32. Bernard Berelson, *Graduate Education in the United States* (New York: McGraw-Hill, 1960), 35.

33. No author is given for this pamphlet dated 1974, but it is attributed to the University Academic Planning Committee at Boston College, ABC. For this quotation, see p. 5. Emphasis added.

34. The rate of growth in all American institutions is startling: In 1940 about 100 universities gave the doctorate and 300 the master's; in 1958 there were 175 institutions giving the doctorate and 569 the master's.

35. William P. Leahy, *Adapting to America* (Washington, D.C.: Georgetown University Press, 1991), 138–139.

36. Ibid., 139. The struggle within the Society of Jesus to try and achieve collaboration among the universities is covered in detail by Fitzgerald, *Governance of Jesuit Colleges.* An excellent analysis of the complex relations between the university presidents and the Jesuit provincials in the 1970s is given in Joseph A. Tetlow, S.J., "The Jesuits' Mission in Higher Education: Perspectives and Contexts," *Studies in the Spirituality of Jesuits,* vol. 15, no. 5 (November 1983) and vol. 16, no. 1 (January 1984).

37. Nathan Hatch, *The Professions in American History* (Notre Dame, Ind.: University of Notre Dame Press, 1988).

38. Laurence Vesey, "Higher Education as a Profession: Changes and Continuities," in Hatch, *The Professions.*

39. The statistics on graduate education, while not always reliable, suggest that this increase in the number of colleges offering master's degrees may have caused a decline in the number of students going to the research universities. For example, in the decade 1968–1977 Saint Louis University experienced a decline from 2,487 graduate students to 1,824, a decline almost entirely in the school of arts and sciences. Within the arts and sciences about 40 percent of the degrees were in education. English had a decline of more than 75 percent and history, 70 percent. See "A Study of Graduate School Enrollment Trends, 1968–1977." This report was compiled by Rev. William Stauder, S.J., Graduate Dean, according to a letter from Stauder to Dr. Edwin G. Eigel, Jr., Academic Vice President, July 17, 1978. Concern was expressed in the report about the fact that SLU was not in line with trends at other doctoral universities, as reported by the Council of Graduate Schools. The conclusion was that graduate education at SLU "has been allowed to erode until it is now in a crisis or near crisis situation." Yet, the basic problem of under-enrollment may be related to the increasingly pragmatic goals of graduate students.

40. For data gathered by ACCU on graduate education, see David M. John-ston, "Graduate Education in Catholic Colleges and Universities," *Current Issues in Catholic Higher Education* 3, no. 1 (Summer 1982).

41. Timothy O'Meara, provost emeritus at the University of Notre Dame, paper delivered at Saint Louis University, May 9, 1997.

42. Nuesse, *Catholic University*, 263, 281–286. Fitzgerald, *Governance of Jesuit Colleges*, 34, recounts the animosity between CUA and the Jesuit institutions when the latter began to develop graduate education in the post–World War II days.

43. Nuesse's history, *Catholic University*, gives a good sense of this change in the role of CUA vis-à-vis the other Catholic colleges and universities. The importance of its individual scholars was emphasized by Rev. William J. Byron, S.J., president from 1980 to 1990. Interview, March 27, 1996.

44. Nuesse, *Catholic University*, 393, quoting from Allan M. Cartter, *An Assessment of Quality in Graduate Education* (Washington, D.C.: ACE, 1966). This was in contrast to the 1934 survey, which had rated ten programs at CUA as "adequate" and only one at Notre Dame (p. 262). See William Shea, "Jesuits and Scholarship: A Reading of the Macelwane Report," in Shea and Van Slyke, *Trying Times.*

45. The growing recognition of Catholic research universities, albeit very modest, can be seen in some of the data studied in Graham and Diamond, *Rise of American Research Universities.* Only Notre Dame is included among those "on the threshold of national ranking," but several others make the grade in various categories: Boston College, Duquesne, Saint Louis, Fordham, and Catholic University. Since the various data depend heavily on financial commitment and reputation among peers, the Catholic university cohort has gotten off to a late start. The authors have attempted to balance the strengths in natural and hard sciences, social sciences, and arts and humanities; traditionally, the Catholic colleges and universities have emphasized the latter, while the funding has been largely in the sciences.

46. ACUA/NCEA. The preparations for this conference were carried on at the NCCB/USCC office in Washington under the direction of Dr. Francis Butler and his staff, which included David O'Brien, Margaret Cafferty, P.V.B.M., Rev. J. Bryan Hehir, John Carr, and Alice Gallin, O.S.U. The overall chairman of the effort was Bishop John Dearden of Detroit, whose leadership was very important, and Bishop James Rausch, General Secretary of the NCCB/USCC at the time. The materials from this project are housed in the NCCB archives and some of them can also be located in the archives at The Catholic University of America (ACUA/NCEA).

47. Burrell and Kane, *Evangelization in the American Context.*

48. A copy of the directory is in the ACCU library. The author was Rev. George McLean, O.M.I.

49. "The Challenge of Peace: God's Promise and Our Response" (1983); "Economic Justice for All: Social Teaching and the U.S. Economy" (1986).

50. The records of the IICR are found in ACUA/NCEA.

51. Report of the FADICA meeting, ACCU office.

52. "Catholic Higher Education and the Pastoral Mission of the Church," Gallin, *Essential Documents,* 147.

53. See Gleason, *Contending with Modernity,* for a discussion of the role played by neo-scholasticism in the integration of the curriculum.

54. See the reference to pre-Vatican theologians and philosophers, especially Weigel's paper in 1957, cited in chapter 1. See also Patrick Carey, "College Theology in Historical Perspective," in *American Catholic Traditions: Resources for Renewal,* ed. Sandra Yocum Mize and William Portier (New York: Orbis, 1997), and Carey's "Changing Conceptions of Catholic College Theology/Religious Studies 1965–1995," a paper given at SLU, May 1997, and published in Shea and Van Slyke, *Trying Times.* See also Patrick W. Carey and Earl C. Muller, S.J., eds., *Theological Education in the Catholic Tradition: Contemporary Challenges* (New York: Crossroad, 1997).

55. Carey and Muller, *Theological Education.*

56. Sandra Yocum Mize is engaged in writing the history of this program at Saint Mary's College, Notre Dame, Indiana.

57. Wilson, "Catholic Colleges and Civil Law." Religion courses had always been required in some colleges, which generally provided Scripture courses for non-Catholics.

58. "Post Vatican Survey," *College Newsletter* 30, no. 2 (December 1967).

59. A selection of papers on the current state of the art in the teaching of theology/religion/religious studies appeared in *Occasional Papers,* vol. 1, no. 2 (December 1975).

60. Text given in *College Newsletter* 33, no. 4 (June 1971). Father Sullivan later served as president of Seattle University.

61. Rev. Gerard Sloyan gave a good summary of the situation in a paper prepared for the CTS meeting in June 1995. Copy in the author's possession. See also the articles by Matthew Lamb and William Shea in Carey and Muller, *Theological Education,* part 4.

62. Information about the establishment of the Graduate School of Religious Studies is taken from the committee files. Papers of John K. Zeender, ACUA.

63. Introduction, *Occasional Papers,* vol. 1, no. 2 (December 1975).

64. This point is at the heart of Gleason, *Contending with Modernity.* The function of neo-scholasticism as an integrating factor in the curriculum of Catholic colleges has never been transferred to another discipline.

65. An excellent analysis of the situation was done by a committee of the American Catholic Philosophical Society and published in *Current Issues in Catholic Higher Education* 2, no. 1 (Summer 1981). The members of the committee were Jude P. Dougherty (The Catholic University of America), Desmond Fitzgerald (University of San Francisco), and Thomas Langan and Kenneth Schmitz (University of Toronto).

66. The questionnaire was prepared and distributed by Rev. Leo Martin, S.J., of Loyola University Chicago. ALUC.

67. CTS endorsed the statement that "religion as an academic discipline" should seek "to promote understanding of an important human concern rather than confessional commitment." Rosemary Rodgers, "The Changing Concept of College Theology: A Case Study," master's diss., CUA, 1973, 250n, 254.

68. Monika K. Hellwig, "Twenty-six Years of Undergraduate Theology," *Conversations*, no. 5 (Spring 1994). Dr. Hellwig at that time was Landegger Professor at Georgetown University. She has since become Executive Director, Association of Catholic Colleges and Universities.

69. Derek Bok, *Beyond the Ivory Tower: Social Responsibilities of the Modern University* (Cambridge, Mass.: Harvard University Press, 1982). Although Bok deals only with the large research universities, the same pressures were experienced by all of higher education.

70. See chapter 6.

Five: Partnership with Laity

1. Information taken from institutional publications and from letters to the author from Charles Ford, an administrator at the university from 1972 to 1978.

2. Several Catholic colleges were later founded by laypersons: Cardinal Newman in St. Louis, Christendom in Virginia, St. Thomas Aquinas in Santa Paula, California, and Magdalene in New Hampshire. The loss of funding caused Newman to close its doors within a decade. The others have continued and have a very clear Catholic identity in the traditional sense of that term. Enrollments remain in the range of two to five hundred. They are described in Mary Jo Weaver and R. Scott Appleby, eds., *Being Right: Conservative Catholics in America* (Bloomington: Indiana University Press, 1995).

3. The proportion, of course, was uneven in the cohort of Catholic higher education. Some particular statistics are given below.

4. Histories of individual colleges or universities tend to focus on the members of the religious community, especially where the president was a member of the community. This bias is not surprising, since the archival material is organized according to administrations (hence, by presidents) and the history of college and community is such an interdependent one. However, there is a need to uncover and celebrate some of the lay leaders and their contributions.

5. While this is generally true, a notable exception was the College of St. Catherine, the first Catholic college to be awarded a chapter of Phi Beta Kappa in 1938. Many of the Sisters of St. Joseph who administered the college had taken Ph.D. degrees at secular universities.

6. The theological reflections of Henri de Lubac, Yves Congar, John Courtney Murray, and others and the incorporation of their insights into the documents of Vatican Council II changed the way in which the role of the laity was understood and presented (see chapter 1). The concept of "mandate" used in the status of

Catholic Action projects was a unique way of expressing ecclesial approval for a work undertaken by laity. It was used later in the revision of the Code of Canon Law in 1983, appearing in canon 812, where the desired relationship of the theologian to the magisterium is described as the reception of a "mandate."

7. Quoted in Charles A. Curran, "The Role of the Laity in the Thought of John Courtney Murray," in J. Leon Hooper, S.J., and Todd David Whitmore, eds., *John Courtney Murray and the Growth of Tradition* (Kansas City, Mo.: Sheed and Ward, 1996), 244. Murray developed this understanding of the role of the laity in his writings on inter-creedal cooperation and church-state relations. But it gave way to the new definition of the church emerging from the documents of Vatican Council II. See Komonchak, "Clergy, Laity, and the Church's Mission."

8. A good example of lay Catholic action can be seen in the life and work of Maisie Ward Sheed and her husband Frank Sheed. Dana Greene, *The Living of Maisie Ward* (Notre Dame, Ind.: University of Notre Dame Press, 1997). Donald Thorman described the layman in 1962 as "emerging," but by 1967 he expressed disillusionment because the church structures could not absorb the changes of Vatican Council II. See Martin H. Work and Daniel J. Kane, "The American Catholic Layman and His Organizations," in Gleason, *Contemporary Catholicism*, 349–371. It was lay leadership that produced two important Catholic periodicals, *Cross Currents* and *Commonweal*.

9. An informal survey of the "first and second generation" of lay presidents produced ten brief memoirs, detailing their experiences. All but one reported a high level of support from the religious community of women and, in general, enjoyment of the situations in which they found themselves. However, several commented on the fact that the dire financial situation of the college was not fully presented to them when they were interviewed for the job. And they were too inexperienced to ask critical questions! They had to introduce a new culture to the campus in terms of their family life and their lay responsibilities. Upon reflection, they all express satisfaction about the richness they found in their work and in the friendships they developed. Responses in possession of the author.

10. Fitzgerald, *Governance of Jesuit Colleges*, 150.

11. *Proceedings of the Conference of Presidents*, January 10–11, 1960, ABC, JEA collection. Emphasis mine. It is also clear from the discussion at this meeting that laypersons were being sought because there were not enough Jesuits to run the expanding universities with their increasing complexity.

12. Notes from Ann Ida Gannon in the author's possession as well as Minutes of the Board of Trustees, Mundelein College, AMC.

13. Karen Kennelly, C.S.J., "Faculties and What They Taught," a paper prepared for a forthcoming book on the Neylan colleges, edited by Cynthia Russet and Tracy Schier.

14. Ibid., 38.

15. It was still assumed that there would be members of the religious community available for the president's position when the incumbent resigned. The typical

tenure of the presidents at this time, such as Theodore M. Hesburgh, C.S.C., Paul J. Reinert, S.J., John Cortelyou, C.M., Raymond Baumhart, S.J., and Raymond A. Roesch, S.M., was fifteen to twenty years or more. Among the generation following them, J. Donald Monan, S.J., Dorothy Ann Kelly, O.S.U., Joel Read, S.S.S.F., Lawrence Biondi, S.J., Edward Malloy, C.S.C., Brigid Driscoll, S.H.J.M., and Ray Fitz, S.M., have also had terms from ten to twenty-five years, but they do not see many of their sisters and brothers anxious to assume the presidency after them.

16. A petition from some faculty to eliminate the restriction of the presidency to Jesuits was presented on November 14, 1969, to the trustees at the College of the Holy Cross. ACHC box 8 folder 4.

17. A study done in 1980 on the presidency of Catholic colleges and universities, based on 146 valid responses, gave the number of lay presidents responding as 32, 30 of whom were male. There were 64 women religious and 50 men religious who responded. See Louis C. Gatto, "The Catholic College Presidency—A Study," *Current Issues in Catholic Higher Education* 2, no. 1: 24–31. Gatto noted that about twelve of the sisters' institutions had recently replaced a lay president with a sister, which puts into question a decided trend in any direction on the basis of lay/religious and suggests rather that qualifications and availability are the determining factors.

18. See, for example, Joseph B. Connors, *Journey Toward Fulfillment* (St. Paul, Minn.: College of St. Thomas, 1986). Although the presidency remained in the hands of clerics and the bishop served as chair of the board, there was a generous representation of the laity among the faculty and administrators.

19. The process by which Manhattanville moved to a "secular" identity occurred between 1968 and 1970, and it was linked to its desire to become academically more respectable and to shed its image as a "Kennedy girls' school." However, a significant factor in attaining this public recognition was the securing of Bundy money, predicated on not being "church-related." Many Manhattanville alumnae interpreted the fact that the college was among the first three Catholic institutions to be awarded Bundy money as a "sell-out" of the Sacred Heart tradition. The president, Mother Elizabeth McCormack, R.S.C.J., explained her position in a letter to the *New Yorker* (December 18, 1971) in response to a previous article by William F. Buckley Jr. Mother McCormack clearly denied that it was *in order to* get Bundy money that Manhattanville became a secular college and stated that the changes she made were necessary if Manhattanville was to be recognized as a peer in contemporary higher education. AMHC, McCormack file. Nevertheless, many alumnae remained unconvinced and angry.

20. Leo Martin, S.J., ALUC. Note that these developments were not related to the Bundy money, since the New York colleges were omitted.

21. All of this information is taken from the minutes of the board of trustees, ABC.

22. Martin Stamm, "The New Guardians of American Catholic Higher Education: An Examination of Lay Participation . . . ," Ph.D. diss., University of Pennsylvania, 1979.

23. Daniel L. Schlafly (1912–1997) was an outstanding citizen of St. Louis who served for twenty-eight years on the City of St. Louis Public School Board during the difficult days of desegregation. In 1967 he accepted Paul Reinert's invitation to be the first lay chair of the newly reorganized board of trustees of Saint Louis University. He was committed to keeping the university Catholic and Jesuit and worked for the eleven years of his chairmanship to fulfill that goal. Edmund Stephan (1912–1997) was the partner of Theodore Hesburgh as Hesburgh thought his way through to a new organizational structure for the University of Notre Dame. Stephan applied his legal skills to drawing up the new bylaws and chaired the board for fifteen years. Until a few months before his death he continued to attend board meetings, commencements, and many other activities. He was part of the story from Land O'Lakes to *Ex Corde Ecclesiae* and never wavered in either his loyalty to the Catholic church or his defense of institutional autonomy.

24. A detailed study of the faculties at Catholic men's colleges, based on a survey in 1960, provides an excellent analysis against which to measure the growth and changes in the three decades we are studying. See John D. Donovan, *The Academic Man in the Catholic College* (New York: Sheed and Ward, 1964). Donovan, of course, recognized that his study did not include faculty at women's colleges, where 30 percent of all full-time faculty were employed (p. 8). He conducted 300 interviews of lay and religious men at twenty-two Catholic colleges and universities. Tom Landy, in his paper delivered at Saint Louis in May 1997, analyzed the data from 1960 to 1990 at the colleges sponsored by women religious. The shift from religious to lay was dramatic at some of these Neylan colleges. For example, at St. Benedict's in 1969–70, 35 of the 52 faculty were members of the religious community; by 1979–80 the ratio was 33 to 123.

25. McGrath and Dupont, *Future Governance*, 11 n. 1. The same study points out that between 1956 and 1966 enrollment in Catholic colleges increased by 71 percent and in some places the ratio of lay to religious teachers became 8 to 1 (p. 24).

26. Ford and Roy, *Renewal*, 123. Philip Gleason noted that in 1958 over 80 percent of the faculties of six fairly representative medium to large-sized Catholic institutions were composed of laymen. "A Historical Perspective," in Robert Hassenger, ed., *The Shape of Catholic Higher Education* (Chicago: University of Chicago Press, 1967), 5n. I presume that these six colleges were all for men.

27. Contosta, *Villanova University*, 149.

28. The St. John's case has been dealt with in detail in chapter 2.

29. One of the tensions on the campuses, even as lay faculty became the majority, was the perception that the religious were an "in group" and the laypersons an "out group" in the matter of policy-making. Where separate norms for hiring

and retention of religious were in effect, tension naturally increased between the two groups. See Paul J. Reiss, "Built-in Tensions," in Hassenger, *Shape of Catholic Higher Education*, 265.

30. Friedman to Membership, October 24, 1968, referring to the American Association of University Professors, "Statement of Principles on Academic Freedom and Tenure," which had evolved over the years from 1915 when AAUP was formed. The Association of American Colleges had been a partner with AAUP in the development of the principles, and Friedman's close association with AAC probably influenced his attitude.

31. Details regarding the role of AAUP are given in chapter 2.

32. "Lay Involvement: La Salle College," *College Newsletter,* June 1967.

33. Ibid.

34. See the treatment of AAUP and the 1970 interpretative comment in chapter 2.

35. Curran, *Catholic Higher Education*, chapter 3, gives an excellent treatment of this period and the acceptance of the principle of academic freedom by leaders of Catholic higher education and, to some extent, by church authorities in the United States.

36. Donovan, *Academic Man*, 173–175.

37. 562 F.2d 246 (3rd cir 1977). NCEA submitted a strong *amicus brief* for St. Francis in which the jurisdiction of NLRB over Catholic colleges was not disputed, but the ruling against including the religious in the vote on unionization was seen as violative of the First Amendment in that it interfered with the right of free exercise of religion by discriminating against the religious because they had made vows of poverty. This position is contrary to that taken by Catholic schools in *NLRB v Bishop of Chicago,* in which they sought and won exclusion from jurisdiction of NLRB on the grounds that Catholic schools were controlled by the bishop and therefore exempt from NLRB rulings. St. Francis avoided using that line of defense since it identified itself as an independent institution, not controlled by the bishop. Most Catholic colleges and universities have followed this line of reasoning.

38. Reiss, "Built-in Tensions," 266. One might ask: Are there not comparable obstacles to scholarship for the administrator or faculty member with responsibilities to his or her family? Reiss, for example, was unable to do as much as he wished in professional publication as a sociologist when he served as academic vice president and executive vice president at Fordham and as president of St. Michael's College, while also attempting to give sufficient time to his wife and nine children (letter from Reiss to the author). Time for research and writing is always at a premium, whether the faculty member is lay or religious. It may be that motivation for scholarly work is weaker among the religious because of the individual's commitment to active apostolic service in non-academic areas and the expectation of religious communities that their members will serve in many different roles.

39. See, for example, the testimonies in Hesburgh, *Challenge and Promise,* and Mark Poorman, C.S.C., ed., *Labors from the Heart* (Notre Dame, Ind.: University of Notre Dame Press, 1996).

Six: Are They Still Catholic?

1. *Ex Corde Ecclesiae,* Introduction. Gallin, *Essential Documents,* 413.

2. David O'Brien, *From the Heart of the American Church* (New York: Orbis, 1994).

3. We have already noted in chapter 2 the talk given by Francis X. Gallagher to members of the NCEA College and University Department while the *Horace Mann* case was still in litigation. He warned them about the use of "sectarian" language in their brochures and in the various internal documents that reflected the Rule of the religious community. Department directors Friedman and Murphy reenforced this message in communications to the membership.

4. In the spirit of Vatican Council II, the emphasis was placed on the authority of the local bishop and regional hierarchy. However, the Apostolic Constitution on the reform of the Roman Curia of August 15, 1967, enlarged the responsibilities of the Congregation for Seminaries and Universities and renamed it the Congregation for Catholic Education. The Congregation was now divided into three offices, the second of which had the responsibility of "regulating" universities "to the extent that they are in any way dependent upon the authority of the Church." See the memo prepared by Frederick R. McManus for the NCEA Executive Director in 1976. ACUA / NCEA, Sacred Congregation file.

5. William M. Shea, "Beyond Tolerance: Pluralism and Catholic Higher Education," *Current Issues in Catholic Higher Education* 8, no. 2 (1988): 38.

6. All of the relevant documents are in Gallin, *Essential Documents.* For the history of their development, see Alice Gallin, "On the Road: Toward a Definition of a Catholic University," in *The Jurist* 48 (1988): 2. An excellent account by a contemporary observer is Ann Ida Gannon, B.V.M., "Some Aspects of Catholic Higher Education since Vatican II," *Current Issues in Catholic Higher Education* 8, no. 1 (1987): 10-25.

7. See chapter 3.

8. See chapter 2. At the same time, the Catholic universities participated in the IAU discussions about the autonomy of the university as such.

9. Land O'Lakes Statement, in Gallin, *Essential Documents,* 7.

10. Kinshasa Statement, in Gallin, *Essential Documents,* 13-16.

11. The American delegates were Rev. Clarence W. Friedman (NCEA), Rev. Robert J. Henle, S.J., Rev. Theodore M. Hesburgh, C.S.C., Neil G. McCluskey, S.J., Rev. John J. McGrath, Brother Gregory Nugent, F.S.C., Daniel L. Schlafly, and Rev. Michael P. Walsh, S.J.

12. This was known as the Rome Statement or "The Catholic University and the Aggiornamento." For the text, see Gallin, *Essential Documents*, 17–35.

13. Letter from the Sacred Congregation to the delegates to the Rome Congress, April 25–May 1, 1969, dated December 11, 1969. The results of the Plenary Session of the Congregation had been approved by Pope Paul VI. ASLU, Henle papers.

14. Response to Garrone, February 27, 1970, and Hesburgh to Garrone, March 30, 1970. UNDA, CPHS 98/09. We see here one of the constant points of disagreement about language: to the Roman canonical mind, "norms" are general principles of universal application but with proper allowance for interpretation and implementation; to the American civil and constitutional law, they are "laws" intended to be kept as written. In practice, however, this benign understanding of canon law has often given way to explicit interpretation by Roman congregations and American diocesan authorities.

15. Executive Committee Minutes, NCEA College and University Department, undated, but presumably summer 1971. ACUA/NCEA.

16. Gannon, "Some Aspects," quoting a position paper by McCluskey.

17. Submitted with the Letter from the Sacred Congregation to the delegates to the Rome Congress, April 25–May 1, 1969, dated December 11, 1969. See note 13 above.

18. See chapter 2 for the discussion of *Tilton v Richardson*.

19. Friedman to Schroeffer, July 30, 1969. ACUA/NCEA, Sacred Congregation file.

20. This dollar amount was, of course, before the Higher Education Act initiated the strong student aid programs which would be steadily increased in the seventies.

21. Friedman to McCluskey, April 2, 1971, ACUA/NCEA, Sacred Congregation file. While appointment of ex-priests was not at issue in the meetings regarding the document to be developed, Friedman obviously viewed it as an example of interference with the internal structures of the universities. In a fairly typical response, the Congregation maintained that it was not a rule emanating from the Congregation for Catholic Education but rather came from the Congregation dealing with clerical life. This issue would arise again in 1975 when the American delegates to the IFCU Assembly in New Delhi met with Cardinal Garrone. It would also be pursued on several occasions by ACCU and by the Bishops and Presidents' Committee, but never resolved. ACUA/NCEA, Bishops and Presidents' Committee file.

22. Friedman to Henle, March 30, 1971. ACUA/NCEA, Sacred Congregation file.

23. Friedman to McCluskey, May 26, 1971. ACUA/NCEA, Sacred Congregation file.

24. Friedman to Henle, July 11, 1972, ASLU, Henle papers on IFCU.

25. A letter from Schroeffer on June 5, 1971, to the presidents of Catholic universities had informed them that the selection of nine delegates from the United

States was very difficult; the delegates should come only from institutions with graduate programs and the presidents should send their votes to President Walton. ACUA/NCEA, Sacred Congregation file.

26. Marchisano to Walton, June 20, 1972. ACUA/NCEA, Sacred Congregation file.

27. Letters from Rev. C.W. Friedman to Rev. Msgr. Terrence J. Murphy of August 28 and 31, 1972. ACUA/NCEA, Sacred Congregation file. There was strong suspicion that Msgr. George Kelly and S. Thomas Greenburg of the Institute for Catholic Higher Education were behind the Roman distancing from NCEA. See note 47 below.

28. Friedman to Murphy, August 28, 1972. ACUA/NCEA, Sacred Congregation file.

29. ASLU, Henle file. Henle moved from Saint Louis University to the Georgetown presidency on June 16, 1969. The response to Rome was in the letter from Hesburgh dated March 30, 1970. AUND, CPHS 98/09.

30. Garrone to Hesburgh, June 22, 1970. ASLU, Henle file.

31. It is difficult to reconcile this statement by Hesburgh with the figures on membership given by Michaud, *Knowledge and Faith* (p. 122), where the number of members in 1965 is given as 51 and in 1970 as 80. The difference may be explained by the nature of the institutions that had recently become members, compared with those that had dropped out.

32. Hesburgh to Garrone, May 17, 1971. ASLU, Henle file.

33. Hesburgh to Friedman, June 2, 1971. ACUA/NCEA, Sacred Congregation file.

34. Garrone to presidents, May 10, 1972. ACUA/NCEA, Sacred Congregation file.

35. Claydon was probably chosen because of her position that year as chair of the College and University Department of NCEA. Trinity was an undergraduate women's college and so would not have been eligible for membership in IFCU.

36. Gallin, *Essential Documents*, 37–57.

37. R. J. Henle, "Catholic Universities and the Vatican," *America*, April 9, 1977.

38. Gallin, *Essential Documents*, 59. The letter was to accompany the document wherever it was published.

39. See the discussion on honorary degrees in chapter 1.

40. All of these documents, with accompanying commentary, can be found in Gallin, *Essential Documents*.

41. John F. Murphy to Cardinal Garrone, May 1, 1975. ACUA/NCEA, Sacred Congregation file.

42. Garrone to John Murphy, June 2, 1975. ACUA/NCEA, Sacred Congregation file.

43. Report of John F. Murphy to the Bishops and Presidents' Committee, October 10–11, 1975. ACUA/NCEA, Bishops and Presidents' Committee file.

44. Several earlier attempts had been made by Father Friedman to convince Rome that laicized priests need not be excluded from faculties. See Friedman to McCluskey, April 2, 1971; Friedman to Garrone, May 10, 1974; and Garrone to Friedman, May 24, 1974. ACUA/NCEA.

45. John F. Murphy to presidents of member institutions, NCEA College and University Department, September 10, 1975. ACUA/NCEA, Sacred Congregation file.

46. Garrone to all presidents, January 10, 1976. ACUA/NCEA, Sacred Congregation file.

47. As early as 1971, opponents of NCEA were involved in convening meetings and reporting to Roman officials. Minutes of the Executive Committee, NCEA College and University Department, April 14, 1971. Mention was made of Dr. S. Thomas Greenburg and Rev. Joseph Cahill, C.M., president of St. John's University, New York, who had set up the Institute for Catholic Higher Education and were attempting to organize presidents who disagreed with the way NCEA was interacting with Rome. A report of visitations to forty-five campuses by members of the Institute and two conferences sponsored by the Institute is given under date of June 14, 1971. There is also a report on a conference held at Biscayne College, October 31–November 2, 1972, but the date of 1972 seems inconsistent with events detailed in the report. More probably it was 1975 and was reported on by Msgr. Murphy to the Bishops and Presidents' Committee on November 11, 1975. ACUA/NCEA, Sacred Congregation file. Published accounts of the activities of the Institute can be found in the newsletter of the Fellowship of Catholic Scholars and in articles and books by George A. Kelly.

48. Gallin, *Essential Documents*, 71–86. The various drafts of "Relations" are in ACUA/NCEA.

49. A delegation from NCEA consisting of Msgr. John Murphy, Archbishop Borders, Rev. Terrence Murphy, and Sister Sally Furay met with Garrone and his staff (Schroeffer, Marchisano, Cerruti, and Bruskewitz) three times during the week of March 29, 1976. ACUA/NCEA, Sacred Congregation file.

50. Response from Rev. Joseph Cahill, C.M., to the draft of "Relations." ACUA/NCEA, "Relations" file.

51. Kelly, *Battle for the American Church Revisited*, 82–83.

52. George A. Kelly, "Charles Curran and the ACCU," *Social Justice Review* 77, nos. 9–10 (September–October 1986): 158. Kelly's general position can be found in his *Why Should the Catholic University Survive?* (New York: St. John's University Press, 1973).

53. All the various drafts of canons regarding universities from 1977 to 1983 are in Gallin, *Essential Documents*, Part III.

54. Gallin, *Essential Documents*, 156. See also no. 64 in the 1978 draft: "Those who, in any kind of institute of higher studies, give courses in theology or courses related to theology require a canonical mission."

55. See, for example, no. 60 in the 1978 draft.

56. A Committee on Property of Colleges and Universities (COPCU), the Center for Constitutional Studies, and a very generous group of canon lawyers combined efforts to critique the various drafts of the proposed code revision on behalf of ACCU. Msgr. Frederick R. McManus, Rev. Ladislaus Orsy, S.J., Rev. James Provost, Rev. James Corriden, and Rev. Charles Whelan, S.J., worked on the drafts from 1977 to 1983. In addition, the civil and constitutional issues involved were ably handled for the association by Charles Wilson of the firm of Williams and Connolly. Besides preparing a scholarly paper for the association at the request of the president of Georgetown, Wilson spoke in an executive session at the annual ACCU meeting to the presidents of the colleges and universities on the potential dangers inherent in some of the proposed legislation. See further for the points he made.

57. "Relations of American Catholic Colleges and Universities with the Church," in Gallin, *Essential Documents*, 71–86; see discussion in chapter 3.

58. Bernardin to Gallin, September 15, 1995. Letter in author's possession.

59. Gallin, *Essential Documents*, 87–127.

60. Letter from Msgr. Marchisano to Alice Gallin, Executive Director, ACCU, October 3, 1980. ACUA/NCEA.

61. Address of Pope John Paul II to the Presidents of Catholic Colleges and Universities. Gallin, *Essential Documents*, 129–133.

62. Ibid., 130–131.

63. Ibid., 137.

64. Timothy Healy, S.J., to Bernardin, August 28, 1981. ACUA/NCEA, Canon Law file.

65. Letter to the American bishops, July 24, 1981. AUND, UPHS file.

66. Bernardin, Memo to Alice Gallin, October 23, 1981. ACUA/NCEA.

67. Their thinking is reflected in the ACCU response regarding canons 762–770. Gallin, *Essential Documents*, 167–174.

68. The sudden death of Cardinal Pericle Felici at age seventy on March 22, 1982, left the dispute unresolved. However, "canonical mission" was not reintroduced.

69. For an excellent commentary on the entire Code of 1983, see James Coriden et al., *The Code of Canon Law: A Text and Commentary* (Mahwah, N.J.: Paulist Press, 1985). The part that deals with higher education is reprinted in Gallin, *Essential Documents*, 175–187.

70. Submitted to a group of "experts" by the Congregation, March 1, 1982. After they responded, the Congregation then extended the consultation on March 9, 1983, still "informal." At its meeting of April 4, 1984, the Plenarium reviewed the opinions of those consulted and then distributed it to all "interested parties" for their review. This became known as the "Schema" of 1985.

71. The term "inculturation" is used here to identify a process of dialogical interaction between the church and various cultures. It is an ongoing exchange in which each party to the dialogue expresses its values and seeks ways to harmonize them with the other party's values, without losing their original strength. In

contrast, "acculturation" means that one culture adapts to another and becomes part of the other's value system. See the explanation in A. Roest-Collins, S.J., "What is so new about inculturation?" *Gregorianum* 59 (1978): 721–738. In the last twenty years much has been written on the subject and the distinction is somewhat fluid. It is more easily explained in Latin than in English.

72. The documents regarding the Schema of 1985 and subsequent drafts leading to *Ex Corde Ecclesiae* (1990) can be found in *Essential Documents,* Part IV. A task force of CTSA studied the Schema and on November 7, 1985, concluded: "The Schema is substantially flawed; despite some valuable insights and phrasing, this task force votes 'non Placet' and seeks a completely new Schema."

73. The bishop-delegates from NCCB were Daniel Kucera, James Malone, Francis Schulte, and Paul Waldschmidt. The presidents' representatives were Dorothy Brown (Rosemont), Patrick Ellis (LaSalle), Paul Reiss (St. Michael's), William Byron (The Catholic University of America), Edward Malloy (Notre Dame), Thomas Scanlon (Manhattan), Joseph O'Hare (Fordham), Frank Kerins (Carroll), Sally Furey (San Diego), J. Donald Monan (Boston College), Joseph Hagen (Assumption), Dorothy Ann Kelly (New Rochelle), Ray Fitz (Dayton), Brigid Driscoll (Marymount), Alice Gallin (ACCU), and Magdalen Coughlin (Mt. St. Mary's, California).

74. In the absence of Cardinal Baum, who was in the United States for medical reasons, the presiding officer was Bishop Jose Sarraiva Martins.

75. Gallin, *Essential Documents,* 381–383. On April 25 the pope addressed the meeting, once again noting how much "at home" he felt with university people and how much he appreciated their work. He spoke of the task that had occupied them during the meeting: "considering ways to give greater efficacy and a better expression to the two-poled entity 'University—Catholic.'" These poles, he pointed out, enrich each other and serve both church and society (ibid., 385).

76. The three delegates chosen by their colleagues to represent the United States were Sister Sally Furay, R.S.C.J., of the University of San Diego, Rev. Edward Malloy, C.S.C., of the University of Notre Dame, and Rev. Joseph O'Hare, S.J., of Fordham University. A key figure in the writing of the final document was Rev. James Sauve, S.J., who was on loan to the Congregation for this purpose. Unfortunately, Father Sauve died suddenly in 1997.

77. There were seven articles under general norms, each with some sub-articles, and three transitional (technical) norms. Gallin, *Essential Documents,* 428–433. The role of the regional bishops' conferences, seen as a recognition of subsidiarity, was swiftly undercut by a list of "directives" for implementation of *Ex Corde Ecclesiae* sent out by the Congregation.

Seven: Confrontation or Convergence?

1. *Priorities for Action: Final Report of the Commission on Higher Education,* 6.

2. Ibid., 23.

3. In a letter to Jesuits engaged in higher education, the American Jesuit provincials made it clear that they no longer were in a position of authority with regard to Jesuit colleges and universities. They addressed not the institutions but simply all Jesuits who were serving in the universities. They expressed a continued commitment to higher education but expected to carry out their mission by influencing the institutions through individual Jesuits and local communities rather than by governing them by Jesuit authority. "The Jesuit Mission in Higher Education," Easter 1978, in Tetlow, *The Jesuits' Mission in Higher Education*, appendix, pp. 81–111.

4. Edmund D. Pellegrino, "Toward a True University, Truly Catholic," March 30, 1979, in *Occasional Papers* 5, no. 1 (Summer 1979): 3–7.

5. Gallin, *Essential Documents*, 135–151. See chapter 6.

6. Ibid., 136, quoting *Gaudium et Spes*, par. 57.

7. Gallin, *Essential Documents*, 137–138; note 4 on 149.

8. Not all Catholic colleges and universities focused on newly arrived immigrants. However, most of them, especially in urban areas, historically had a large proportion of second- and third-generation men and women who were the first in their families to attend college.

9. Ann Fecher, ed., *Recruitment and Retention of Minorities, Ten Case Studies from the Neylan Minorities Project* (Washington, D.C.: ACCU, 1991), introduction. The ongoing goals of the Neylan Minority Project were (1) to increase the pool of minority students with potential to move from the secondary level into college; (2) to increase the enrollment of minorities in college, especially in the four-year colleges of the Neylan group; and (3) to increase the proportion of minority students who graduate from these colleges. For more on the Neylan colleges, see chapter 4.

10. An ACCU committee later modified the inventory to deal specifically with Catholic colleges and universities. See *Current Issues in Catholic Higher Education* 7, no. 1 (Summer 1986): 20–30.

11. The four volumes produced after the Congress were distributed to all of the institutions represented. They are entitled *Church and College: A Vital Partnership*, with subtitles for each volume: *Affirmation, Mission, Accountability*, and *Exchange* (Sherman, Tex.: Austin College, 1980). They quickly went out of print, and since they had been distributed without cost, there were no funds for reprinting. The fellowship generated at the meeting continued in the Executives of Church-Related Colleges and Universities, a group which met twice a year in subsequent decades. The Bishops and Presidents' Committee was supportive of the effort leading to the Congress and held its June 21–23 meeting at Notre Dame in conjunction with the National Congress; Minutes of the Bishops and Presidents' Committee, February 15, 1979, ACUA/NCEA. The papers of the National Congress are housed in ACUA/NCEA.

12. George M. Marsden, *The Soul of the American University: From Protestant Establishment to Established Nonbelief* (New York: Oxford University Press, 1994).

13. Riesman, *On Higher Education*, 175.

14. James Tunstead Burtchaell, C.S.C., "Decline and Fall of the Christian College," *First Things* (April and May 1991). See also his presentation of case studies
in *The Dying of the Light* (Grand Rapids, Mich.: Eerdmans, 1998). A continuing
criticism of Catholic higher education for becoming "secularized" has been offered
by the *Fellowship of Catholic Scholars Newsletter*. See especially a summary of their
position in vol. 3, no. 2 (February 1980). For an opposite view, see O'Brien, *From the
Heart of American Church*, chapter 6.

15. This is the basic concern in George Marsden's *The Secularization of the
Academy* and *The Soul of the American University*. A different perspective is found
in Alice Gallin, "American Catholic Higher Education and the Experience of Inculturation," in Shea and Van Slyke, *Trying Times*.

16. Harry E. Smith, *Secularization and the University* (Richmond, Va.: John
Knox Press, 1968), 93.

17. Memorandum to Fordham Board of Trustees from Edmund G. Ryan, S.J.,
on "Secularization," July 31, 1968. AFU, PML3.

18. *Fellowship of Catholic Scholars Newsletter,* February 1980.

19. Pettit, *Enrollment and Finances*. The Carnegie classifications are used here
by Dr. Pettit. The enrollment numbers come from Fall 1988. For much of the data
in this chapter consult Thomas Landy, "Demographic Snapshot: Catholic Higher
Education 1960–90," paper delivered at Saint Louis University, May 9, 1997.

20. Landy, "Demographic Snapshot," points out that 1970–1989 was the period
in which the fastest enrollment growth took place in colleges founded by women
religious. In 1959 there were 51,860 students, while in 1989 the number was 169,670.
There were, by then, fewer colleges of this type and most were coeducational. By
1998 the number of single-sex colleges had dropped to twenty-seven. During the
same years, the enrollment at colleges founded by men religious went from 162,535
to 297,072, and at diocesan colleges from 16,693 to 49,579.

The terminology can be confusing. For a transitional period, the Women's College Coalition and the American Council on Education (two sources generally
referred to for statistical data) agreed on using an 85 percent figure as a criterion for
being identified as a women's college. However, since the late eighties the policy
seems to be to let individual colleges decide if they want to be considered as a
women's college. While the formerly men's colleges, in becoming coeducational,
quickly added numbers of women, the formerly women's colleges did not add large
numbers of men to their student bodies. Landy uses a cut-off figure of 10 percent
rather than 15 percent.

21. Fecher, *Recruitment and Retention*. The ten case studies in this project were
Alverno College, Barry University, College of New Rochelle, Emmanuel College,
Heritage College, Madonna University, Mount St. Mary's College (California),
Mundelein College, Our Lady of the Lake University, and The College of Mount
Saint Joseph. The project included the development of tools for assessment of the
degree of success achieved by individual colleges and was partially funded by the
Ford Foundation.

22. See the study of Catholic students done by Rita Scherei, based on the data collected by Alexander Astin at UCLA for incoming freshmen. A copy of her UCLA dissertation is in the ACCU office library. A summary appeared in *Current Issues* 2, no. 2 (Winter 1982).

23. Telephone interview with Brother Theodore Drahman at the Christian Brothers Conference in Hyattsville, Maryland, May 21, 1998. He also pointed out that currently the College of Santa Fe reports 229 Catholics in a student body of approximately 1,400. Geography obviously plays an important role in demographic data. The University of Notre Dame, on the other hand, reported 87 percent Catholics in 1996.

24. See Boyer, *Control of the Campus.*

25. See chapter 4 for a description of the different associations.

26. The internal NCEA matter was resolved in a memorandum developed by ACCU in conjunction with the Bishops and Presidents' Committee, January 29, 1981. ACUA/NCEA, Bishops and Presidents' Committee files.

27. Concurring opinion of Frankfurter and Harlan as quoted in Boyer, *Control of the Campus,* 4–5. A somewhat different situation exists in New York State, where the Board of Regents has the responsibility of approving the master plans and new programs of *all* higher education. In a recent controversy about admissions policies at CUNY, this authority was challenged (*New York Times,* August 14, 1998). In New York the private institutions of higher education constitute the University of the State of New York, an entity distinct from the State University of New York. They are, therefore, subject to regulation by the Regents.

28. For the various anti-discrimination laws, see Wilson, "Catholic Colleges and Civil Law," 39–53.

29. For data on student attitudes, see Alexander Astin's annual survey of incoming freshmen which began in 1966 (UCLA-ACE). For trends, see his *The American Freshman: Thirty Year Trends* (UCLA, 1996).

30. Horowitz, *Campus Life,* 252.

31. Quoted by Horowitz, ibid., 254.

32. See chapter 3, p. 179 and note 19. A later reflection on the experience of women at Notre Dame is given by Regina Coll, C.S.J., "Women at Our Lady's University," in Mark L. Poorman, C.S.C., ed., *Labors From the Heart* (Notre Dame, Ind.: University of Notre Dame Press, 1996). The Notre Dame decision for coeducation was, of course, linked to the failure of plans for a merger with Saint Mary's College, and so the reasons for the change are a bit difficult to disentangle. AUND.

33. Examples of this can be found in trustee discussions at Holy Cross, Assumption, Fordham, and Loyola of Chicago. See, for example, Charlene Longhi Martin and Maureen Ryan Doyle, "Coeducation and the Assumption Experience," in *Assumption College Magazine* (Spring 1998): 25. It is interesting to note that in the women's colleges the transition to coeducation was not as simple. Alan Simpson, the president of Vassar in 1964, was opposed to coeducation, saying, "A coed campus is a male-dominated campus," but after the trustees rejected a merger with

Yale, he went along with a move to coeducation in 1969 (*New York Times*, May 8, 1998). The economics of the situation were determining at Vassar as elsewhere, and it took several years before a good balance of male/female could be achieved. Catholic women's colleges had similar "conversions" to coeducation when they were hit by the loss of students to the men's colleges. Some of them have been very successful, while others still attract very few men.

34. For data see Bartell, *Project 80* and "Catholic Higher Education: Trends," and Pettit, *Enrollment and Finances*.

35. See *Current Issues in Catholic Higher Education* 2, no. 2 (Winter 1982): 6–28.

36. ISACC was the brainchild of Dr. Sandra Estanek, Vice President for Student Affairs at Ursuline College. The three-year program was supported by Ursuline College, John Carroll University, the Lilly Endowment, and ACCU. For a description of ISACC, see Sandra M. Estanek and Martin F. Larrey, "ISACC: Integrating Student Affairs Practice and Catholic Identity," *Current Issues in Catholic Higher Education* 18, no. 2 (Spring 1998): 51–63.

37. Borders' address is in *Delta Epsilon Sigma Bulletin* 23, no. 2 (May 1977).

38. The final report on the seven pilot colleges is in *Current Issues in Catholic Higher Education* 1, no. 2 (Winter 1981). Included were Aquinas College, Holy Names College, California, Iona College, St. Mary-of-the-Woods, University of Notre Dame, Villanova University, and Wheeling College. They were chosen as pilots to indicate the wide variety of institutions that could embark on such a program. In 1998 Iona College sponsored a celebration of twenty years' growth of these programs. While the extent of commitment varies from campus to campus, in 1988 there were 155 Catholic institutions that at least had a "coordinator for peace and justice education," and 105 reported that they had some kind of program. See O'Brien, *From the Heart of the American Church*, 192, quoting a study by Loretta Carey at Fordham University.

39. For the text of "*Ex Corde Ecclesiae*: An Application to the United States," approved by the American bishops on November 13, 1996, by a vote of 224 to 6, see *Origins* 26, no. 24 (November 28, 1996). The Observations from the Congregation were sent to the bishops' conference and to the members of the Implementation Committee in April of 1997 and were published in *Origins* 27, no. 4 (June 12, 1997). A subcommittee, chaired by Cardinal Bevilacqua, is attempting to reconcile the differences, as of summer 1999.

Eight: Tolerance, Pluralism, and Beyond

1. Marsden, *Soul of the American University*, 436.

2. Richard T. Hughes and William B. Adrian, *Models for Christian Higher Education* (Grand Rapids, Mich.: Eerdmans, 1997). This book was produced under the aegis of the Lilly Endowment and became the basis for several denominational gatherings and a national conference at Notre Dame in the summer of 1998.

3. See, for example, the many papers presented at a conference at the University of St. Thomas, St. Paul, Minnesota, August 1995. This conference was the result of a collaboration with ACCU, and the papers were published as *Occasional Papers* 1, no. 1 (November 1995): 38.

4. One example of this is the project of the International Federation of Catholic Universities on *University, Church and Culture*. A first symposium on this topic was held at Saint Paul University in Ottawa on April 19–23, 1999.

5. Address at St. Thomas, *Occasional Papers* 1, no. 1 (November 1995).

6. Marsden, *Soul of the American University*, 437.

7. On this point, see Giuseppe Alberigo, Jean-Pierre Jossua, and Joseph A. Komonchak, *The Reception of Vatican II* (Washington, D.C.: The Catholic University of America Press, 1987). For the papers prepared for the Synod of 1985, see *Origins* 15, nos. 15 and 27 (1985). The paper by the Most Rev. James Malone, president of the NCCB at the time, is of particular interest for those seeking to understand the implementation of Vatican Council II in the United States.

8. Avery Dulles, S.J., "The Reception of Vatican II at the Extraordinary Synod of 1985," in Alberigo et al., *Reception of Vatican II*, 350.

9. Ibid., 353.

10. See the document on Episcopal Conferences in *Origins* 28, no. 9 (July 30, 1998): 152–158.

11. This symposium celebrating twenty years of specific programs on Catholic campuses coincided with the issuing of a document by the American bishops at their June 1998 meeting on the theme: "Catholic Social Teaching and Catholic Education." Archbishop John Roach, the chair of the task force which prepared the statement, spoke at the symposium and expressed his appreciation for the progress already made by the Catholic colleges.

12. On this topic, see the thoughtful address given by Archbishop Rembert Weakland at Saint Louis University, February 24, 1997, entitled "Aesthetic & Religious Experience: A Neglected Aspect of Contemporary Evangelization."

13. Carey and Muller, *Theological Education*. It contains a good bibliography compiled by Pamela C. Young, C.S.J., pp. 375–400, which could be extended by reference to *Current Issues in Catholic Higher Education* and the Jesuit periodical, *Conversations*.

14. *Occasional Papers* 1, no. 1 (November 1995): 5.

Index